2

Evening Telegraph

DERBY

OUR CENTURY

BY THE PEOPLE WHO LIVED IT

Emma Atkin

Evening Telegraph

DERBY

OUR CENTURY

BY THE PEOPLE WHO LIVED IT

Emma Atkin

The Breedon Books
Publishing Company
Derby

First published in Great Britain by
The Breedon Books Publishing Company Limited
Breedon House, 44 Friar Gate, Derby, DE1 1DA.
1999

ISBN 1 85983 168 0

Printed and bound by Butler & Tanner Ltd., Selwood Printing Works, Caxton Road, Frome, Somerset.

Colour separations and jacket printing by Green Shires Group Ltd, Leicester.

Contents

Introduction

Our Century is a piece of living, breathing history. Published as part of the *Derby Evening Telegraph's* Millennium celebrations, it looks back at Derby and Derbyshire over the greater part of the last hundred years, telling the story of the places and personalities that made Derby the city that it is today.

Unlike traditional local heritage books, *Our Century – By The People Who Lived It* does not carry detailed historical records which have been researched from the archives.

Instead, it is packed with evocative eye-witness accounts by you – the people who were there.

Buildings have been bulldozed. The face of the city has changed. People have passed away. But your memories live on. And now those memories have been preserved through the pages of *Our Century*.

Your stories are divided into chapters which focus on specific aspects of Derby life.

There is a chapter about your schooldays, recollections of your youth, whether you were a pupil at Central School or Bemrose, Parkfield Cedars or Rykneld.

Another chapter turns the spotlight on your leisure time, whether it was spent at the theatre, cinema, playing sport or shopping.

Other chapters look at the world wars, your life at work and memories of your families.

And, of course, no book about Derby would be complete without a chapter devoted to the fortunes of Derby County: the ups, the downs, the trials and tribulations.

The result of your work is *Our Century*: a unique record of our city's rich and varied history.

by Harold Richardson, Trowels Lane, Derby

Harry Sykes – 'the friend of all poor children'

ON the face of it, the 20th century did not have a good beginning. In 1900, Britain was at war against the Boers in South Africa. And in London alone, an influenza epidemic was killing 50 people a day. There was unrest in Ireland. The Boxer rising against Westerners in China was nearing its bloody climax, and Queen Victoria's long reign as head of the world's greatest empire was drawing to its close.

But it was still a Britain confident of its place among industrial nations of the globe.

Motor cars were beginning to be seen on the roads, but were little more than toys for the wealthy, and horse-drawn traffic continued to clog urban streets. It was the age of the railways by then and with the railways had come a new and expanding prosperity.

For the masses, however, the evil courts of the back-to-back houses became no sweeter, disease still held sway, hunger went unappeased, the workhouses remained open, and the country continued with its class-dominated normality. Yet for some of the children of Derby's West End and other deprived areas of the town, brighter times came in with the last years of the Victorian era.

The Great Northern Railway had a branch line to the east coast, and it was at a village called Skegness that Harry Sykes had founded a charity renowned and unique to the town of Derby. To give his parties of ragged children a holiday by the sea, Harry Sykes rented accommodation in the High Street. A board fixed to the wall declared it to be 'Derby Poor Boys' Home'.

It was a struggle to keep going, and only when the father of one of Harry Sykes' friends, ex-MP for Derby, Sir Henry Howe Bemrose, took an interest, was the future of the home secured.

Harry Sykes, the founder of the holiday home.

The home in Roman Bank, Skegness (circa 1895), renamed Derby Children's Holiday Home.

The young Harry Sykes makes a speech to the Duchess of Rutland at the opening of the home in 1898.

Enlisting the support of other worthies of the borough, Sir Henry proposed buying a piece of land 'for the purpose of founding a permanent home at the seaside for the benefit of the poor children of Derby and the county of Derby'. On what was then open land on the edge of the village, a holiday home was built at a cost of £1,020, and opened by the Duchess of Rutland in 1898.

To generations of poor children it became known affectionately as 'Sykes' Home' and a cause for much excitement around the lively streets of those times. To many old people today Harry Sykes was the Santa Claus of their childhoods – as is remembered of a day in 1926: "I was ten years old and my father had died, and I think it was from the schools they got to know who to send to the seaside. It was Mr Sykes himself who would come round to the different houses and it only had to be said 'Mr Sykes is about!' for all the children around the West End to be on the lookout, hoping he would be going to their house. He was always dressed in a smart suit, a bowler hat and a dickie-bow, and carried an umbrella which he used to rap on the doors. The first thing your mam wanted to know was: 'How much is it going to cost?' Well, you know, for the really poor people there was no cost at all, many children went to the seaside for nothing …"

Memories stretch back to the days when indoor sanitation was undreamed of and piped water was a luxury, when Saturday night drunkenness and violence was part of childhood.

"My dad just left us and we never saw him again. It must have been the headmistress of the school where we were going who noticed how poor we were and it didn't cost my mam anything to send me to Sykes' Home, but she had to scrape around to find clothes for me to take. It was the LNER station in Friar Gate and I went with my little case and there were other children waiting on the platform. My mam kissed me and I got on the train. I was only seven and I remember thinking at the time: 'Is Skegness at the end of the earth?' and 'Will I ever see my mam again?' It was the first time I had ever been on a train, of course, and after all the years I have never forgotten the smell of engine smoke and the rattle of wheels that seemed to go on all day. When we got there it was all so different for me. I never knew the world could be so nice, just wonderful to me as a child. When the time came to pick up my case and the big front door closed on our little group of children, I cried for the first time, because I didn't want to go back."

Even in the slums, childhood summers were always blue, clear and sunny.

"It was 1939 and a sunny morning when the form came. I was 11 at the time and all the talk was of war. Dad had been out of work for a long time and he told mam it would cost six shillings to send me for a fortnight's holiday to the seaside. I think my heart stopped beating and I was ready to hold back my tears. But dad said: 'We'll manage somehow.'

9

The original holiday home in High Street, Skegness.

now, with lots of white hair and a white moustache, he wasn't tall. Sometimes he'd wear a cloth cap, but always a grey suit. He would walk with his hands behind his back and a spring in his step. He'd often laugh and play jokes on us and he could whistle like a bird. I remember him stopping us outside a gift shop while he went to talk to the shopkeeper. Next thing, the shopkeeper came out with little gifts for us all. Mine was a waist chain with a tiny lock – I kept it for years and years. He was a wonderful man. Some memories stay with you all your life and Mr Sykes especially. If I were an artist, I could draw it all, even now, after all this time.

"A fortnight's holiday, even in childhood, is not forever and my first and unforgettable holiday had to end. When we left I rather think we were the last batch of children the home would see for many years to come.

"My last memory of Mr Sykes is with his hand raised in farewell on the platform of Skegness station."

The Second World War began in September. The seaside had suddenly become a dangerous place and children were no longer sent there. Renamed evacuees, they were given a cardboard box containing a gas mask, labelled, and sent

"The day came, Saturday it was, and mam walked with me to the station. I carried my little case. It wasn't heavy because we hadn't got everything it said to take with me. Waiting on the platform were a lot of other girls. I have never forgotten the excitement when the empty train came in and we piled into the carriages. We crowded to one side of the carriage to look over Brook Street as the train crossed the bridge and I caught sight of the old West End. It looked different from above, its streets neater I thought, and for a moment I thought I was going to cry, as if I was leaving forever.

"We got to Skegness and we walked in a crocodile along what I think is Roman Bank. I remember my first sight of the big double-fronted house on the corner of Scarborough Avenue. I thought it was ever so posh, not a bit like a children's home as I had imagined, it was just a lovely big house.

"Some days, Mr Sykes would take us out. I can see him

The 'new' home, which opened in 1898, and was built at a cost of £1,020.

The home reopening on Saturday, April 4, 1998.

off to the remoter parts of the country.

Toys and playthings were put away, the staff completed their last chores, and for seven years no more children passed through the doors of the home.

Harry Bates Sykes died at his home in Osmaston Road, Derby, on December 30, 1940. He was 72.

The 20th century will claim many success stories – victorious wars, atom bombs, computer technology, flights to the moon, but can any of this compare to the simple humanity of a man whose epitaph was attached to a wreath of flowers? It said it all: 'Friend of all poor children'.

**by Joyce Bennett,
John O'Gaunt's Way,
Belper**

Grandparents' corner shop was godsend to the locals

AS the grand-daughter of the late Mr and Mrs Cooper I feel there are many people who will remember the shop they kept on the corner of Drewry Lane and Talbot Street in Derby.

It literally was an open all hours corner shop. It was taken over by my grandparents in 1902. They had seven daughters.

Later, it passed to the youngest daughter Minnie (Mrs Kinson) and then to her older sister Edith (Mrs Newbold)

until in the early 1960s she retired when the shop had to close to supposedly make way for the inner ring road. But the site is still an open space today.

The Talbot Street/Drewry Lane east corner, showing Edith Newbold's shop, in around 1962.

Edith Newbold (right) and Minnie Kinson.

Joyce Bennett's grandmother Sarah-Ann Cooper.

We can still picture the shop, which had a wooden ceiling with all cup hooks screwed into it, and cards hanging from them with little boxes of back and kidney pills, and 'This is it' foot paste. People used to bring in a cup for 1oz of Indian Brandee or liquid paraffin.

Tea was sold in 2oz packets and people came in for half a pound of sugar, a quarter pound of Echo margarine or lard, an egg or a penny Oxo cube.

Also biscuit tins were labelled and held black and white cotton, boot and shoelaces, pins, press-studs and buttons.

In the Talbot Street window were cups, basins and hardware, with bundles of sticks for fires stacked underneath.

As well as groceries, the children came in for a halfpenny of sweets, and Woodbine cigarettes would be sold singly with a match.

There was a barrel of vinegar under the counter, which was sold in small quantities. And bread and cakes were delivered from Buxton's Bakery three times a day.

It was a close-knit community and the people had hearts of gold, and to thank all her customers, my aunt (Mrs Newbold) gave them all a dinner party with a band for entertainment at the Iron Gate Hotel on her retirement.

Sadly, Minnie (Mrs Kinson), now 93 years old, is the only surviving daughter.

Edith Newbold and Minnie Kinson wheel Joyce (nearest to the pram handles) and her late sister Brenda along St Peter's Street more than 70 years ago.

Death of a Princess

by Ivy Ryalls, Strathmore Avenue, Alvaston

ON the morning of August 31, 1997, I woke up at about 3am and switched on my small bedside TV.

On the screen was a picture of a mangled car in a tunnel, and the caption read something like this: 'Dodi Fayed killed in auto crash, Diana Princess of Wales has concussion and a broken arm'. Instantly I got out of bed and hurried downstairs to switch on my colour TV.

The picture seemed to be constantly on the wreckage, with people wandering around the car, but I didn't see anyone taken from the car, and so assumed all the occupants had been rescued. At 4.50am the message came on the screen that Diana was dead … I was dumb-founded… it couldn't be true. I switched off the TV and looked through the window to see if my son who lives next-door-but-one, was collecting his car (which he parks on my drive). He leaves for work at 5.30am. I decided against telling him in case it took his concentration off his driving on the way to his work at Nottingham. I thought that he would soon hear the news once he reached there. He was told, and he was as shocked as everyone was when they got up that morning. He works continental shifts – that's why he was at work on a Sunday.

In all my 74 years I have never seen our nation moved so much, and so swiftly, it was as if the nation had dissolved into tears, and folded up into a ball of quiet sorrow.

This great shawl of grieving muffled all of the days. I tried to watch the TV channels showing normal programmes but it was impossible. I just had to go back to the crowds on TV and join with them all… I found a degree of comfort in that. When you live alone, there is no-one to turn to and exclaim.

Going back to that early Sunday morning … I eventually went back to bed, and went to sleep, and I dreamed that I was with the two princes, and I put my hand on the top of Harry's head, but his hair was red, like blood.

All through that week I waited for my newspapers to come through the letterbox each morning, but as soon as I started to read them the tears would flow, and I couldn't see through my glasses. I haven't read them yet, but I have saved them all to read in days to come, and I will save them all for my youngest grandson.

How wonderful it was to see all of the flowers. People needed to give a personal offering to Diana, a hand-held symbol of their love and admiration for the person she was.

Almost all of the mature people realised what an unhappy life she really had endured, except for the two months of the year she spent with her beloved sons.

I think she had been used to furnish the Royal family with heirs to the throne. The fact that she knew before her wedding day that Charles was still seeing Camilla must have broken her heart.

Very few people had had actual contact with Princess Diana, but almost everyone in the land felt that they knew her. They, especially women, could identify with her anguish. That is why it felt so natural to take flowers, gifts, poems, and visit a place to pay homage to a brave and courageous young woman.

On Monday, September 1, I walked down the main street in Derby. It was crowded, but there was no sound of voices anywhere. And that is one of the things that struck me whilst watching TV … there were thousands and thousands of people gathered together, but not a sound could be heard, and then a dog barked, and that sound rang through the air.

I thought that the St Paul's Cathedral service was brilliant … so now, so us.

I listened spellbound as Charles, Diana's brother, painted an exact word picture of his sister. It was so refreshingly true, so funny at times, and so utterly

Diana, Princess of Wales.

The mangled wreck of the Mercedes in which Diana and Dodi died on August 31, 1997.

damning of the way she had been treated by those who had used her. In that short space of time he told the whole world about her, and the hordes of people listening, and watching the service on huge screens put up in the parks surrounding the cathedral, rose to their feet and applauded his words, and the applause spread to the people sitting in the congregation, and the whole of the building rang with their own reaction. It was wonderful to realise that almost all of us, unknown to one another, understood his text exactly.

I wasn't surprised that her path was strewn with flowers, that flowers were thrown at the hearse ... what love, and admiration prompted those actions. I have never seen anything like it before, and I don't suppose I ever will, there is no-one else to match her popularity.

I was uneasy when it was announced that Diana was not to be to buried with her family ancestors because the site would become a shrine, and that the villagers would not be able to cope with the millions of visitors.

Instead, she was to be buried all alone on an island in the middle of a lake. I felt so sad. I thought that the poor girl had been really so lonely all of her life, and even in death, she was being isolated.

When my 50-year-old son saw the beautiful pictures in the newspapers of the flower-strewn island, he said that he doesn't believe that Diana is buried there at all, and

that the flowers were strewn so that there was no sign of the ground not being disturbed. He believes that Diana will be put in the family vault secretly ... I do hope so.

I do really feel that the reactions of the Royal family, or should I say the silence in the beginning was very detrimental to their image. I was shocked to see the young princes paraded to church so soon after the death of their mother. And not one reference to the death of the Princess during the service ... it is almost unbelievable.

I have felt for a long time that the Queen needs some new advisors to bring her, and the family, into the same era that we all are living in.

Britain has changed so much.

All this curtsying and bowing to Royalty should stop, the silly garden parties, and command performances too.

It will be the young people, and those of Diana's age that will keep her memory alive for a long time. The title 'The People's Princess', will live forever, it might even be carved in stone. When she said in her interview on TV that she would like to be the Queen of people's hearts, I thought that was a bit silly, but by golly how right she was.

The whole world had taken her to their hearts.

I have a feeling that fate has a hand in our destiny. Diana was desperate to belong to a family, to feel secure, but Dodi Fayed, although he was rich in his own right, and belonged to a close family, he wasn't the right mate

Diana's coffin covered with the Royal Standard and flowers from Princes William and Harry on the catafalque in St Paul's Cathedral.

for Diana … that's how I feel about it. Dodi's loss is just as keen to those who knew him and belonged to him. I did send a sympathy card to his family.

I do hope that the two princes will be allowed to have some fun in their lives and not be brought up in the stilted fashion that their father was. It is a kind of comfort that William looks so like his mother.

Something else that came to mind very strongly as I watched the hundreds and thousands of people thronging the different places in London, and queueing to sign condolence books and place flowers in towns and villages all over the British Isles … It was PEOPLE POWER.

The power of love, sorrow, homage, and pilgrimage was enormous … I'm sure that it was so intense it could have moved a mountain, and it was all generated by one 36-year-old woman.

The thought crossed my mind, that if the power of the people could be harnessed against war, corruption, and all things evil, the world could be a wonderful place for us all to live in, and everyone would be cared for. But it seems it needs a Diana to generate this power, and they are very few and far between.

I went to a dinner party last night, and Diana, and the Royals, was one topic of conversation. I love listening to other people's opinions, especially when they often coincide with my own feelings and thoughts.

It seemed to be a general feeling that the Royal family was on the way out because they hadn't kept up with the changed and modern Britain of today. One comment was why have they still got all these castles and costly homes to go to when the majority of us have a struggle to maintain one home.

Another comment was that the family should have come straight back to London to be near to the Princess's body, and the mourning nation. It was also mentioned that Diana's body, or coffin, should have been available for the public to file past. She shouldn't have been left all alone.

Two of the people present at the dinner said they didn't believe that Diana was really dead at all. And several of the men voiced their opinion that Diana was not buried on that island, but would secretly be put in the Spencer vault. It was even discussed how it could be kept a secret because it would need many people to carry that lead-lined coffin, and who would not divulge a secret for a vast amount of money?

Only time will tell.

Pre-war boom in affordable housing hits Colwyn Avenue

by Peter Saunders Manor Road Hoylake Wirral

DESPITE economic slump and unemployment, life changed for the better for many people in Derby during the 1920s and 1930s as they moved from congested streets to the new private housing developments on the leafier outskirts of town.

More than 2,500,000 houses were built for private sale in Britain during the years between the two world wars,

and many of them were modestly priced, with mortgages available on fairly easy terms. Deposits on new houses could be as low as £25, particularly towards the end of the 1930s when competition was keen in the building industry.

My parents met on the tennis courts at Normanton Park, married in 1929 and moved into Colwyn Avenue, one of many such quiet roads of neat semi-detached houses with generous gardens which formed the new outer suburbs of Derby.

The house cost around £600 and gained the builder an encouraging subsidy from the Government. My parents, Guy and Doris Saunders, the son of a doctor with a general practice in Derby and the daughter of a railwayman, were among the first couples to move into Colwyn Avenue, just off the Derby ring road and close to Normanton Park. My mother, a widow since 1956, was probably the last of the original residents still living there when she was obliged by failing health to move into sheltered accommodation in 1992.

When I was growing up, Colwyn Avenue was the preserve of white-collar office workers who trooped up to the nearest bus stop on Carlton Road between 8am and 9am every day. Few of them had cars, and during the Second World War their usage was limited anyway. Some were jacked up and covered in dust sheets for the duration.

One figure who went to work in the opposite direction was the briskly striding manager of the Cavendish Cinema, built in the 1930s, a typical brick suburban 'dream palace' of the period. I often wondered why a cinema manager went to work as I was about to go to school, but I suppose he had the cleaners to supervise. It was a long day for him. He would return home in the afternoon and change into a dinner jacket and black bow tie for the evening performance, standing in the foyer to wish patrons good night after the credits rolled.

Colwyn Avenue residents were proud of their gardens, spending much time cultivating them. They featured as the background to many family snapshots. Ours was fairly typical, with a small front garden lawn, shrubs flanking the path at the side of the house, a larger lawn at the rear – with an herbaceous border and rose pergola –

and the remainder devoted to vegetables and fruit, including two apple trees. It was heavy clay soil, a back-breaking job to turn every autumn before the frosts splintered the clods. Dad selected seeds from a mail order catalogue and planted potatoes, onions, carrots, parsnips, cabbages, Brussels sprouts, runner beans, peas, beetroot, lettuce and radishes.

A row of poplar trees, which provided a major pruning job for dad, separated our garden from Adcock's nursery, fringing the eastern side of Colwyn Avenue, and providing fruit, flowers and vegetables for Adcock's greengrocer's shop in Babington Lane. There were apple, pear and cherry trees just over the fence – a tempting target for a boy, and one I could not resist on several occasions, although there would have been hell to pay if old Mr Adcock had caught me as he patrolled with his stick.

A wooden garden shed was used for the storage of tools and bikes. It was also a childhood den. Despite the closeness of the park, Colwyn Avenue gardens and sheds were much used for playtime 'make believe' games – and it was safe to play cricket against a lamp-post in the street because there was so little traffic.

Memories of the West End

by John Buckland, Broadway, Derby

I WAS born and lived in Lodge Lane in the late 1930s, on the fringe of the West End; the street effectively dividing the West End and an area of housing bounded by St Helen's Street and Orchard Street.

Quigley's newspaper shop was within this divide and provided a source of sweets and my weekly comics (at various times, the Beano, Dandy, Hotspur, Wizard, Film-Fun, Knockout and the Eagle). One only mentioned with shame was the Girls' Crystal which I had seen at someone's house and had asked my mum to secretly buy for me each week. Needless to say, none of my friends knew this.

The annual bonfire always took place on some wasteground behind Quigley's shop and was often the scene of pitched battles between opposing factions of boys (and the occasional girl).

This always began with verbal insults, thinly-veiled threats and was soon followed by a full-blown fight when stones would be hurled (and the occasional firework) and fists used to gain the advantage.

On one such occasion, I tangled with a boy whose father had been in jail for swiping a cut-throat razor across someone's face. Honours were fairly even and we

finally broke off our fight by arranging for our respective fathers to meet in combat. I don't think my father slept easy in his bed for some time afterwards.

Further up the street from the shop was a cattle transporting business run by Mr King, which was based in a former public house called the Brown Bear. I used to play with Mr King's children and I can still remember the farmyard smells which emanated from the yard at the back where he kept the lorries together with various farm animals and equipment.

That small farmyard was a little bit of a country in the town and Mr King must have been very patient to allow most of the neighbourhood kids to invade his domain.

Pocket money had to be earned, and one lucrative and money-making exercise was to scour the area for old newspapers and cardboard boxes and take them to Robshaw's in Brook Street in exchange for cash. The money, of course, was always spent on sweets or small toys, but sometimes we would buy a box of matches (if we were able to convince the shopkeeper that they were for a grown-up) in order to set fire to bits of card or paper. As the best source for this was a shop in Agard Street, we often adjourned to Brook Walk, which was nearby, where we would make paper boats, ignite them and float them downstream in the brook.

One person who was an influential figure in the area was Captain Blake, who ran a boys' club. I was a member of that club, where boys engaged in various character-building pursuits such as boxing. On one occasion, I remember being pummelled all around the makeshift boxing ring by a boy called Herbert Benjamin until I managed to recover and save face, even if it was somewhat battered. I can still remember his boxing gloves 'popping' me in the face to this day.

Another figure worth mentioning is a lady called Miss Smith who took it upon herself to tour the local streets in search of children. Once a selection had been found we were all ushered to the Church Army hall, which was underneath the railway arches at the corner of Willow Row, where we would look at magic lantern slides of Jesus and drink cocoa.

Football too was very important, and there was a solid following for the local West End team, whose home ground was Brook Street Rec. The crowd was sometimes two or three deep at the touchline and the team was always well-placed in the league and cup competitions. Notable players were the King and Parker brothers, with Roy King, in particular, being a demon centre-forward. It was always a point of one-upmanship that the only training the West End team did was to have a couple of pints in the local pub just before a match (this also provided a changing room) whilst their opponents were limbering up prior to the game and inevitable defeat. A local unnamed supporter with a limp used to collect money from the crowd in a collection box with the cry, 'just for the lads'. However, at the end of the season he absconded with the cash, never to be seen again!

Brook Street Rec was also used by Nun's Street School for football. We used to clatter up from the school in our football boots (or, at least, those who could afford them, did) in order to play matches against other schools. The pitch we played on was opposite that used by the West End team, but instead of being composed of grass as that was, the surface was black cinders and many cut knees and grazes ensued.

My football teacher was called Mr Wibberly and as I was tall for my age I always played at full-back. The rules were simple; I wasn't allowed, for any reason, to cross the half-way line and when the ball came to me I was supposed to kick it upfield as far as I could. If I was a little slow to spot the ball, Mr Wibberly would shout and say, "Kick it, Buckland" whereupon I would thwack the ball upfield in the best traditions of my Hotspur heroes. The rest of the time I was allowed to engage the goalkeeper in conversation, secure in the knowledge that Mr Wibberly would let me know when it was in my direction.

We used to play football in Lodge Lane too, as cars were almost non-existent, and I can remember playing a frenzied game with about a dozen players on each side who were hurling themselves in all directions. The local bobby was spotted coming down the street so we stopped playing, and one quick-thinking individual hid the ball. The policeman ambled past as we all stood in mute silence whilst gazing nonchalantly into space. As he turned the corner into Willow Row the game restarted but he reappeared around the corner. We all froze on the spot, but he only smiled and said: "What's the score, lads?" before he disappeared again without waiting for an answer.

Nun's Street School was a happy place for me and I've fond memories of being a pupil there and especially taking part in the school recorder band. It wasn't possible to buy recorders in those years, at least not for the average pupil in a school like Nun's Street. So, the music teacher, a lady called Miss Brown – hair scraped back into a bun and rimless glasses – with great ingenuity, decided that we would make recorders out of a length of bamboo with drilled holes for the finger movements and a cork fashioned to form a mouthpiece. We also painted the recorders and I recall painting different-coloured diamond shapes on mine with great care. When Miss Brown saw my attempt she said: "Very good and I do like the coloured splodges". Notwithstanding that slight setback, I did make the recorder group and we performed at many schools and at music festivals with some success. As a footnote to this story, I was outed from the school choir a few months later when my voice broke and Miss Brown said I sounded like a frog.

Sherry for a shilling at my father's shop

by William C Burton, Farnway, Darley Abbey

THIS is a photograph (on next page) of my father taken outside his shop, 111 St Peter's Street, Derby during the 1940s. The shop was originally opened by my grandmother Ada Burton at 9 London Road, probably not long after her husband's death in 1900.

My father trained for the wine and spirit business at Upton-on-Severn. His mother died in 1930 and he continued the business until 1947 when the property was sold to the Singer Sewing Machine Co and the wine and spirit business was sold to Burrows and Sturgess. A kitchen at the back of the shop was used by my father and

Joshua Arthur Burton outside his wine and spirit business in St Peter's Street, Derby.

his sister for lunch during opening hours.

I can well remember members of the family watching the annual hospital carnival in the 1930s and the procession of King George V and Queen Mary in July 1933 to open the Royal Show at Osmaston Park. This was the last visit by the King to Derby.

Overlooking St Peter's Street, the upper floor of the shop had floor-to-ceiling windows. There was a house adjoining the rear of the shop let to a tenant, and a long single-storey building where my father did his own bottling. Each Christmas Eve the shop was packed solid with customers, and several members of the family helped behind the counter. British sherry was 1s (5p) for a small bottle and whisky was 12s 6d (62 and a half pence) a bottle.

The premises (much changed) are now occupied by Going Places travel agent.

All mod cons

IT was the hottest day of the year, August 1, 1908, the day my grandmother was born in Church Street, Derby. She was the fourth child to be born into the Hall family: Ivy, Iris, William and now Charlotte Ann.

The house they lived in has now been demolished, and unless you saw it, it would be hard to imagine. There is little trace now of the Derby my grandmother grew up in. I can tell you that it was a three-up and three-down terrace, which shared an entry with the three houses next door. In the living room there was a fire, with a boiler for water on one side, and an oven on

by Colleen Herbert
Broadway Park Close,
Broadway, Derby

the other. Her mother would spend hours black-leading and emery-papering the steel parts of the grate until you could see your reflection in it. As it grew dark the lamp would be lit and set in the glow, though not enough to read by.

There was one tap at the top of the entry and this had to be shared with the three neighbours for a good many years. Great was the family's joy when a cold water tap was installed over the sink in their own kitchen. No more tripping out in all weathers for every drop of water, although of course, it put an end to the neighbourly chats, gossips and, no doubt, scandal-mongering.

After the water tap came the greatest modern conven-

Charlotte Ann as a young bride on her wedding day in April 1930.

ience of all: gas lighting was installed in the house, just in the front room, which was kept for special occasions, and the living room. Candles still had to be used in the kitchen and upstairs.

The gas mantles, like tiny pieces of thistledown, were sold in little square boxes and the greatest care had to be taken if they were not to be broken as they were lifted out. On either side of the lamp was a chain, one to release the gas and one to adjust the flame once it had been lit. The glow would gradually creep up until the mantle gave off a brilliant light, which seemed wonderful to the children. Light also entered the room from a street lamp, just outside the window. The lamplighter would place his ladder against each lamp-post and with his long stick – like magic, the children thought – he would light each lamp.

Many of the sights and characters familiar to my grandmother are now long gone. A swarthy man leading a large black bear on the end of a rope would make it dance in the street in the hope that people would throw money. Others sang in the street, and one particular couple used to come right to the back doors. Apparently they made such a dreadful sound, they were given money to make them go away! A much more welcome visitor was the hurdy-gurdy man; every Tuesday morning he would come along, and play some very cheerful tunes with his little monkey on top of the barrel organ. Everyone was pleased to give him a few pence.

Saturday night was the highlight of the week for my

grandmother. All the children would go with my great-grandmother to do the shopping for the weekend joint. The shopkeepers along Peartree Road would be calling their wares from the open fronts of their shops, stalls displaying goods would be arranged outside on the pavement.

My great-grandmother would always stop to have a chat with Mrs Yeomans, the fishmonger's wife, with whom she was on first name terms. Mrs Yeomans had formerly been Miss Laura Green of Greens Mill and my great-grandmother one of the first workers there.

It may seem strange to write of being on first name terms now, when even new acquaintances of greatly differing age are introduced by their first names, but my grandmother was to have neighbours of whom she was very fond for more than 50 years and still refer to them as Mr and Mrs Pegg, and Mr and Mrs Jones.

Sometimes on a Friday night my great-grandmother used to take everyone to the Morledge market. Now that was something. All the stalls were down the centre of the road and we would sit on benches and have a tuppenny mix, consisting of peas, chips and a small piece of fish, enough to satisfy quite a hunger and all for less than what is now 1p.

There was a slaughterhouse in the street where they lived and droves of sheep and crows would be herded up and down. Occasionally one would stray into the entry and look into the house. Even though she didn't know what a slaughterhouse was, my grandmother always found it disturbing. In later life she resolved to become a vegetarian, although as far as I remember she never quite managed to give up meat altogether.

It is hard to imagine the changes that people born in the early 1890s lived through, but reading my grandmother's notes I came across a passage in which she recalled an Easter outing to Little Eaton to visit the fair.

With several members of the neighbour's children and some brothers and sisters, she made a packed lunch, loaded it on to a pushchair which already had a small occupant, borrowed her mother's washing line and skipped her way to Little Eaton. One person on each side of the road held the washing line while the rest of the group skipped over it as they turned. Occasionally the rope had to be dropped to let the traffic over: the traffic she refers to was the bicycle (you were very lucky if you had one) and the horse and cart. There was very little for

them to spend at the fair, but they enjoyed seeing everything that was going on, and then skipped home again just as they had come.

Sunday school played a very important part in the lives of the young family – and Whit Tuesday played a very important part in the life of the Sunday school. All the pupils and teachers would assemble outside Rose Hill Wesleyan Chapel. After first having tea in the school room, the older ones would walk in procession behind a huge banner proclaiming the name of the Sunday school, and the younger ones would ride on horse-drawn drays and, accompanied by the band of the Boys' Brigade they would join up with seven or eight more schools and proceed to Normanton Recreation Ground. There, after one or two rousing hymns, each group went to its respective field for a sports day. My grandmother was a very good runner and in later life used to worry her neighbours when she ran for the bus at the age of 65.

**by Peter Yates
Bretton Avenue, Littleover**

Fond memories of Little City

I WAS born in Grey Street but moved to Burton Road. I attended Christ Church School where the head-master was a Mr Musson.

The fruit shop on the corner of Britannia Street was owned by my grandfather and I had two aunties living in Britannia Street and two on Burton Road, the Askfords, the Woolleys and the Butlers.

I lived at 20 Burton Road and next to us was Poyser's Poultry and next to them was Buxton's Bakery.

The paper shop on the corner of Waterloo Street was Mr and Mrs Talton's and on the other side of the street was a fish and chip shop.

On the opposite side of Britannia Street lived a scrap

A view of Waterloo Street from Burton Road.

Britannia Street during demolition.

metal man, Amos, and his wheelchair-bound son who I used to take to the Picture House at the bottom of Babington Lane. I also knew Betty Childs and Kenny Dean.

I had a very good time in Little City and have lots and lots of memories. The little alley was where I met my first love, who lived in Forester Street.

It's a family affair

IN 1946, my parents took over my grandfather's herbalist shop in Normanton Road, Derby, on the corner of Leonard Street. They were no strangers to the business as my Aunt Margaret had a similar shop in Osmaston Road, Uncle Fred was established on Curzon Street and, of course, my mother and her sister had helped my grandfather in the shop while they were growing up.

Normanton Road was a wonderful bustling place to live in in those days and I had many good years to look back and reflect on. Looking out of our living room window you could see the brick-built communal air raid shelter which would be standing there for a few years yet. It smelled pretty awful but you soon got used to it and it was a good place to explore.

Beyond this, on the other corner of Leonard Street and Normanton Road was the Iron Tent, a gospel hall which in those early days was mainly made up of iron sheets. It is still there but rebuilt in modern brick. It drew a lot of

by Lon Houlston, Pritchett Drive, Littleover

children to its services including myself and my sister, Margaret as, in addition to their bible classes, they encouraged us to take part in a lot of outings which we all enjoyed very much.

I think the minister was Mr Parkinson at the time, but the mainstay of the mission was a grand old lad in his 70s who did an awful lot for all of us – Mr Wright. He taught me to write shorthand, which must have taken a lot of effort on his part. Despite his age, Mr Wright had a heart as big as a lion's and went everywhere on an old sit-up-and-beg bike which made creaks and groans everywhere it went. He was one of the few people I have met in my life who truly loved his fellow human beings, and I wish that I had appreciated him more at the time!

Past the hall and going up the road was a petrol station and then the Alexandra picture house which we visited regularly, about twice a week. Naturally, there was very little television, and we all thoroughly enjoyed our excursions to the silver screen. There was a full performance then with a main film, a B-film, trailers for the next change, the news, adverts, a cartoon and even, if you were lucky, a travelogue. The performances were continuous so you could slip in at any time and just wait until you reached the entrance point. It was all a bit different to the modern multi-screens! In later years – the 1950s I think – the Alexandra changed its name to the Trocadero and became a roller skating rink in the afternoons and a dance hall in the evenings. It was where Barbara, my future wife, and myself spent a lot of our spare time. (I think it was originally set up as a roller rink in, or about, 1908).

I can see Sammy Ramsden, the owner, now – dressed in one of the light-coloured suits he used to wear, walking down Normanton Road with his usual flower in his buttonhole and a cigar in his mouth or leaning over the shop counter talking to my mother and discussing the topic of the moment.

Going back to our shop, the ice cream freezers were still operative although we should not be using them for a year or two yet when the 'makings' would be available. My father was still turning out the healthy drinks, however, such as sarsaparilla, raspberry, ice cream soda, peppermint, orange, lemonade and several others the names of which I have since forgotten – but I still have the recipes somewhere. These were kept in clayware kegs and displayed behind the counter. They were very different from the chemically-impregnated liquids churned out these days and seemed to be well liked by our customers.

The receipts were run through a huge brass till embellished with a plethora of keys which mum and dad both played with much gusto and expertise. A part of the shop was devoted to a small area with iron-legged tables where customers could order their drinks. I remember Horlicks was very popular, when you could actually get it, apart from the health drinks. In my grandad's day, glass jars stood on the counter filled with various kinds of chocolate biscuits wrapped in gold and silver paper. It would be a long time before we would be able to repeat that.

Leonard Street was where we met up with most of our friends. Edna Shardlowe was my sister's best friend and lived not far down the street.

Next door was Miss Brown's sweet shop where we usually arranged to choose one and a half ounces of sweets each, twice a week ready for consumption at the pictures. Sweet rationing would not end until 1953, so we sucked our choice very carefully, making it last as long as possible. (Of course, whenever we ran out of sweet points we substituted with cough sweets or Spanish root).

When rationing was finally over Margaret and I had great difficulty in coming to terms with the fact that we could actually walk next door and buy unrestricted quantities of confectionery. Then there was Mr and Mrs Jones' newspaper shop where I bought my Wizard and

Adventure comics ready for swapping later on with my mates for a Rover or a Champion. A barber's shop occupied the rear of the premises which was looked after by the son, Bernard Jones, when he was demobbed. I had my hair cut there for many years!

Next, bubbling and steaming away, was Humes's Fish and Chips which was so popular that a lot of our time was spent queuing up and waiting for our dinner. There was one more shop which I am sure sold electrical appliances and where I bought my first portable radio. The Old English public house was the last building on the road, although I was not to have much personal knowledge of this for some years yet.

Actually, the Old English stood on the corner of Normanton Road and Grove Street, and not far from here lived Michael 'Ginger' Heaps, who was one of our gang and with whom I played a lot of street cricket. Dougie and George lived in Twyford Street just down the road, and Roger Mansell lived round the corner just in front of the lodge gates near the entrance to the Arboretum. My best friend at the time, Peter Leany, lived in Depot Street and we were fated to share many interests and some girlfriends together.

Over the road was John Bottom's fruit and vegetable shop where we bought an apple for one old penny. Mr Bottom's mother used to sit in a chair in one of the windows looking out and was ever ready to give advice on any of the games in vogue at the time. John Bottom was a good family friend, and in later years, when I tired of being tossed over the handlebars of my secondhand motor bike when attempting to start it, I would prevail upon him to help me get it going.

The establishments in Normanton Road are too numerous to describe, but one or two others I recall well are Bird's the bakers on the corner of Belgrave Street, and Palin's Motorcycles on the other. It was from there that my father bought his beloved Silver Bullet in the early 1950s. Not far from there, on the corner of Dashwood Street, was the other chippy which we used to frequent in the evenings – real chips were always wrapped in newspaper in those days. Back on our side of the road and further down was the Home and Colonial, a lovely old-fashioned store where we bought some of our provisions.

The trolley buses rattled their way past our windows at frequent intervals, but we got so used to them that we never noticed the noise and they were cheap so we used them a lot. They were also reliable, apart from the poles which often slipped from the wires at transfer points and had to be replaced by the conductor using a huge bamboo pole which slid into a repository along the side of the bus. I am sure that as kids, we never paid more than a penny a ride.

The Offiler's Brewery horses used to put in an

appearance on high days and holidays and always looked magnificent with brasses gleaming like gold, manes plaited and tied with ribbons blowing in the breeze and the cart paintwork sparkling in the sun. It seemed that every day was full of sunshine, but of course it wasn't! Their huge hooves clattered away as they were urged into a trot and the metal-rimmed wheels spun round. It was really great! Was it Moore Street or Ambrose Street where the brewery was located? No matter, as you walked by, that lovely, malty, yeasty smell grabbed hold of you as you took a deep breath and there were always plenty of new bottle tops lying about the yard entrance to pick up and turn into badges.

The Arboretum was a big part of our life then and was beautifully maintained by the town council, unlike the situation today where it appears to be in a state of steady deterioration. But that is another story ...

Leaving for another land

THIS photograph was taken on the day that the family emigrated to the USA. The shop at 43 Grove Street, Derby, was owned by Tom Walmsley and his wife, Helen.

Harry was a farrier in the Army during the First World War, then he emigrated to Ohio, USA, where he also worked as a farrier. On the day the photograph was taken Harry was told to remain sober, but instead

by P. J. Nicholson, Stanley Road, Chaddesden

visited the Old English Gentleman pub (on the corner of Grove Street and Normanton Road). His wife, Lizzie, was very cross and didn't want him to be on the photograph, but eventually allowed him to to stand on one side.

Lizzie visited England in the 1960s, to see relatives in Tansley, near Matlock. Harry Junior died about four years ago. Marie is now 83 and has two children, Peter and Carole, and two grandchildren, Samantha and Nicholas.

The photographer's reflection can be seen in the shop window.

Helen Walmsley, Lizzie Ludlam (née Walmsley), Tom Walmsley, Marie Walmsley (now Nicholson), Harry Ludlam junior and Harry Ludlam line up for the camera outside T. Walmsley's fruit shop on the day they were emigrating.

Pantry a safe haven during air raids

by Mrs Esme Stone, Azalea Avenue, Alfreton

WILLIAM Powditch, my dad, and the son of John and Agnes, was born on November 30, 1906, at Boothgate, near Heage. He married Esme Hazlewood at St Peter's Church in Belper on March 5, 1934. Esme was born on February 8, 1906, at Well Lane, Holbrook, in Derbyshire. Bill died on January 30, 1983, at Derwent Hospital in Derby and was cremated at Markeaton. His ashes were buried in St Werburgh's Churchyard at Spondon.

Their children were: Esme born on October 16, 1937, at 110 Overlane, Openwoodgate; Enid was born on July 5, 1941, at the same address, and also Anthony, born on January 12, 1947.

William was a coalminer and first went down the pit at 13 or 14 years old at the Denby Drury Lowe Colliery (Old Denby) where his brothers George, Tom and later John, worked.

Esme Stone (née Hazlewood) with husband William (Bill) on their wedding day, March 5, 1934.

In 1956, whilst at Denby Hall (New Denby) pit, the coalface fell on him, crushing his ribs. As a result of this he was in Derbyshire Royal Infirmary for three months.

After his stay in hospital he went for convalescence in Etwall and Ashbourne for a few weeks. I believe it was this accident that caused arthritis and chest problems as he grew older and became much more painful before he died.

He was a very good singer and was in St Mark's Church choir at Openwoodgate with his brothers Tom and John and sisters Gladys and Agnes.

When we were small, my brother Tony, sister Enid and myself lived with my parents at 110 Overlane which was a smallholding rented from a Mr Innes.

I can remember dad letting us help in the cowshed and getting the eggs from the fowl shed, and seeing and holding the little, new chickens.

We had a pig shed and all the children helped feed the pigs. Mum used to boil their food and mash it in an old copper.

My mum liked being in the garden and she had lovely flower borders. My dad had the kitchen garden with potatoes, beans, peas and the like, together with the greenhouse. At the bottom of the garden was a small orchard with apple and damson trees.

I remember once finding some eggs and taking them into the house thinking I was very clever until my dad told me that they were old ones that had been there for ages! I just screamed and dropped them!

Another time I climbed on to a little wooden stool at the sink and was playing with the cold water as we had no hot water. The stool slipped and I fell over and banged my eye on the sharp corner of the bread tin my mum had put to cool on the floor. It made quite a bad cut and I still have the scar nearly 40 years later.

At nights we used to help by cutting up bits of old jumpers and other old clothing and mum sat and pegged rag rugs. This made dints and blisters on our fingers because the scissors were not very sharp.

During the war, I can remember hearing the air raid warning sirens and then mum and dad brought my sister and me downstairs and put us under the stairs in a little stone pantry. My Auntie Aggie and Uncle Jim lived in the next cottage to ours and they and their son Barry would come in to see us. I still remember sitting wrapped in blankets on the stone slab and being frightened almost to death until the all-clear siren went and we could go back to bed.

We had a kitchen with a red brick floor and one step up into the living room which had a stone floor covered with lino and rag rugs, two more steps led into a narrow, little room leading to our stone stairs.

Dad bought a piano and I started to play little tunes on this when I was about five and began music lessons at the age of seven.

Another memory is of playing at the piano for my one-hour practice as it was turning dusk in the summer evenings with moths and daddy-long-legs flying in through the open sash window and all around my head! I was terrified of them and sat crying whilst playing.

All the hard work paid off in the end as I gained a Grade VI Royal Schools of Music Examination at the age of 16, and as well as enjoying many an hour playing classical music at home I have earned quite a lot of money over the years entertaining people in local pubs.

My sister Enid and I helped our mum on washdays during the school holidays. She had a huge mangle with wooden rollers and a large handle which she let us turn whilst she put the clothes through. Then we helped to do the washing in the big tub with the dolly peg and ponch. All the pillowcases and the bolster cases and best white shorts were dipped in a cold water starch after the last rinse. Quite often they dried really stiff and hard, especially in the summer. They were very hard work to iron as they had to be dampened with cold water before ironing with our flat irons which mum had heated up on the gas cooker. During the damp winter months, I remember the smell of wet clothes drying over clothes horses around the coal fire.

One of the best Christmases I can recall is the one when mum and dad bought me a bike. I do not know exactly which year it was but I would have been about 10. I had kept on and on about how much I wanted a bike, and on waking up before daybreak I saw in the gloom this lovely black bike propped up against the bedroom wall. Really it was only a second-hand, old fashioned, sit-up-and-beg bike, but my dad had lovingly painted it a nice shiny black. To me it was the most marvellous thing I had ever had – I was very proud of it.

The school holidays seemed to last for ever and ever. One of my friends used to come and visit her granny who lived on the main road at the top of our drive. She had what we thought of as a posh brick house. I always used to try and get the girl, Kathleen, (who came from Shottle just outside Belper) to play on her granny's yard as it was a smooth concrete one and the house walls were brick which made it ideal for playing whip and top or a game where we used to play with two balls, bouncing them off

the yard and on to the wall. If her granny refused we had to play down our drive which was an uneven dirt track. Mum would put the cold ashes out of the coal fire on the drive so that in wet weather it would not be too muddy.

Another of my friends visited her granny who lived next door to Kathleen's granny. Her name was Yvonne Harman. Her brother used to come as well and another brother or sister, I forget which. They were well off compared to us and spoke posh English compared to our Derbyshire dialect, but for all that we were friendly with one another and used to like playing together.

I enjoyed it especially when she came to our house and we went upstairs to my bedroom where Yvonne would

Agnes and John Powditch (Esme Stone's grandparents) outside the Colliers Rest pub, Kilburn Lane, Belper.

act, dance and sing, dressing up in the different clothes my mum had let us borrow. Yvonne was very good at it and I must admit that I was envious of her, wishing I could be as clever as her.

Oddly enough, after Yvonne's granny died we moved into her house which was number 114 Overlane at Open-woodgate, so we did not need a removal van, but between us we carried the furniture, bedding, clothes and pots down our drive and along the pavement. Although, like the cottage, it did not have a bathroom, there was a proper water lavatory outside and the rooms were big, light and airy. It had three good-sized bedrooms, a

A young Esme (left) with brother Anthony (Tony) and sister Enid.

pantry, a cellar and a garden which was hidden partly by a brick wall and a tall wooden gate. There were two lovely linden trees behind the wall. They used to hang over and were covered in bright yellow flowers – hence the house was called The Lindens.

We thought that house was a palace as it had electric lights upstairs as well as down, and we were only disappointed at having to leave all the animals. I think my dad sold them to Mr. Thompson, a farmer whose land joined on to ours.

During our stay in the smallholding we had spent many happy hours playing with Mr. Thompson's children – Brian, Harold, Alan and Margaret. We played either in our fields or in Open Wood at the bottom of the fields or Morrell Wood at the side of Mr. Thompson's fields. At other times we would play in Thompson's farmyard or on top of the hay inside the big barn. We went out after breakfast, taking a bottle of water to drink and some bread and jam to eat, disappearing all day until it went dusk. We went deep into Morrell Wood and made dens among the trees and bushes or played hide and seek for hours. Neither Margaret's parents nor ours ever used to worry about us as they knew that eventually we would come home tired, dirty and hungry, with our legs and arms covered in scratches from the bramble bushes or from climbing trees.

You had to be smart to dodge Sunday School

SUNDAY was the day of rest in the 1930s. And Sunday was another day you got rid of the kids. How? You sent them to Sunday School.

Sunday would start off in the normal way with breakfast then washing the pots, and wiping of course, then I would go out to play in the back yard (we had no garden). Come dinner time, it was indoors and wash hands, sit down and eat your dinner.

After dinner it was washing up and wiping time, yours truly of course. Then when everybody else sat down but me, Joe Soap had to get ready to go to Sunday School, with nice clean shoes (I only wore them on Sundays) a clean shirt, clean short trousers and coat. My mother would take me up the street to the Queen's Hall, see me into school and then leave me. This was the only way she could make certain that I went there, otherwise I might turn around and walk to Alvaston Lake to watch a

by Walter Ford, Yew Tree Close, Alvaston

football match or I might go to the Five Arches and watch the trains go by, or I might go down the meadows to watch football. If I did these things I would have to run like mad to get back to the Queen's Hall in time to be met by my mum or dad, and then it was home as though nothing had happened.

Once home it was upstairs to take off my Sunday best and change into my weekday ones. This would just give me time to come downstairs and get my hands washed before tea.

After tea when everything was tidied up, we used to wait for the people to come out of evening church. Then the people at the top of Canal Street had a treat. A few people would come out of church, bring the organ with them, and all the ladies would get a chair and sit by the front door with nice white aprons on (well-starched) and we would have a sing-song, a short sermon and prayers. Then we would all go indoors, switch on the wireless and settle down for the night. I would be packed off to bed.

That was Sunday in the 1930s. The time I went to bed was between 7.30pm and 8pm, and no arguing or my mother's long arm would come and send me to bed!

Just looking for attention

I WAS born in 1934, the second son of Reg Cope, a master butcher, and his wife Nellie, at 61 King Street, Derby. The actual place of my arrival was Portland Street Nursing Home.

Of my very earliest years I can remember little, but I am informed that I spent many hours in my pram in the sunshine, outside the shop front, throwing

by Barrie Cope Valerian Close Buxton

my toys on to the pavement to gain attention whenever the opportunity presented itself.

My later years up to 1939, are recalled as a happy sunny period with regular Wednesday (half-day closing) shopping excursions to Nottingham or even Leicester and occasional weekend trips to Skegness. One memorable trip took us through the newly-opened Mersey Tunnel and returning via New Brighton fairground, where a collapsing Ferris wheel narrowly missed father's Vauxhall 14 saloon.

With the declaration of war in 1939, a sombre mood descended on the family, with the uncertainty of how we would be affected and also the knowledge that should matters be prolonged, my brother Reg, then aged 15, would inevitably be conscripted into the Armed forces.

The King Street shopkeeping community was very close and friendly, all seeming to struggle without animosity to earn a living.

This spirit was brought sharply to our rescue one night during the bitter winter of 1940, when Pickford's garage, next door, caught fire. The conflagration spread through the roof to the upper bedrooms in our three-storey home, filling my bedroom with smoke. My brother Reg, woken by the noise, alerted my father, who rescued me and sent for the fire brigade.

The fire was difficult to deal with, because the severity of the weather had frozen the hydrant covers, but water was finally located outside The Flower Pot pub, on the corner of Chapel Street, 100 yards away. I returned home to see a large hole in the roof, water pouring down the staircase and the smell of smoke, which to my mind never left certain parts of the house.

I was taken on the night of the fire and for the next two days, to stay with Mr and Mrs Hart, the shoe repairers, three doors further up on the same side of King Street.

As the war progressively invaded our lives, the cellar was reinforced with heavy beams as an air raid precaution, and barrage balloons could be seen on the skyline and close to Derby Cathedral.

Father's beloved Vauxhall was laid up in the garage, with blocks under the chassis. We could only look at it and remember days gone by. The car was later requisitioned for war purposes, and the surrounding gloom deepened further.

Air raid precautions, black-out curtains, carrying your gas mask, the apprehensive wailing of sirens, listening for the Home Service news proclaiming war progress, food rationing, the home economy, make do and mend, dig for victory; the watchwords became part of our daily routine.

Grandpa George Smith, a retired tram driver living in Almond Street, invested in a reinforced dining table as an air raid precaution, while my schoolfriend John Donnelly's parents, had an Anderson steel shelter built in the garden.

Father joined the local firewatch group, later becoming a special constable sergeant, joining the Flying Column of the St John Ambulance, driving a converted three-ton Austin horsebox to bomb-damaged areas.

By 1942, adding further to the family gloom, brother Reg received his call-up papers and reported to RASC, Aldershot. Would our situation ever improve?

In the meantime, daily life in King Street appeared to continue unchanged.

Mr Gilbert, from his dairy on the corner of St Helen's Street, delivered the milk every morning. He was a slightly-built, older man who always wore leather gaiters, he used to lead his horse and dray against the traffic selling bottles with cardboard lids or loose milk from a churn into your own jug.

Mr Busfield, at the sweet shop at No.59, next door, always resplendent in dark suit and grey spats, continued to sell sweets on coupons from his lock-up shop.

Arthur Newton, across the road at the gent's hairdressers, was still dispensing his short, back and sides, followed by a generous application of board mixture to hold down his styling masterpiece.

Arthur Fox Furnishers had furniture and carpets on show for sale on dockets. The shop exuded a wonderful smell of carpets, mahogany and polish whenever the door was opened. George Fox, at the King Street forge, was incessantly busy, blowing clouds of smoke and ringing out with the incessant hammering of hot steel on the anvil.

Ominously, further down King Street at Albert Looms scrapyard, discarded R-R Merlin aero-engines were being piled up for dismantling.

However, with the passage of time, I too was growing up and education was beckoning. This started for me at a nursery class at St Mary's Catholic Church. This was quickly followed by Kedleston Road Primary and Infants' School, in September 1940.

After three years I transferred to Ashbourne Road Junior School, where, in schoolboy parlance, the 'Ashy Road bucket bangers' chided the 'Keggy Road closet cleaners'. The banter never stopped.

Eventually, we were upgraded to Mrs Jelley's class of 40 pupils, whose edict 'You will pass your 11-plus' spurred us on to success.

Life at home was dictated by the needs of the shop. The dining room/living room was directly behind the shop, on the same floor level. At times when business was quiet, the shop could be monitored from the dining room and this room, my dining room, became an extension of the shop, a meeting place for privileged customers, favoured representatives, immediate friends and nearby shopkeepers.

In one corner of the dining room was the radiogram, and amid the clamour of the dining room I would sit on the floor with an ear to the loudspeaker listening to Toytown with Larry the Lamb (Mr Maaayor-sir) or play the new record Run Rabbit Run.

Because the shop produced a range of cooked meat products, like sausage, pork pie, savoury ducks, haslet, black pudding and home-cured bacon, father employed a helper, and much-remembered was Bill Goulding (from Stockbrook Street). Besides all the making-up work, he was capable of woodwork, repairing most things, making toys and cutting my hair with hand clippers – ouch!

In the making-up room was a meat chopping machine, operated by a gas engine with a large flywheel, and this was started manually by turning the wheel until it ran on its own.

Outside, at the rear of the making-up room, was the baking oven which was coke fired. On my school holidays, a delightful job was to help push the handcart down St Helen's Street and Ford Street to the coking plant and gas yard, and return with a supply of coke to the rear of our premises in Orchard Street, next door to Nelson's grocer's shop.

Mondays at the shop were always special. For some reason there were few customers and, therefore, it became a cleaning day when I could help while the display window was polished, scale weights Brasso'ed, fridges defrosted, chopping blocks scrubbed and the shop clock wound up, prior to resumption of normal trading on a Tuesday. Wednesday was a traditional half-day closing, with meat being delivered early afternoon by Castledine's, 'Casso' himself staggering into the shop under the weight of fore and hind-quarters of beef.

In the meantime, the war was progressing more favourably and at one point father came rushing into my bedroom, waking me from my slumbers, to tell me that the British Navy had sunk the Scharnhorst, a mighty German battleship. We were surely making progress.

As time moved on, my brother Reg was occasionally allowed home on leave, and for me the highlight of his time at home with us (when he could be prised apart from his girlfriend!) was a game of war. This comprised two sets of lead soldiers, a wooden fort and my brother and I knocking down each other's soldiers with paper bullets fired from rubber bands, until one side was completely knocked down. I could never understand why my brother always won!

Other childhood pastimes were simple: a trolley bus trip to Mundy Park, with its pool to sail toy boats (I once fell in and went home dripping on the next bus), making and driving push carts with pram wheels and a packing case wood platform, endless games of two-man cricket, shove ha'penny football using real football team names, lots of reading, long visits to Derby museum and library, three-wheel, then later two-wheel bike rides, eventually leading to tram-spotting on the Three Arches Bridge, London Road, in later years.

One regular outing with mother that I particularly enjoyed was to Home Economy, the cooking exhibition at the electricity showrooms in Iron Gate. There were usually warm tasty morsels to eat.

A walk down town from our shop would take you past Pickford's garage (Humber and Hillman dealers), Shelton's hardware shop, Dunnicliffe's butcher's shop, Frank Pratt, the oak furniture producers, Albert Looms scrapyard, King Street Methodist Church with its untidy graveyard frontage, and further on at the junction of King Street/Queen Street, Roome's Corner, with its wonderful aroma of deep sea wet fish.

I mentioned earlier about father losing his car in the interests of war, and without wheels he wasn't the same person, so to improve his lifestyle he purchased pedal cycles for himself and mother, but somehow it hadn't the same charisma as the car, and the bikes were quietly dropped off until father could somehow procure a set of motorised wheels.

The King Street/Queen Street area was a cornucopia of thriving small shops and businesses which were destroyed at one blow with the coming of the underpass/relief road scheme of the 1960s.

by Richard Wood, Bowbridge House, Mackworth

Richard gets in a right mess before a trip to Skeggy

I AM nine years old and my sister is seven, and we are off to Skeggy for the day. I have been to Skeggy before. My dad is a Loco man and so we are going on his free pass. We should really be at school today, but mum has written to the school to ask for us to have time off because the

Loco always breaks up for its fortnight before the schools do.

It is funny being up so early but dad insists that it is late. He sets off for work at this time every day, him and Mr Kirk walking up Abbey Street and then Spa Lane, in the middle of the road. Janet Kirk is my girlfriend – she is going to Skeggy on Friday with her mum and dad. My dad says not all Loco men use their passes on the same day.

Mum insists I put on my best trousers, the others are in the copper. She says they smell, and my sister agrees. We both sat on the barrow up to the allotment yesterday.

I had better explain. We live at 217 Abbey Street, opposite Billy Boden's haulage company. Billy Boden has three wagons and six shire horses, he also has a horse-drawn mower that he uses to cut the grass at Nottingham

Road cemetery. Little Billy always has the best collection of frogs from going to help his dad at the cemetery. The horses always deposit some manure just as they come out. We live at the side of the entry, so we can usually get to it in the street before Michael Macglinchy. The only time Michael Macglinchy or David Campbell get the hoss-muck first is when they cheat and come out of their front door. Dad saves the hoss-muck until he has a barrowload and takes it up to the allotment. He covers it on the barrow with sacking and when we are draughted to go up to help him with the weeding, we often sit on the sacking. So my pants are now in the copper. Mum says that I will have to do the dolly-pegging and mangling myself.

Dad's allotment is at the top of Boyer Street, near the rec. Rykneld Rec is a fantastic place with a big paddling pool and every year there are loads of taddies in it. There are swings and a roundabout.

Mum bought my best trousers for the Coronation. We had a street party in Little Stockbrook Street, and my sister went dressed as Britannia and I went as a Roman soldier pushing her in a wheelchair. We won first prize. Mum and dad had bought a television set for the Coronation from Townsand's on the never-never. Dad had always said he would never go on the never-never, but mum insisted that we have a television for the Coronation. The whole yard came in to watch.

The train arrives at Friar Gate station at 7.30am, so all of us will be on the platform by 6.45am. Mum has already made the sandwiches and these are now wrapped up in greaseproof paper. In a few minutes time we will be setting off down Abbey Street towards Stafford Street to go the back way into the station. Every year we have been to Skeggy, the train comes in ten minutes late. I wonder if it will be any different this time.

**by Don Farnsworth,
Greenland Avenue,
Derby**

'33 and two thirds

BORN in 1933, I have lived almost exactly two-thirds of this century, all of it in Derby, and the one abiding impression of my life that overrides all others is of the ever-increasing rate of change in virtually every facet of life.

Over thousands of years man has gradually improved his living and working conditions with the occasional advance in technology from stone and metal tools to the plough and the loom. More recent centuries have seen the industrial revolution with the building of those dark, satanic mills and a little over 100 years ago the invention of the internal (or should it be infernal?) combustion engine (and, yes, I do have one); the drastic effect of the latter on society no-one could possibly have foreseen.

All of these seemed to evolve quite slowly, yet in the last 50 years there has been a technological explosion, with a major new breakthrough occurring almost every day. While it must be admitted that many of these have added considerably to our living standards, they have also changed our way of life almost beyond recognition.

I once had a ride in a car with a fold-down top and a round bonnet like a boiler. That was a real treat as my parents, like the vast majority of people, could never have afforded a car of any sort and there weren't very many around. Now there are so many it is not uncommon for ordinary working families to have two or even three.

Along with the old cars there were chain-driven lorries, even steam lorries still chugging along the roads. Many carried a circular plate with the figure 20 on it to show they were limited to that speed, while for local deliveries of bread, milk and coal there were still plenty of horse-drawn drays and vans.

Local public transport was mainly by trolley bus; these picked up power from overhead lines which stretched along every main road out of Derby with a complicated system of points and cross-overs in the town centre. Being fuel-less they were environmentally friendly and reputedly were capable of very great acceleration.

Mixed in with all this, I have seen cattle being driven down Ashbourne Road to market with the traffic tolerantly accepting their right to be there. Imagine that happening today! Gridlock would indeed be a reality and the cattle would probably die from the fumes. And there were steam rollers and railway engines! Great smoking

A 1931 view of one of Derby's first trolley buses. Introduced on to many routes around the town, they were normally trouble free, but could face spectacular problems if the overhead power cables iced up in the winter.

An atmospheric early morning picture of the wholesale fruit and vegetable market showing some of the delivery vehicles in use.

monsters that made fascinating watching for a young lad. Which shall I drive when I grow up?

I remember being taken in 1939 to the opening of Derby Airport at Burnaston and how impressed I was with a beautiful bi-plane airliner, the Handley-Page Heracles. It seemed enormous, yet its fuselage would have fitted easily inside some of the modern wide-bodied jetliners. Today the airport has gone, sacrificed to the production of still more cars.

Not far from where I lived in Windmill Hill Lane was an area of Derby which had no mains electricity until the late 1940s, less than ten years before television came to the town. Prior to that my parents did actually have a valve wireless set that plugged into the mains while many people still had battery models. The batteries were made of glass and had to be recharged quite frequently, often at the nearest corner shop. Even then they had a knack of fading at the crucial point of a programme! As far as I can remember the only programmes available were the BBC Home Service and occasionally Radio Luxembourg from where I was encouraged to protect my teeth with Gibbs Dentifrice. Subversion of the young is nothing new!

Another, more recent, invention which is having a truly dramatic effect on all our lives in so many ways is the microchip. I went to work at Bemrose and Sons, the printers, where I was apprenticed as a photographer operating a large process camera as part of a team of

Burnaston airport at its peak. This was the layout of facilities as the airport was outgrowing itself in the 1960s.

highly-skilled, time-served craftsmen to produce printing cylinders. As late as 1954 I had to be able to hand process negatives by the wet plate method, the same as that used by the Victorian pioneers of photography more than 100 years earlier. New materials and equipment, along with improved working systems, came from time to time, but all depended on the manual skill of the craftsman. Forty-two years after I made my last wet plate I lost my job to a computer operated by a 20-year-old who did my job (and those of my colleagues) faster and better. I know I am not unique in this as there are thousands of people from all sorts of trades and professions who have been through a similar experience, and I, at least, was lucky in that I was very near retirement. But what a change!

What of my home town during this period? In many ways it is certainly a better place to live, but in some respects it isn't. Large areas of old, low-grade housing like

the West End and Little City have been cleared and the people rehoused in modern dwellings, but unfortunately with the clearance died the community spirit that sustained them. People today seem to be too self-centred to care abut their neighbours.

My Derby had a shopping centre that was largely Victorian and Edwardian with a scattering of converted older buildings, some quite grand and imposing, such as the former town house of the Dukes of Devonshire in the Corn Market; a motley collection maybe, but without exception they had character. Shops with long, polished wooden counters and mechanical tills with a bell that rang when the cash drawer was opened; and assistants who really seemed to care about customer satisfaction. Many of these old buildings have been swept away or altered in the name of progress. Even as I write, Derby's unique bus station is under threat. Today's replacements are mainly bland and tasteless although there are one or two reasonably good ones. One positive improvement is the introduction of traffic-free zones.

No longer can we wander round the open market, so full of atmosphere and bargains, although the modern indoor one and the shopping malls do give protection

Sheep being driven down St Peter's Street near its junction with Babington Lane. Although the picture was taken early in the century this scene was witnessed well into the 1930s.

from the weather. Wonderful characters like Mad Harry and those of his ilk are gone, as has Cockpit Hill where they traded. The town centre has been moved south and the old Market Place is now occupied by theme bars and restaurants, many aimed at the student population as Derby now has a university.

With the insurgence of many hundreds of students came the need for accommodation, and much building has been done to this end but, without exception it, like the new work in the city centre, is purely utilitarian and utterly without character. Our prison was better looking and even the St Christopher's Railway Servants' Orphanage shouted its own classic individuality.

Having said all that, I admit that Derby has been, and still is being, good to me and I have far more good memories than bad ones. I am retired and happy to be so while acknowledging that life is ever for the young. I know some young people who think that modern Derby is a marvellous place to be, even to the extent of one student from elsewhere already buying a house here whatever the results of her degree course may be. This city is their inheritance and if they like this new Derby as much as I liked the old then so be it, but please, don't demolish any more of the old simply for the sake of change. So much of the new is unworthy of our city. I wish the future generations good luck and hope that the speed of change, which eventually outpaced me, does not do the same to them.

On reflection

by Norman Holman, Bethulie Road, Derby

I WAS born in Dorking, Surrey, in 1929. My father was transferred to Derby with his job as GPO linesman. We came to Derby in about 1933.

We lived in Kedleston Road for about two years. I can remember the trams rambling along. We then moved to Suffolk Avenue, where I started school at St Mark's Road Infants.

I remember seeing King George V and Queen Mary when they visited the Royal Show at Derby. Sometimes we would watch the racehorses from one of the roads near Beaufort Street.

While at Suffolk Avenue my interest in the cinema began. My brother and I started going to the children's matinees at the Gaumont on Saturdays. Of course, I was hooked. In 1937 we moved to Rupert Road, Chaddesden.

I went to the opening of the Gloria and Majestic. You could see a different film every night of the week, between the two cinemas. During the war years the Gloria became very popular for its Sunday night concerts, which featured well-known stars of radio, like Norman Evans, Anne Shelton, and Jevel and Worris.

King George V and Queen Mary visit the Royal Show at Osmaston Park in July 1933.

During the war I delivered newspapers for Mr Sanders of Chaddesden Lane, although the papers were often laid up during the war. I would often pick up pieces of shrapnel from gunfire on my round. Two or three bombs fell in Chaddesden Park.

Sometimes I would be late for school because of my paper round. I used to go to Spondon House school. We used to catch the bus outside the Wilmot Arms.

I remember the Cheshire Regiment was stationed in tents on fields by the side of Chaddesden Wood. Some of the soldiers went into billets around Chaddesden.

On leaving school I worked at Halfords at The Spot for about 15 shillings (75p) per week.

We often served people who were appearing at the Grand Theatre. They came in for number 8 batteries

The former Gaumont cinema in London Road, Derby.

which were very scarce. People used to queue for them. Everybody had a torch during blackout days.

When the war finished I was working at Coles Cranes in Slack Lane. With not much work left, I had the job of painting the stores, which led to my next job as apprentice painter and decorator with Les Hague of Spinney Road,

The demolition of the former Plaza ballroom in London Road.

Chaddesden. It lasted about 12 months. But Les had to give it up, owing to a severe winter during 1946 and 1947.

I then went to work for A.B. Marriot and Son, in Wilson Street. I stayed there for about three years. When you turned 21, they gave you the sack. I don't think they liked the idea of paying an apprentice top money.

Many of my old workmates have died, Alan Morley, Colin Moran. I wonder if Joe Burrows is still about? I know Harold Richardson still is.

I was quite active in those days, playing football for Morley Road, and Cherry Tree Hill Youth Club, until I was injured and had to give it up. So I took up cycling in 1948, which I really enjoyed.

My brother Colin and I were among founder members of Derby Wheelers, which was involved in all aspects of cycling, including touring and racing. By this time – 1952 and 1953 – I was working for Wimpey on the Mackworth Estate. We got paid more bonus money than wages. I was saving money for a youth hostelling holiday in South of France.

I left the Wheelers in 1954 to pursue the art of courting! I met my future wife Renee Morley at the Plaza Dance Hall in London Road on New Year's Eve 1954. The music was provided by Jimmy Monk and his band. The Plaza had a string of well-known bands playing on a Friday evening, including Ted Heath, Joe Loss, Oscar Rabin and Jack Parnell.

We visited all the dance halls in Derby – King's Hall, the Churchill Hall, Albert Rooms, Ritz, Rialto and Bosworth School.

Back to the house that held so many memories

AS a girl growing up, soon after the turn of the century, my mother had lived in cottages in the Church Broughton area. She was one of nine children, and had thoroughly enjoyed her childhood.

She thought nothing of the four-mile journey to school, when she would run across fields, jump over brooks and finally make her way along Watery Lane to the small school house in Foston. She did this until the age of 14, when it was time for her to earn a living. She worked first at Nestle's factory, and later, 'in service', as a house-maid, as was usual in those days.

In contrast, I was an only child, and in the 1950s and 1960s, we were living in the centre of Derby, where I walked, and later cycled, through streets of terraced houses to Dale Infants School, then Hardwick Junior Girls and finally Homelands Grammar School. When I left, in the 1960s, it was to read mathematics at London University – something my mother would never have dreamed of.

My mum, though widowed, was one of the few who owned her own home in our street, but being still a country girl at heart, thought it essential that we head out of town to green spaces whenever possible.

So, at weekends in the summer, we would pack a picnic, and with my best friend Josephine, would set off from the bus station on a single-decker red Trent bus to Swarkestone, Dovedale, Tutbury or wherever a bus would take us. The summers can't always have been sunny, but those were the days I wanted never to end.

by Jennie Wood, Bowbridge House, Mackworth

About once or twice a year, however, we would go on a different outing. We would catch the Ashbourne bus, and a few miles outside the city boundary, as we dropped down the small hill from old Mackworth village, a house would come into view over the hedgerows: Bowbridge House, my father's home. It stood then, and still stands today, a Georgian country house, facing Derby, surrounded by overgrown gardens containing ancient tall trees, with the land in front, sloping down to the wood, containing the brook. We alighted at the top of the drive, and walked down the gravel path into another world.

We always went in at the back door, past the old pump in the back yard, which provided spring water for the house, and into the high-ceilinged kitchen. This was the entrance with which my mother was most familiar. Kate, the housekeeper would always be there. "My, how you've grown, Jennie," she would say every time she saw me until I was well into my 20s. Then she would announce our arrival to my step-grandma, known to me as Aunty Nancy, and we would be ushered through the tiled hall, with grandfather clock and winding staircase, into one of the main reception rooms.

Apart from a succession of lodgers in the north wing, the lady of the house and housekeeper were now the only occupants of the house, but they were separated socially by the class system, and physically by green baize doors. Each knew her place. During our visit, we would often walk the black labrador to the wood, to collect watercress which we would hand to Kate to wash and make into sandwiches. The path through the wood and the rest of the gardens bore traces of the landscaping reputedly carried out by William Emes, the landscape gardener, and first occupant of the house, and perpetuated by, amongst others, the nine gardeners, employed at the end of the last century.

Bowbridge House, off the A52 near Kirk Langley.

When we were settled in the Victorian conservatory, Kate would be summoned to bring tea on a trolley, by means of a rope-pull attached to a series of wires and pulleys, connecting it to a little labelled bell in the kitchen area. All the main rooms had been connected in this way, so that the servants would know where to attend. What the house lacked in modern sanitary arrangements, it made up for in beautiful antiques. I particularly remember the full-size billiard table, and the grand piano in the drawing room.

My mother had joined her sister and brothers to work for my father's family in the 20s. When my father lost his mother and 19-year-old elder brother to TB, within six weeks of each other in 1926, my mum naturally felt sympathy for him. Sympathy turned to other feelings, but it was not until the war years, when social structures had broken down, that they were able to marry. The marriage was to be short. My father died when I was three, in 1950.

And so we would make the yearly pilgrimage to where it all began. Aunty Nancy continued to live in the house until it became too much for her in 1977, when she was in her 80s. We were told that the furniture was all shipped to America, where it would fetch the best price, and the house stood empty for six months, and was vandalised. The roof leaked where lead had been stripped off; brass light switches and other fixtures, including the huge kitchen dresser, were stolen; the conservatory glass was smashed. Such a large house in such bad condition naturally had limited appeal. So finally, and with the understanding of my husband, when it came to the auction, we were able to buy it!

So that is how our three children came to be brought up here, in the house which their grandfather had owned, and their grandmother's family had worked. It was a struggle. We were both country house owners and general dogsbodies. My mother and two aunts both moved back to their former place of work, and spent their remaining years there – having lived through two world wars, and many changes.

Fortunately, my husband is a keen gardener, and when we open the garden to the public for charity, occasionally people will come up to us and tell us of an association with the house. One lady was evacuated there as a pupil of Friar Gate House School, during the last world war. Another had played tennis there in his youth. Now, also, students who have lodged in the attics, return to visit a house which has meant much to them.

Our family home was built in about 1760, but this century has perhaps seen the greatest changes.

Lost at the cattle market

by Dail Seaman, Spondon

MY name is Dail, and I am the baby of five in the family of Annie and Tom, and we live in Abbey Street in Derby.

My sister Carrie gave me my name because she was so pleased to have a sister at last – already having three younger brothers.

She is very clever: she has a wonderful sewing machine and makes me lots of pretty dresses. Richard, who is 18 months older than me, only has boring trousers and shirts though, but she does buy him nice presents for his birthday or Christmas. Last Christmas Carrie bought me a great big Teddy bear; I called him Rupert – he's nearly as big as I am, so there's not much room in my little bed for both of us. Richard had a lizard once.

It's a Friday night in the middle of a nice hot summer, and after a lot of persuasion from Richard, Mum said we

Traders inspect cattle at Derby Cattle Market.

could both go for a walk 'round the square'. This meant going up Abbey Street and into Grey Street, along Gerard Street, back down Wilson Street and then walking back up the other half of Abbey Street. I had a tiny green doll's pram, and so I put my dolly in and off we set – this time down Abbey Street and up Wilson Street – we then turned left into the other bit of Gerard Street.

It was a lovely evening, the sun was shining, my dolly was being good in her pram and Richard said he knew the way......we just kept on walking. After a little while I was a bit afraid, I was getting tired and thirsty – but Richard said he knew the way...... and we were going to see the moo cows.

Most Sunday mornings our dad and Mick used to take us down to the Cattle Market to see the moo cows – we did enjoy this. I think that sometimes there were a few pigs and lambs there too.

Mick was what people called a 'lodger' – he had come to live in England from his home in Ireland just after the war – and he had made our family into his family. He worked at the Railway (as we then called it) along with our dad, and although ours was a big family anyway, mum and dad gave Mick a home too. He used to buy us sweets, so we were happy. Anyway, after our trips down

to the cattle market, dad and Mick would carry us home for our lovely Sunday dinner. This was always very good, with everything fresh. We kept chickens and they were fed on potato peelings and other scraps which were boiled up on the back of the coal fire. The chickens always tasted great.

This Friday night, I was wishing I was sitting having some of Mum's lovely cooking. I was now quite scared. There were no cows at the Cattle Market tonight, it was just full of empty pens. It just wasn't the same as on a Sunday morning!! We set off back and Richard said he knew the way...... After what seemed a very long time I saw Corden's greengrocery shop where Mum used to get some vegetables from (not many, as dad grew most of them in the garden – dad's home-grown tomatoes were sweet and lovely). I looked at my big brother and we both smiled. He was so clever – he DID know the way after all.

All of the neighbours were out in the street looking for us. Mum was crying, but she was so pleased to see us safely home that we were allowed one of her homemade cakes, a nice cup of tea (mum thought pop was bad for us) and then it was 'off to bed'.

I was so glad at last to be tucked up with Rupert that I fell straight to sleep. What an adventure!

Memory of a childhood tragedy

by Dorothea Keeling (née Buxton), Deeres Bank Road, Swanwick

THERE were six children in my family at the time. We lived in cramped conditions in a house with no running water – an environment which spawned the diseases and illnesses prevalent in the 1930s, from the minor ear or throat infection to the sinister polio and TB. Infectious disease would go through families like a hot knife through butter in the close-knit community in which we lived.

Over the years the older children in our family had measles, chicken pox, mumps and scarlet fever at various times, and all recovered fully with no ill after-effects, so when the two youngest, Ida and Mickey, developed measles there was nothing really to worry about, was there?

Both were admitted to the isolation hospital at Breadsall because mum was due to have her seventh baby. Both of them came home supposedly well again, but Mickey developed breathing problems. He was rushed back into the children's hospital in North Street where, a few days later, he died from complications associated with measles. I could not understand in my young mind how we could all get well but Mickey had to die. I thought kids died from TB and diphtheria, not measles.

We were a happy family, and then came all this sadness. A good friend of mum's, Mrs Bates, came to stay with us on the day of the funeral. A pathetic group of four people – mum, dad, Aunt Lil and Aunt Dot, dad's two sisters – who carried the tiny coffin, made up the so-called cortege. My mum had given birth to my sister Ena just two weeks prior to Mickey's funeral. A new life, but my baby brother, just 22 months old, had gone forever.

Now I was seven. The summer was hot, dry and very exhausting – one of those summers in which infectious diseases thrive.

An outbreak of diphtheria hit our Traffic Street school. Not an epidemic by any means, but scary nevertheless. We all had swabs taken and I tested positive. Not that I had developed the disease – no – I was a dreaded carrier. I was not happy at having to be isolated at home, only allowed to play outside on my own during school time, but when school was over I was banished to an attic room where I had to remain until the morning. Mum would scrub and swill out every day with strong-smelling disinfectant.

The public health doctor, Dr Haigh, was a regular visitor to our house over the next few weeks to swab my throat. Mum and dad tried to make things easier for me – in fact I felt special – they bought me comic books and a needlework box. I even plucked up the courage to ask for a doll's pram, something I'd always wanted but never got.

I knew that they couldn't afford to buy me one, so I had to make do with a wooden box on wheels, a kind of wheelbarrow really, which Dad made for me. Ah well, it was usually a doll and pram but for me it was a doll and wheelbarrow.

I was delighted when Dr Haigh came to tell me that I was in the clear and his praise for my mother spoke volumes for the way she had handled the situation – no-one caught diphtheria from me.

* * * * * * * *

"Be sure your sins will find you out" These were the foreboding words spoken to me by Sister Lang of the DRI. I felt sure that when I died I was destined for the other place.

You see, I had already been forbidden to swing on the rusty rails which surrounded the yard at the side of the Gaumont on London Road for obvious reasons. But, I was unable to resist one last chance even though I was in charge of my small sister in a pushchair. I swung over, legs high in the air and down I came, the metal Blakeys on the heel of my shoe, jagged from wear, caught my baby sister Ena on the head, inflicting a deep gash. Blood was spurting everywhere – I thought she would die.

Horrified and in shock, I ran all the way with her to the DRI, by-passing Hill Street where we lived. By this time blood was running down her face and neck, she was sobbing and bewildered. I pushed her up the incline to casualty, almost collapsing as I reached the door. I was then confronted by a stern-looking sister and was crying so much I could hardly get the words out. Eventually she got the picture.

Does your mother know?

"Oh no," I said. "I daren't take her home."

They soon stitched and cleaned her up. I was only eight years old, but it wasn't unusual for me to visit the DRI. I'd had grit removed from my eyes, had a deep splinter removed and loads of cuts and grazes attended to. In fact we kids from the area would go regularly for treatment – without adults – just popping in really. Living practically on the doorstep made it easy and even at our tender ages we were treated like VIPs. It was so simple then.

Yes, I was chastised by my mother, though not as severely as I thought, and I learned a lesson for being disobedient. I have heard the words uttered by Sister Lang many, many times since then, but hers were a first for me.

I am still reminded by my sister, even 60-odd years on, that I'm responsible for the bald patch which she still has to this day.

Children's Hospital stay proved a sweet success

by Dail Seaman, Spondon

I WAS about four and was told I had to go into hospital to have my tonsils out. Mum and my elder sister took me up to the Children's Hospital which was in North Street, Derby.

We must have caught a bus as it was quite a way from where we lived in Abbey Street and not many families had cars. I would have liked some sweets but was told that the rationing coupons could be better used once I was better. The Second World War had been over for about five years, and although some things were no longer rationed, coupons had to be handed over for sweets and chocolate, so these were really a treat.

The children's hospital had high ceilings and was an old building – and I didn't like the smell. Visitors were only allowed for about an hour every day, so I was soon left in that large ward without my mum. I began to cry until the girl in the next bed spilled her Oxo drink – she laughed and said she didn't like it anyway. I also started to giggle a little bit then, especially when I looked at the tin mug that had been placed on my locker, and it was full of the same brown liquid.

The next day, I was wheeled out on a trolley and a lint-type mask soaked in ether was pressed down on my mouth and nose to make me go to sleep – it was very very frightening for a little child like me. Soon, though, I was awake again and sitting up

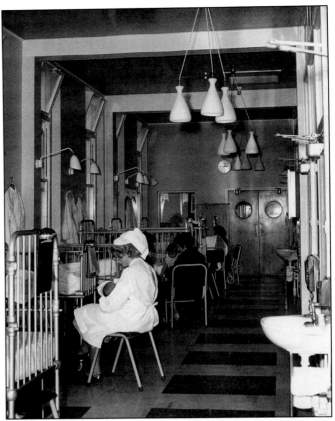

A ward at the old Derbyshire Children's Hospital in North Street, Derby.

eating jelly and ice cream – things didn't seem quite so bad now.

Once I was home the lady from the White Sweet Shop, which was just across the road from our house, bought some sweets over. That soon cheered me up. The little shop had such a lovely selection: there were tiger nuts, Pontefract cakes, toasted teacakes, Maltona drops, and black jacks, which made your teeth very black. All the sweets were stored in large jars and weighed out into little square white paper bags, unless you had a sherbet dip and then it was a pointed bag with either a lolly or liquorice to dip in.

Joan Mathers (née Blackshaw), Glanffynnon Road, Llanrug, Gwynedd, North Wales

Our garden gate bolstered war effort

I WAS born in Crewton, Derby, in 1921, and attended Brighton Road School, then the Central School, Hastings Street. When I was 15 it was Coronation year for George VI.

The *Sketch* ran a competition for children of various ages. We were asked to write an essay on why we would like to see the Coronation procession.

I was fortunate enough to win a trip to London with the following:

"I would like to see the Coronation procession so that in future years I could say I was there. The dry bones of mere facts and dates in the history books would come to life for me. I should be able to see again the pageantry of the procession, the colourful uniforms and cloaks of the soldiers and pages, and feel again the quickening of my blood at seeing and hearing the soul-stirring procession which was the cynosure of the eyes of the world.

"Instead of merely seeing decorations at Derby, how wonderful it would be to see the riot of gorgeous colour made by the procession that all the world had come to see.

"I have never seen the King and Queen, and would be very proud to think that I had seen them in one of the happiest moments in their lives!"

I could take either my father or my teacher with me. My father won the day, although I know Miss Witt my teacher deserved the chance.

I had my photograph taken by the *Derby Evening Telegraph* and felt very excited.

We travelled by train to London and had rooms at the Ensleigh Hotel. Early next morning we were on the balcony of the top floor of the Galeries Lafayette. Unfortunately, though we saw all the procession, we were too high up to see the people in the carriages.

After the procession Dad and I went round the sights. On returning home, Dad never stopped talking about his trip.

In those days I used to catch the tram, then in later years, the trolley bus from Brighton Road to Midland Road, then I would walk through the Arboretum and about three streets, to Hastings Street.

We never expected or received any trouble en route. The most wicked thing we did was occasionally knock on doors and hide nearby!

We played hockey in the fields at Homelands, but I left school before the move there.

My father was out of work when I was born in 1921 but was given a few weeks pay by helping to build Alvaston lake and park.

After working at the Whitehall Cinema for years, my aunt, who lived with us, managed the Douro Wine Shop in Green Lane. At Christmas, my father helped her, and they used to bring the considerable takings home on the bus for safekeeping and counting until banking the next day. What days of innocence!

At the outbreak of war in 1939, my cousin Dot and I joined the Air Raid Precautions Service as wardens.

My saddest memory was helping when a bomb hit a trolley bus on London Road and people were killed and injured.

When working in the offices of the LMS Loco Works during the war, if the station went dark, there was an alert. On walking home in the dark, it was past evil-smelling

Derby Market Hall is decorated for the coronation of King George VI in December 1936.

drums of smoking oil, placed to act as a smoke screen in hopes of hiding the station from the enemy bombers.

For the war effort my parents had their iron railings and gate taken off the front of the house.

On the first night of the war an alert was sounded, all the family sat on the cellar steps, my mother giving us tots of whisky to stop our limbs shaking! We all had our gas masks at the ready as we did not know what to expect.

I remember when I was young paddling in my wellingtons to put a shilling in the electricity meter when the cellar was flooded, as happened before they re-routed the River Derwent.

When I was very young we all had to put on our coats to go to the toilet at the bottom of a very long garden, then later on we went very modern by having a loo built on the back of the house. We never did have a bathroom; we had a zinc bath (up from the cellar) in the kitchen on Friday nights, and hot water boiled, in the beginning, in a brick copper, and later, in buckets on the gas stove.

On writing this, at the age of 77, I realise how very much life has changed. Living conditions are vastly improved, the war is long since over, but I feel that trust, honesty and caring for others have sadly deteriorated.

by Dail Seaman, Spondon

Ridding ourselves of those washday blues

BY now, Mum had a fridge and a twin-tub washing machine, Dad had stopped keeping chickens – we had great big shops called supermarkets – but the chickens from them didn't taste half as good as ours had.

There were adverts on television which interrupted the programme just at the wrong time, and sadly for Richard and I, the Cattle Market was no longer down by Cockpit Hill. Mad Harry (as he was called) still sold his pots and pans from his stall down there, though: he was a real character and the shopping took much longer because people just wanted to stand and listen to his jokes and silly tales.

Soon the bulldozer was to erase Cockpit Hill also and

Cockpit Hill showing the Morledge market, the bus station and the Council House in March 1962.

now there is a car park and Eagle Centre shopping area. Although this is all covered over somehow it has lost a lot of the warmth and charm of the old Cockpit Hill!

But then, on a Monday it doesn't matter if it rains because I have an automatic washer and tumble dryer. Well, we do have to have some changes, don't we?

Cockpit Hill, looking from Morledge, with East Street on the right, towards the Eagle Market. The original Castle and Falcon pub – still selling Offiler's Ales in the 1960s – is on the corner.

Nelson cakes were a childhood delight

by Ivy Ryalls, Strathmore Avenue, Alvaston

THIS century was just 29 years old when my family came to live in Derby. I was six.

We lived in a corporation house in Glossop Street. I think that they were quite new. The kitchen walls were uneven brick painted dark green at the top, and brown at the bottom. My dad plastered the walls with layers and layers of newspapers before he put on the final flowered wallpaper in an effort to make it more homely, and less like an institution. The Ryalls family lived next door. They had two sons, Victor and Horace. My brother Syd and I would sometimes go out to play in the street with Victor but it was Horace that I married at St Augustine's Church, Upper Dale Road, 16 years later.

On the opposite side of the road lived the Wilsons. They had moved to Derby from Barrow-in-Furness, Cumbria. Their daughter was one of my playmates, I think her name was Lena. Next to the Wilsons lived the Bantons, Eunice was my playmate. Next came the Robinsons – was it Gwen who joined in our games? The old memory is not so good nowadays.

The streets were spotlessly clean. The privet hedges enclosing the gardens of the houses were clipped to perfection, and the gardens all cultivated.

The only car I ever saw belonged to Dr. Mary Elmitt when she came to visit my mother. We could safely play out in the street, and stretch our long skipping ropes right across the road. The fastest vehicle we had to look out for was someone on a bike.

The butcher's boy delivered all the meat to the homes on his bike. The milkman pushed a handcart with a churn on it, and he scooped the milk from the churn with a ladle into our jugs.

There weren't any fridges in our homes then, so to keep the flies out of the milk a little net with beads around the edge was placed over the jug.

In the hot summers, the meat and bacon went bad very quickly, it had to be used almost straight away.

The baker delivered the bread in a horse-drawn vehicle, and the coalman used a horse and cart as well. Mind you, we children were glad about that because we would follow the horses around with our shovel and buckets just waiting for the horse to answer the call of nature. We sold this rich by-product for tuppence a full bucket, and a penny for half a bucket.

This was our Saturday picture money. Our dad gave us each a penny a week pocket money which we usually spent on sweets. Oh, the joy of standing outside the sweet shop scanning the boxes and jars trying to decide what we would get most of for our money.

Sherbert dabs lasted a long time but often made our tongues sore. Liquorice root was so sweet and stringy but one could only swallow the juice. Pear drops were a favourite, and everlasting sticks, a long, thin, strip of toffee. And locust beans with their dark brown shiny shells that collapsed between your teeth and let the sweet centre escape on to the tongue. Acid drops, hundreds and thousands, Black Jacks, tray toffee, crispets, marzipan teacakes, and gobstoppers, just to name a few of the wonderful selection that teased our eyes each week.

I can't remember any vandalism or burglaries in those days. Bobby Gadsby always patrolled the streets.

Most of the children went to Nightingale Road school. I was in the infants in Amber Street until I was seven, and then I moved up into the big school. We were put into teams for the rest of our school days there I was in Rossetti team, and at games and sport we wore green bands. I can just about remember the names of two of the teachers. Miss Sutton, and Miss Goodhand – she was my favourite, even if she did smack me across the head for talking in line. My pride was hurt much more than my head was.

I loved school right up to the day I left at 14, to start work. By that age I was at a different school. Whilst I was still at Nightingale Road School, every Thursday I had to take a basin and some money to school with me which I hid behind the vaulting horse in the hall, then at home time I would walk into Allenton to buy hot faggots from the butcher's and then I would run all the way home before they got cold. My mam would have the vegetables ready cooking on the stove, the table laid, and the gravy made.

Elton Road then was not much more than a lane. Apart from a few houses on the left-hand side, the fish and chip shop and the boot menders, all the rest was fields stretching right down to the few shops near to the bridge foot. There was the dairy, a newsagent, and a general store which sold biscuits from tins on a slanting display unit. The smell was mouth-watering.

I'm almost sure this shop also sold bars of washing soap. My mam always used Sunlight to wash the clothes. One day I noticed that Fairy soap had a halfpenny coupon on the side of the packet, I tried to persuade my mam to buy that instead, but she pointed out to me that the Fairy soap was a halfpenny dearer to buy than the

Sunlight. That was my first lesson in the power of advertising, and how to resist it.

On the opposite side of Elton Road was Tilly Bracy's shop. Apart from anything else, she sold the most wonderful Nelson Cakes, two squares of pastry with a wedge of glutinous, dark brown, fruity, jaw-clamping confection, about half an inch thick, keeping the pastry pieces apart.

They cost two weeks' pocket money, or one full bucket of horse manure, because they cost tuppence each, but were worth every halfpenny.

Round the corner from Bracy's in Crowshaw Street was the fish and chip shop. In those days a fish cost tuppence, and chips a penny a portion. When we had no money at all, we would watch from outside for the lady to run the sieve through the fat, dredging out the tiny pieces of batter that had dropped from the fish as it cooked. She would bang the big sieve on the edge of the fryer to shake off the dripping fat, then throw the crispy bits into a side compartment. That was our cue, and in we went for the scratchings. She would scoop some into a newspaper for each of us, and off we would go with a hot greasy paper in one hand and the other, depositing glorious crispy morsels between our teeth.

I can never remember going into Derby town on the bus. Mum and I always went over the bridge from Elton Road into Princes Street.

At the other end of Princes Street at the junction with Dairy House Road was the Normanton Picture House. To go there cost fourpence (or two buckets of manure) or two weeks' pocket money. If there were no horses about we would go to houses to see if they had any empty bottles or jam jars that wanted returning. It was usually a halfpenny returned on each item.

The Allenton Picture House cost only tuppence to get in. To compensate for the long walk we often bought a half-penny of peanuts in their shells, from the greengrocer nearby. There were very few shops at Allenton in those days. I can just about remember Sol Lux the gents' out-fitters, the Maypole grocery store, and Buxton's bread shop.

To walk up Pear Tree Road and Normanton Road was a real treat. I can remember Bradford's Home Made Sweet Shop, Clarke and Pearce home furnishers, and Boots the Chemist on the corner of Rosehill Street. And you could smell the beer being brewed in Amber Street. There were butcher's, draper's, florist's and furniture shops, and before you knew it you were in the town.

Although we never went inside public houses, I can remember the one on The Spot opposite the toilets. It's called The Neptune now. The name didn't mean anything to me, but the coloured lights fascinated me, they seemed to run in coloured waves across the front of the building advertising Bass. Another pub at The Spot opposite to the

Gaumont Cinema, was The Green Man. Further down St. Peter's Street, on the same side, was a tiny fronted pub called The Cheshire Cheese with a little alleyway at the side where you could walk down past the houses into Albion Street – it was a short cut to the Co-op offices, and to the Regal Cinema. The two pubs, houses, and the cinema have all been destroyed to make way for shopping centres.

Also quite near to The Spot was Moults haberdashery, a lovely black and white facade of which a tiny portion is still visible if you look towards the roof. On the opposite side was Peacocks the hardware store, with its bare wooden uneven floor which seemed to undulate as you walked into the back of the store.

It smelled clean of turpentine, paraffin, matches, polishes, stepstones, firelighters, and wooden clothes pegs, to name just a few. Hunts, a fabulous arcaded shop selling ladies' fashions was about opposite the bottom of Babington Lane, as was Silky's the bridalwear shop. Boots the Chemist was on the corner of East Street, and it had a wonderful cafe.

On the opposite corner of East Street was the Midland Drapery, a shop split in two by a little street that ran in a half circle into St Peter's Street. There was a little pub down there too. Thurman and Malin was another arcaded, prestigious store in St Peter's Street. It sold ladieswear and soft furnishings. I loved to go into Woolworth's, the 3d and 6d store on the corner of Victoria Street, it had an upstairs and a downstairs. I can't remember Marks and Spencer when I was a child, but I've just learned that the first store was opened in 1933 in Derby. I do know that it had a cafe in it in 1947.

Our wireless, when I was a child, had an accumulator which provided the energy to make it work. When the accumulator ran down it had to be taken to the garage at the bottom of Nightingale Road to be charged up again. We had another one to use in the meantime. If dad was at work when the accumulator needed to be changed, then it was my job, being the eldest of three, to take it to the garage, and bring back another one.

I didn't mind the walk at all because it meant I could come back home by way of Osmaston Road and turn into Abingdon Street. At the corner of Abingdon Street were the tram sheds where the trams were housed overnight. It was the terminus. I loved the sound of the wheels as they grumbled along in the steel grooves in the road. I can remember riding on a tram into town, but not on a bus. Almost every day the Rolls-Royce car engines on a skeleton framework would be driven around the streets, but not at a breakneck speed.

My dad was a driver on the LMS trains. If he was not at work on a Sunday, the whole family were taken on a walk in the afternoon after we had been to Sunday

School at Davenport Road Congregational Church.

Sometimes we would walk over Sinfin Moors, another walk was over the Long Bridge on Osmaston Road, right across the fields and coming out on London Road just about where Ascot Drive is. There used to be a very old church, and a gloomy old house where we children said that a witch lived.

A short walk brought us to Alvaston Lake. A beautiful park, sadly, no longer a place of wonderment. Two gate pillars stand forlornly at the front of the park now. Once upon a time they graced the entrance to Carnegie Library. When you walked right into the park there was a lovely tea house not far from the boating lake.

The boating lake had an island in the middle of it where the ducks nested. Rockeries full of beautiful flowers surrounded the lake. There was a separate paddling pool for young children. It is a pathway now.

People who worked on the railway could have one free travelling pass a year, also four quarter fares. The free pass took us to Yarmouth for one week. And the quarter fares were used to take us on day trips to places of interest such as London, Bristol to see the suspension bridge and time how long it took for a stone to reach the water when dropped from the bridge, and, of course, on journeys back to Stratford to see our grandparents.

In 1934, our family-of-five moved to live in Grange Street, Normanton, next door to the home of Cowlishaw's the butchers.

A community wrecked by the bulldozer

THE street is Freehold Street in Derby's Abbey Ward. The year is 1976, but the debris and dereliction of demolished buildings could be mistaken for a 1940 war-time scene.

Within the shadow of St Luke's Church, Freehold Street is contained in the vicinity of Upper Boundary Road, Parliament Street, Franchise Street, Stockbrook Street, and is the subject of a council housing clearance area.

by Eric Richards, Millbank Avenue, Belper

This compulsory purchase order, which involved some 350 dwellings and properties, was one of Derby's major re-housing programmes of the 1970s.

The underlying theory behind this somewhat massive undertaking was the provision of up-to-date housing with mod cons which would encourage a higher standard of family life.

Many houses were in some state of disrepair, and declared unfit, most in the area lacked the basic concept of bathrooms and indoor toilets.

Composed of terraced dwellings, Freehold Street possessed a nice amenity style. At one end was W.H. Williamson's shop and bakery, opposite was the Freehold Tavern, with the adjacent Whitehall's greengrocery, and at the other end was Parliament Street post office, opposite Brough's General Stores and Off-Licence.

As can be imagined the issue created numerous problems, such as compensation payments, re-housing difficulties, residents who wished to remain and have dwellings and the whole area upgraded and improved, and those who preferred to leave an area which was being run-down.

My family resided at No.41 (classified as a fit property), which was a passaged, spacious, family house, featuring a wide two-stage stairway, sporting a fixed shower, kitchen units, washing machine, etc. cellar/basement, storeroom, with large garden and outbuildings.

Several homes in Freehold Street escaped the bulldozer, sadly ours did not. The site remains an off-street parking space today.

Perhaps the saddest part of the upheaval was the disruption and widespread dispersal of a long-established community.

We moved to Etwall Street, still in Abbey Ward, for a number of years and now reside in Belper.

Threepence for a rabbit skin

I WAS born in Thorn Street, Normanton in 1939 and my name was Smith. I have so many happy memories – one of my earliest was when I was about two or three years old.

My mam took me to see the big hole at

by Nadene Shrigley, Derwent Gardens, Ashbourne

the top of Derby Lane where a bomb had dropped and demolished some houses.

My dad had a little seat on the crossbar of his bike for me to sit on and I went everywhere with him. He took me to see some 'ack-ack' guns and barrage balloons, I think they were somewhere along Osmaston Road.

I was always singing and I must have been about four when I used to go

Debris is strewn over the back gardens of a council housing estate in Derby Lane after a bomb exploded during an air raid on January 16, 1941.

shopping with my mam along Lower Dale Road. There was a butchers at the bottom of Co-operative Street. He always asked me to sing a song and gave me a penny. I can remember getting quite a few pennies, sitting on his step, singing for the customers.

I also remember going to Normanton Rec with my mam and singing for the soldiers who were billeted there at that time. They had little gardens in front of their tents and used to give me a bunch of marigolds.

I can still remember our Co-op Divi number (45483). Every time I was sent round the corner, at the bottom of Stonehill Road to the Co-op which was there, I was reminded: "Don't forget the check number".

When mam got a marrowbone and some nice meaty bones I was sent to the corner shop with tuppence for a penny Oxo and a penn'worth of pot herbs (an onion, a carrot and a parsnip or little turnip) to put in the soup. She added potatoes and a packet of Symingtons tomato soup and I've never tasted anything quite so good.

Sometimes my dad brought us a rabbit for Sunday dinner. He skinned it in the yard and always gave me the rabbit skin. I took it to Mikey Babes (the rag yard) in Upper Dale Road where they gave you threepence for it.

I can remember VE Day vividly. The barrels of beer and singing and dancing at the street party. A piano was pushed into the street and we were allowed to stay up late.

People were drunk but happy and mam even took off her turban and pinafore and put on her best frock.

There was a fancy dress competition and I remember crying my eyes out because my friend Christine Logan was dressed as a bride in her mam's wedding dress. My mam dressed me up as an old fashioned lady with a cushion pushed up the back of the skirt as a bustle and a straw hat, steel rimmed glasses and a basket of flowers. I was only six and I cried and cried and refused to go out of the house as I wanted to look beautiful like a bride.

One treat I remember well was when my mam used to take me to catch the trolley bus on Upper Dale Road. We sat on the top deck at the front and rode all the way to the terminus, then home, a great adventure for a little girl.

The trolley arms often came off the overhead wires and had to be put back with long poles.

Another treat was when my mam met me from school with my tea in a paper bag, a bottle of pop and a bar of chocolate and we went to the pictures (The Cavendish, Normanton or Alex).

I always went to the Saturday morning picture show with my friends. It was sixpence downstairs and if you were well off, ninepence in the balcony upstairs.

Flash Gordon, The Lone Ranger and Johnny Mac-Brown were some of the films shown.

It was a bit of a bun fight sometimes with the kids in

the balcony dropping all sorts of unmentionables on the kids downstairs.

We were never fed up as we had so much to do – hopscotch, snobs, marbles, swapping comics, ludo, snakes and ladders, whip and top, ball games, and playing in the Anderson shelter.

It was very rare to see a car, so we had a skipping rope (mam's clothes line) from one side of the street to the other. We had to lie it down in the street if a bike came by.

Most people had a jigsaw puzzle on the go and anyone who called round to the house managed to put a few pieces in. We were always swapping jigsaw puzzles so it cost very little to entertain ourselves.

We listened to the radio a lot and my mam let me stay up and listen to 'Appointment with fear' on Saturday nights. It used to frighten me to death so I wouldn't go to bed till mam and dad went too.

My dad was a policeman and one day when I was small I got myself lost (on purpose). I was taken to Peartree police station. I was given biscuits, pop and chocolate by the policemen.

Then my dad walked in, as he was stationed at Peartree – I didn't half get a smack when he took me home. I didn't do it again.

Our summer holidays between 1946-1953 were always taken at Mablethorpe with my Auntie Mabel and cousins Pauline and Keith. My dad showed us two white five pound notes before we went, which was spending money. I'd never seen so much money.

We had half a crown each in pennies and halfpennies each night to spend on the slot machines and yes! it did last all night.

We went by train from Friar Gate station which was really exciting. The beach had barbed wire on it and notices saying 'Beware of Mines'. Just a small area had been cleared for people to sit on.

We always had a lovely time and sunny weather. One year my mam knitted me a bathing costume. The only problem was when it got wet it dropped down to my knees – I never wore it again.

Friday night was bath night when we fetched the tin bath in from the back yard where it was hung on a nail.

It was put in front of the fire and I went in first. Dad went second and poor old mam went in last, you just added a kettle of hot water in between – I'm glad I wasn't mam.

I was also given my weekly dose of sulphur and treacle

Crowds gather in Derby Lane, Normanton, to see roofs blown off and craters in the road, air raid damage in 1941.

which was golden syrup on a spoon mixed with a little sulphur powder. It was supposed to clear the blood and I loved the taste of it.

My hair was also checked for nits – it was quite a busy night was Friday night, then we were all clean for the weekend.

I'm really glad I grew up in the 40s. We may not have been rich in money and possessions but we were certainly rich in love and in other ways.

The trouble with public transport

by Margaret Hill, Queen's Park, Bournemouth, Dorset

BUSES – They frequently didn't turn up at all. Living in Spondon, I would cross from the Trent to the Barton platforms in the hope of catching anything at all. Then I'd find one bus full and myself at the back of the queue when the other one turned up, so I didn't catch that one either.

Buses with windows painted sickly blue with criss-cross tape to stop them shattering and the air always thick with cigarette smoke often made for a very queasy journey.

Boneshaker single-deck Trent buses failing to negotiate the steep Willowcroft Hill, and passengers frequently having to disembark and often push to get them going again.

Buses crawling along with someone walking in front as a guide during the thick pea soup fogs that were frequent along the Derby to Spondon route by the river.

**by Jerome Perendal,
Quarn Drive,
Allestree**

Hard times in Queen Street in the early 1900s

HAVING been born in Queen Street (No 14), and living there for my first 14 years, it is not surprising that I remember much about St Michael's Lane, where I played so much.

As a little boy, who was not in danger when out alone, I was able to wander down to the smithy and watch the blacksmith shoeing the horses, many of them shires. He would be blowing up the embers with his overhead bellows while the steel of the shoes became red hot, and then hammering them into shape on his anvil.

Further down on the other side was a place of mystery, the workshop of an 'inventor' we were told – and believed, because he was an unusual looking chap with long hair. Inside his place, from what we could see, anything could have been invented.

Next door, I think, was a basket-maker. A little higher up on that side was the old Wesleyan Chapel where those great Christians had preached. It later became the workplace of the well-known organ builder, Mr Adkins, who lived in St Alkmund's Churchyard, not so very far away.

Then, coming up towards Queen Street, there was a wide yard, as they were generally known, with many small dwellings and a good number of families whose lives would horrify us today, as would the means on which they had to live, or should I say survive? But they were good people and many of their children lifted themselves up to be very different from their beginnings.

One lady I remember well. Mrs Whittingham was a great friend of my mother and as a little one when mum had got everyone off to school and work she would pay her a visit. She was a real Victorian lady who worked long and hard to survive. I seem to remember that having returned from her cleaning work, she would be preparing her breakfast and it always seemed to be fried potatoes. How I wished she would give me one, so brown and smelling so good! But in those days I would have had a good smacking if I had dared to ask!

Next to her little clean house was the entrance to the rear of No.14. We did not have gardens or even a yard, but shared a little one with the Nottingham Castle hostelry

Iron Gate looking up towards St Alkmund's and St Michael's churches, showing the Midland Railway parcel receiving office, All Saints' post office, the Nottingham Castle pub and Bennett's the harness-maker at number 49.

and its neighbour in Queen Street, Whiston's tripe shop – probably the best tripe in Derby.

On the other side we have St Michael's Church and at its rear the churchyard, now the Cathedral car park, where there were church houses, including the home of the Merry family.

There is not much more I can say about St Michael's Lane. One lady I remember well from down one of the wide yards, the mother of one of my pals, she always wore a man's style flat cap and smoked 2d-a-pack Woodbines, and of course the churchyard was ideal for playing fag cards, marbles and whip and top – a real playground.

And at the very bottom of the lane, which was cobbled with granite sets and had a double track of granite slabs to make the lives of the cart horses easier on that quite steep hill, was Watson Sowter mill. I remember the Tilling Seven steam drive, solid-tyred wheeled lorries, chuffing their way up from the mill, with their loads of flour. Many a horse failed to make that pull and fell.

I had friends in Darley Lane, too. I remember a family living in a very large house with an equally large garden with lots of opportunities to make dens and use our imagination – it was in their back door, shared with the organ builder, Mr Adkins, where I trapped my finger and took the nail off and bear the scar to this day. Also there was the Ellis family on the corner, again a house which took little imagination to picture it from the Harley Street days.

I remember its upstairs toilet with its large mahogany seat and its boxes for the toilet paper, in those days in squares.

The Lamb Inn of the McGowrans and the Keenans was next door to the home of Alderman Arthur Hind and his family – Arthur Hind Close, off Kedleston Road, was named after him. I remember Liza's, the greengrocer, where two penn'worth of pot herbs produced a carrot and onion, a parsnip, some greens, perhaps part of a swede, turnip and a couple of potatoes for a family dinner.

The sweet shop nearby was where we saw our first home-churned ice cream. Our sweets were 2d a quarter (better ones were probably 4d) and quite good chocolates were available at 6d – beyond my finances.

Of course, in my 82 years there are many things to remember. Having started in Abbey Street Municipal Secondary School, I moved up in 1930 to Bemrose School under the frightening disciplinarian W. A. McFarlane. He only had to appear in a school corridor for complete silence to result, but he was a just man, and appreciated by us all.

The Nottingham Castle pub, which dates back to the 16th century, closed in 1962 and was demolished in 1964. Some stonework on the ground floor was believed to have dated back to 1250.

Lessons Learned

In the class of 1933-37

NOW that the old school (Alvaston and Boulton C of E School, Elvaston Lane, Alvaston, Derby) has been laid to rest, I would like to make a few comments about my time there between 1933 and 1937.

The teachers at this time were Miss Smith and Miss Belcher for the infants, Miss Fletcher and Miss Hanson for the juniors, and Mr J K Peach was the headmaster over the seniors. Later Miss Gibson came and took the senior girls to Nunsfield House in Boulton Lane.

by Gordon L Webb, Watermeadow Road, Alvaston

All the teachers were able to teach on any subject. Mr Peach was into gardening, poultry keeping and sport and I also had a lesson in woodwork from him, when the garden gate fell off its hinges. His favourite sport was cricket, in as much that in maths once, when he wanted to show us that we could work out the height of a tree by its shadow, he knocked a cricket stump into the ground and stated as stick is to shadow so tree is to shadow.

In Miss Hanson's classroom I remember a picture of nurse Edith Cavell who was shot by the Germans as a spy in the 1914-1918 war. Also in the same classroom was a roll of honour board with the names of the pupils who had passed scholarships etc. I was not on the board, being too thick.

Mr Peach was also a big believer in reading. He asked us to read all the classics, his favourite being Lorna Doone, but he said if we were not capable of reading the classics, to at least read comics or even the labels on sauce bottles.

Sports day at school was always a success. The Reverend Webb used to open the sports and his wife would present the prizes. Mrs Webb was an invalid and was pushed from the vicarage in Church Street to the school in a bed on wheels.

The school borrowed a white lining machine and if I was fetching it, I would try it out on the way back to school; probably the first roads in Alvaston to have white lines.

On Ash Wednesday we all marched down to church in the morning for a service, except for the Roman Catholics, who stayed at school with a teacher.

We had allotment gardens at the back of the school, where the girls grew flowers and the boys grew vegetables, we also ran a business selling eggs. We had six white leghorn hens and sold the eggs to anyone who wished to buy them at 13 for a shilling (five pence).

The school children who wished could buy shares in the business at three old pennies a share.

At the 1936 Alvaston and Boulton horticulture show a number of prizes were won by the school's pupils. I won two first class prizes for parsnips and beetroots and also had the largest potatoes.

The school was in two parts, the left hand side was the home of the caretakers and the right hand side was the four classrooms. A passage ran the length of the school.

Every day we had a third of a pint of milk, except in very hot weather when we were given Horlicks tablets to suck (there were no fridges in those days).

I returned to the school in 1940, having joined the home guard and been posted to the school in the caretaker's old home.

I stayed there until I was sent to company headquarters in 1942 as a despatch rider at two houses in Brighton Road.

Even the toughies were silenced by literature classics

I STARTED school in Clarence Road Infants during the year of Munich. Mother took me the first day and afterwards I walked to school with a slightly older pupil, Barbara Twigg. There was minimal traffic on the route and our parents had no fears for our safety. What a difference today. Beds were set out in the school for an afternoon nap under blankets. I wonder when this practice ceased in Derby's infants' schools?

Moving on to Hastings Street Junior Boys, I remember wartime 'dog fights' in the playground, as we pretended to be RAF fighter planes and Luftwaffe bombers, chasing each other with arms outstretched and mouths contorted into machine gun and aircraft engine noises. There were no teachers' cars (or petrol coupons) available to ferry me to the clinic on Mill Hill Lane when I took a nasty tumble in the newly-asphalted playground and tore a hole in my knee, serious enough to warrant official exclusion for

by Peter Saunders, Manor Road, Hoylake, Wirral

The old Central School.

six weeks and a scar which remains with me today. I had to limp all the way to the clinic on my own, a handkerchief tied around my knee.

Miss Chatfield, our grey-haired no-nonsense class teacher, who may have been called back from retirement due to the demands of the war, introduced us to the wonderful world of imaginative fiction with her Friday afternoon readings from Charles Kingsley's The Water Babies, Robert Louis Stevenson's Treasure Island and John Buchan's Prester John.

There were some little toughies from deprived homes at that school, but they sat in rapt silence as Miss Chatfield opened her desk lid and took out the book of the week. Most of us joined Peartree library and queued in the entrance hall for opening time, filing upstairs to the junior section to choose Richmal Crompton's hilarious and anarchic Just

William stories and Group Captain Johns' Biggles adventures.

There was food rationing in the 1940s, of course, but I do not remember feeling hungry. We had our vegetable garden at home – and I am sure my mother often went without to make sure her children had enough to eat. I did not have school dinners until I went to the Central School – which had been evacuated to Darley Park at the start of the war – and I recall the excitement when there was a rumour that bananas would be on the menu for our sweet one day. We only knew them from pictures in books, although there was understood to be a banana tree out-of-bounds in one of the park glasshouses. The reality was disappointing – an island of reconstituted brown mush in a sea of bright yellow custard. Was this what all the fuss was about?

by Ken Liversage, Causeway, Darley Abbey

Days of scrumping and cow-dung missiles

I WAS born in Derby in 1928 and my first school was Hargreaves House School in Burton Road, which is now the International Hotel. Until the age of about ten I went to the Judy Cholerton School of Dancing and appeared in a tap dancing routine as a page boy at the Grand Theatre and Central Hall.

I also remember a man playing music on wine glasses outside the Grand.

My father, Bill Liversage, was a prominent commission agent and had three offices, his first being in Carrington

Street. He was a friend of Johnny McIntyre, player and assistant manager at Derby County.

He was also friends of George (old scholar) and Alice Baker, licencees of the Royal Standard and the White Horse Hotels. The Bakers were relatives of Reg Parnell, the famous racing driver.

In the 1930s my grandparents Charles and Mary Roberts were licencees of the Rising Sun and the Duke of Cambridge in Whitecross Street.

During World War One my father served with the Seaforth Highlanders and was gassed.

We lived in Leopold Street, where my father drew a horse in the Irish Sweepstake for £1,527 (a very large amount in 1936). We then moved to Prior Rigg, Duffield Road, where my brother Bill and I played in fields at the back.

My brother was always Peter Doherty and I was Raich Carter. We, with others, formed a club known as The Crows and held meetings in a garage. Members included Colin Bewley (prominent chiropodist) and Gordon Bewley (theatre critic).

I remember my mother gave me money to have a hair cut at St Andrew's Church choir practice, I instead spent the money on chips and plastered my hair down with water. But my mother was too cute for that. I locked myself in the cloakroom for two hours but my mother sat outside and dealt out the ultimate punishment.

I remember during World War Two hearing the anti-aircraft guns on Derby Racecourse. I also remember seeing the barrage balloons catching fire during an electrical storm.

We had an air raid shelter in the garden which filled with water when it rained. Sometimes we would shelter in the larder. My mother used to put a saucepan over my head during the air raids.

I went to Derby Grammar School at St Helen's House, then was evacuated to Amber Valley Camp, Woolley Moor, for four years. At the camp I remember that I and George Young were due to be caned (swished) so we ran away. We walked to Stretton station and walked along the railway line towards Ambergate.

We reached South Wingfield when the air raid sirens went. We took shelter in a nearby Army camp. We told the officer that we were on a nature study walk from Derby. He promised to arrange transport to take us to Derby which suited us.

Instead of the driver coming to fetch us the headmaster Mr York fetched us – he was not very pleased but he was relieved to find us and forgot the original caning.

During our stay at camp we had infrequent visits from our parents on two Trent buses. I remember my mother embarrassing me by looking behind my ears to see if they were clean in front of all the other pupils when she got off the bus.

Instead of radios we had crystal sets. We also built dens in the woods and had small allotments, but unfortunately my marrows grew no bigger than the size of my finger.

We played sports and athletics on the playing field which is now the Ogston Reservoir. We lived in dormitories which were named after Derbyshire villages. We used the local chapel and pub, the Napoleon Inn, as classrooms and would go scrumping for apples from the local farmers' orchards.

I remember being chased once. To escape we waded through the river Amber and the farmer threw cow dung at us.

Among the pupils at the camp were Ted Moult (the late TV personality) and A. J. H. (Sandy) Morrison (now retired judge).

Soon after the outbreak of the war my parents took over the Neptune Hotel on The Spot.

When my father died, Florrie 'Flo' Liversage took over the licence. She was small but always commanded respect.

Whilst at the Neptune I remember seeing the shadow of the bomber cross my bedroom window just before the attack on Rolls-Royce.

During the raids we would shelter in the wine and beer cellar.

I also remember big queues outside the Gaumont Cinema which used to go as far as Palings Motors on Osmaston Road. I also remember the large contingency of American Servicemen (Yanks) in Derby.

I can also remember Hoar's Camera Shop, Eastern's Furniture Shop, Dalton's Radio Shop, the Derwent Hotel and The Spot Milk Bar.

I went to see the Rams play in the 1946 Cup Final at Wembley against Charlton Athletic, where the star of the match was Jack Stamps.

We stayed overnight and bought every Sunday morning newspaper. Whilst in London we went to the Old Windmill Theatre.

When I left school I and six friends went on a motor boat holiday on the Norfolk Broads. The boat was called Bounty and a plaque on it showed that it had been used in the evacuation of Dunkirk.

Whilst at Yarmouth we went to a show staring Frankie Howerd. Afterwards we spoke to him and he asked us where we came from. We said Derby, to which he said 'Never mind'.

In 1946, I joined the Army (National Service) at Budbrook Barracks, Warwick, headquarters of the Royal Warwickshire Regiment.

I met Ernie Cripps (who later became the organiser of the Derby Ramathon Race). I went across France on the Medlock Route. There was only one toilet on the troop train. We went first to Ismalia and Cairo, then to Athens.

I saw the scuttled French fleet in Southern France. Whilst stationed at Case-el-Nil Barracks in Cairo the students threw missiles at us and overturned trams. When I had been in Athens for only two days I saw the funeral of the King of Greece – it was quite a spectacle.

I saw an operation in the Army hospital and paced Ernie Cripps in the Olympic Stadium. I hasten to add that we were the only ones in the stadium at the time. I was demobbed at York.

After the war I played football for Derbyshire Amateurs, Derby Casuals, the Old Derbeians and Rosehill Methodists football club.

Amongst the players I have played with were two Derby Mayors, Jack Bussell and "Dickie" Keene. Other players were Bernard Smith (President of Derby Opera Company) and John Dunning.

George Dunning was a referee and was also president of the Derby Opera Company.

I also played cricket for St Augustine's and Rosehill Methodists (one of our players being Gordon Guthrie of Derby County FC).

I have sung with the West End Choral Society, Rolls-Royce Opera and Male Voice Choirs, St Helen's Singers and the Royal British Legion Allestree (Glee Club).

I have been a local football referee, and one highlight was refereeing a cup final at Belper Town's ground and also being a linesman in a Derbyshire Senior Cup Final at the Baseball Ground.

Until an injury, I played badminton until I was 65, and at present play bowls for Breadsall BC. I formerly worked for British Railways (as divisional operating superintendent) and for Derby City Council (in the city Treasurer's office). I have now retired. Even today, 55 years later, we still hold reunions of the Derby Grammar School and Amber Valley Camp.

How many legs does a cow have?

by Robert (Bob) Bates, Werribee, Melbourne, Australia

I WAS Derby born and bred and for much of my life I lived in Dorchester Avenue, Chaddesden. I moved to Australia in April 1974 with my wife and four children. My parents send me the *Derby Evening Telegraph* almost every week and I enjoy Bygone Derby very much.

I would like to write about my days at school. I started off at Morley Road infants and juniors school in 1946. There weren't enough classrooms in those days to cope, so the chapel at the top end of Main Drive, Chaddesden, and the Memorial Hall a bit further down, on Chaddesden Lane, were used for classrooms.

The headmaster of Morley Road school was Mr Kaye. He used to visit each class at least once a week and had with him a ventriloquist's doll. He used to stand in front of the class and ask us questions through this doll. One he asked me comes to mind – how many legs does a cow have? Of course, I said five (counting the tail as a leg).

My first teacher was Mrs Emery. She was very old even then, and lived in a house up Morley Road. When it was time to move into secondary school, we had to go to Spondon House which was situated in Lodge Lane, Spondon. I can remember either walking to school via Chaddesden Park or using my push bike. This went on for two years until they built a new school up Morley Road called Chaddesden Secondary Modern, and we were the first class to use the school.

Whilst still at school I joined the St John Ambulance Brigade. We used to meet each Thursday night at the Cherry Tree Hill school. Here we were taught all aspects of general first aid. We had a new hall built at the entrance to Chaddesden Park and this was the beginning of the Chaddesden and Spondon Division of St John Ambulance Brigade. A few names come to memory and I would still love to hear from any of them: John Sawyer, Johnne Manners, Daniel Bull, Reg Cooke, Paul Hayward, Terry Alcock, Geoff Yeomans, Robert Beatany, Tubby Sheehan, Tony Hardling.

Teacher had a nasty habit

M Y earliest recollections of school life were in 1919 at the age of five. I was taken by my mother to Gerard Street School for Boys, it being the nearest school to where I lived in Drewry Lane at the bakery, my father being the local baker.

by Jack Antliff, Harewood Road, Allestree

My first teacher, as I recall, was Miss Whitworth in the infants department, but it is a long time ago to remember details of that tender age.

As I progressed later into the junior school I came under the influence of Mr Ravensdale, an excellent teacher whom I admired very much. In later years my teachers were Mr Morris and Mr Balkwill. Mr Morris was always smartly dressed and came to school on his bicycle. He was too dignified to be seen mounting it in the normal manner. He mounted it by stepping on to an extension fitted to the hub of his rear wheel whilst gripping the handlebars and then sliding forward on to the saddle. Much more dignified whilst his scholars were watching. Also he wore spats. I suppose young people of today would say: "What are spats?" Well to those who do not know, they were cloth or leather gaiters, shaped to fit over the ankles and top of the foot, fastened with buttons and straps and worn with boots.

Derby Junior Art School class A. Jack Antliff is pictured third from the left on the back row.

He was liked by his pupils, which is more than I can say for Mr Balkwill. Although he was a good teacher, he had a nasty habit of walking amongst the desks and rapping us on our knuckles for no other reason than perhaps to remind us who was in charge.

In 1927 I was recommended by our headmaster Mr Townsend, (Towser as we called him) to move to the Junior Art School which at that time was in Green Lane, together with my friend Jack Horobin. There we found we were having to endure general education lessons, apart from art, which we had already received at Gerard Street, thanks to the excellent tuition we received there. I found myself being very inattentive at times, much to the annoyance of the teachers. Mr Kent, one of the general education teachers, had a face which was easy to sketch, and if he had lifted the lid of my desk, several cartoons would have been found there, which I do not think he would have liked.

Then there was Miss Rogers, Polly as we called her – but not to her face – who took us for other general subjects.

Our sports teacher, Mr Palmer, took us for football on Normanton recreation ground and I cannot forget the kick I received from him during a game. The mark I am still left with on my shin always reminds me of him.

Another of the so-called art classes we had to endure was to learn country dancing. Urgh! This took place in the Unity Hall at the corner of Burton Road and Normanton Road, now demolished. The girls enjoyed it but we chaps thought it was cissy as we performed our 'set and turn singles'. Our headmaster, Mr Simmonds, was the father of Miss Millicent Simmonds who at that time was the owner of a School of Dancing, and I remember he was keen on us young people joining his daughter's dancing school, but I wasn't interested in that! Mr Simmonds was always immaculately dressed, always wearing striped trousers and a black tail coat and his tie unknotted but held in place by a tie ring. He was a strict disciplinarian but very fair and got on well with his pupils.

Mr Sadler took us for technical drawing, that is for those of us who aspired to become draughtsmen. I remember we had to measure various items of machinery in the building and draw them to scale on cartridge paper. Then we had to trace them on to tracing paper in order to produce a blueprint. This was achieved by fitting the tracing into a frame together with a sheet of light sensitive paper and placing it in a sunlit window and hoping the sun shone! The light changed the background blue leaving the lines white and so we produced a blueprint. That's how it was in those early days. After leaving school I submitted the drawings and blueprints to prospective employers, and so my studies in draughtsmanship came in useful.

The subject I liked most was calligraphy, the art of writing, particularly with relation to the old English style of hand printing of manuscripts which I still enjoy doing now.

The boys could take woodwork or metalwork. I chose metalwork, whilst at the same time the girls would be being taught needlework. I cannot recall the names of the teachers but I do recall Mr Yeomans was the assistant master taking us for metalwork. I managed to produce an enamelled brass box, a copper chalice which was later silver plated and a copper coffee pot. I don't know what happened to the pot, I have an idea it went on exhibition to show the pupil's capabilities, but I still have the box and chalice at home. In retrospect, I wish I had taken up woodwork – it would have been much more useful to me in later years.

All new boys arriving at the school were initiated by the older boys, that is they were ducked in the wash basins. Of course the following year it was my turn to inflict this on the unsuspecting newcomers. I never found out what the girls got up to, but they disliked stink bombs thrown into their cloakrooms.

In the summer, we could wear boaters, that is, straw hats emblazoned with the School of Art badge on a blue-and-white ribbon, the school colours. Again the older section took great glee in snatching the hats from our heads and impaling them on the hat pegs in the cloakroom and of course damaging them. That was the idea and we had to wear them in the damaged condition. However as soon as the autumn term ended, we changed back into our caps. We were not allowed to attend school without headgear.

We had a longer school holiday in the summer than other schools but whilst on holiday we had to produce drawings, paintings etc. of some aspect of art, at least one item for each week of the holiday to be produced for examination on return to school.

Subsequently I had the opportunity to stay on a further year, gaining entry into the Senior School of Art where at evening classes, which I also attended, I was lucky to meet my late wife at the age of 16 – happy days.

Such are my memories of school life 70 years ago.

Nourishing dinners and formidable teachers

by Dulcie Morley (née Caygill), Spondon, Derby

I BEGAN my school life in 1945, leaving in 1955. Like many, I started at the relatively new school, Roe Farm, Chaddesden. I lived on Northwood Avenue which at that time was blocked off from Renfrew Street by a small wooded area, which seemed quite large at the time when we used to go and sit inside it. I knew many of the lovely people mentioned in past Bygones, going that route often to school. Roe Farm was a lovely school, surrounded by fields and to the back farm land, and to the left the Derwent Isolation Hospital. Estates and other schools wouldn't appear for some years.

We all, or most of us, seemed to enjoy school, and all got on well together. I can't recall nasty ways or bullying. If, on occasions, boys disagreed, they went down the field, had a few pushes, shoves and a punch, on a one-to-one basis, and usually emerged from the circle round them with arms around each other, having settled their differences. I always thought this odd, but then I was a girl! We didn't have so-called 'girl power' in those days.

The school was fronted by an open verandah. Milk crates were stacked up, ready to be distributed by milk monitors at first play time. I hated milk, but we had to drink it, the benefits being felt in later life. I'm sad this was stopped, as this, and good nourishing old-fashioned dinners gave all the balance that was needed in a child's diet. There were no snacks in those days, sweets (all unwrapped) were on ration and we didn't have money anyway. We did, I remember, eat 'chewing wood' where you sucked a sweet-tasting juice from the wood, and locust sticks – awful-tasting stuff, but we ate those, also small hard liquorice sticks. I'm sure these were really medicinal, but we ate them anyway. Sometimes we ate yellow sherbet which made the tongue sore! We started and ended the day with prayer, had a nature table, did gardening once a week, and country dancing, all as well as the three Rs.

Our headmistress was Miss Richards or Richardson, and I'm sure many will remember Miss Forceph. A ramrod-straight tall, ginger-haired lady, very strict but kind and fair, she lived on Wiltshire Road, and on retiring, always welcomed visits from pupils past and present.

I seem to remember writing on slates for a short time, I don't know what the reason was, other than paper shortage due to war. Also, I remember most of us, being poor, due to shortage of money and availability, having to wear wellingtons when there were no shoes, and I do recall being the proud owner, later, of a pair of clogs, wooden and studded.

Our playtime activities went with the seasons, whip and top, Easter, stripping, two ball, tick and hit games, hop scotch and singing.

A nursery school joined the infant and junior schools (it still exists). This was a full-time free nursery school, and I think it was for working war mothers at first (my own daughter was to go there in later years, free and full time, she loved it).

The junior school was run by Mr Moseley the head, another very strict but kind teacher, very respected. We had a decorative pond on the St Andrew's View side with a grassed area, where we used to sit and talk at dinner or play time. I think this was filled in due to the polio outbreak in the 1940s, as was Chaddesden Park paddling pool and other water areas.

We had lovely school dinners. I'm sure the caretakers and cook were Mr and Mrs Walmsley, a Mrs Woods and others I can't remember the names of. All kind, sensible, caring people. I don't know how they produced such food with rationing.

The cane was still used, but very rarely, and a few pieces of chalk flew through the air at times. I can't say I agree with these methods, but it didn't seem to do any harm. One didn't run home with tales, as mothers didn't seem to go complaining in those days, it was left to the teachers.

The world seemed much quieter after the war. I can't recall people shouting so much. We were lucky, without the traffic, children were usually taken to school for three to five days to get to know the route and afterwards went with other members of family or friends, the fear of strangers unheard of. We were very fortunate with our freedom. We belonged to the era where most mothers were at home all the time.

We lived simpler lives then, with no electrics as such, and we still had a flat iron. Most of the cooking was done over the fire, and we used to blacklead it. The bath, which had a heavy wooden lid and was kept on a hook on the wall, was kept in the back kitchen. There was a sink and cooker, but money was needed for the meter, so the fire served two purposes. This was the only form of heating (most people changed these in the 60s).

It was very cold getting up for school in winter, and we only had lino on the floor with a few 'peg' rugs. Everyone helped to make these using clean sack cloth, and a bag of cut-up pieces of cloth or wool, a design was put on and pegged through. These were done on winter evenings in front of the fire, while at the same time playing guessing what pictures one could see in the flames and all talking together. Can anyone remember the liberty bodice, with its small buttons down the front? It was put on at the end of autumn and never taken off until June 1.

Moving on, I went to Derwent School Seniors on Beaufort Street, Chaddesden, another wonderful school run by dedicated teachers. This was two separate schools in one building, and another relatively new school. I'm sad it's not used as a school now. The infant and junior school disappeared to be replaced with a nursing home. Many of us would go to the youth club there from the age of 13 onwards. When I visit a relative in the home, I can squint and almost see us all laughing, talking, sharing sports and dancing, summer and winter.

Back at school, the girls were upstairs, and the boys down, the playgrounds separated by a white line dividing them on each side of school. Woe betide anyone crossing this line, although all being aware when playing netball or stoolball, that we were being watched by the boys. The girls' school was headed by Miss Bryant, a formidable lady, way ahead of her time in my opinion when I look back. She was very strict, and very respected, but we were a little in awe of her. Her deputy was Miss Richardson, and our class teacher for three years at her request – Miss Moor. Other names, (forgive me if I've forgotten anyone) were Mrs Scott, Mrs Clarke, Mrs Snow, Mrs Roberts, Mrs Chambers, Mrs Truscott, Mrs Stanley, Mrs Brown, Miss Hawks, Mrs Beard, the latter (née Miss Williams) our cookery teacher who taught us well.

I remember having a few clashes, as I thought I knew it all with cookery, but we had fun with learning as well. We first made our apron and hat, then had to take apart and clean the cookers, then clean and stock the pantry, then we cooked good food, the amount depending on how many people were in the family. We all learnt everything – the three Rs, and crafts etc, first at a basic level, moving on to what one was capable of. And we always took home a good nourishing and edible meal for the family.

Mrs Jobey, our drama and classical reading teacher, was a wonderful character who made all forms of literature come to life. I used to see her from time to time in later years in Brindley's Cafe, and with a flourish of her arm she called one over to chat with her. Lastly, (and I apologise if I've forgotten anyone) was our dance teacher Miss Kinner, who I thought so beautiful, so slim and graceful. She also gave up every lunch time to teach us ballroom dancing, and on Wednesdays the boys came up for mixed dancing, I only went to Wednesdays twice, as no-one asked me to dance, and I was shy.

Our teachers were all extremely dedicated, and taught us so much more than just academics. We learnt much regarding morals, and health care, social behaviour, and had fun and friendship and were very disciplined at all times. All the teachers gave and commanded respect. We have much to thank them for.

Our head and teachers all wore cap and gown for morning assembly every day. We began with prayer and singing and a few words from the head. We stood or sat on the floor, with our eyes to the front at all times. We stood when a teacher entered a room and sat when we were told to, and we also stood when saying something. I've noticed that this doesn't happen today, but I feel that apart from others hearing what is being said clearer, it gives the speaker confidence.

On starting school, we were divided up into four

houses named after famous women, and were told their stories – they were Astor, Fry, Nightingale and Macmillan. We then gained or lost team points, on manners, posture, good work, etc. Looking back, I'm amazed at the honesty with this, as we had a team leader who put plus or minus points in the book. Life was simpler then: no outside influences, TV was just being obtained by most families, but TV only ran from about 5.30pm to 10.30pm. The battle of the sexes and political correctness were unheard of. I'm sorry I have no photographs to show for these happy years. I started my school life and finished it with the same set of girls, we keep in touch and some of us are close friends. Our school hymn was Jerusalem, and it was sung with pride on speech days at the Queen Street baths, with boards over the baths.

We got an all-round education and much more, realising we were very lucky to be in an era where you all left school with a job to go to. Sadly that is not the case nowadays. I feel this makes such a difference to how one copes with the time from leaving school to reaching maturity.

Every Christmas, the boys put on a pantomime for the girls and teachers to go and watch, I remember these to be very professionally done, especially Cinderella in, I think, 1952 or 1953, which was one of the best and funniest I've ever seen.

We had a gym, but for outdoor sports we went over to the racecourse. For swimming, we walked crocodile fashion into Derby, to Queen Street baths. We sometimes went or came back a different route, learning about Derby's history on the way.

I have many wonderful memories of my school days. Although both my parents died during these years, I can only remember kindness from school friends and staff. I have much to say thank you for. We were all quite poor moneywise, but very rich in friendship. I wonder what today's memories would read like, I only hope they're half as good as the ones I recall.

The magic of school camp by the sea

by Harold Richardson, Trowels Lane, Derby

WHILE for those who were schoolchildren in the 1920s and 1930s, the name Derby Borough Education Committee Schools' Camp may not ring many nostalgic bells, mention of a town on the north coast of Wales would most certainly evoke affectionate reminiscences.

Each summer throughout those otherwise grim years of 1930 to 1939, about 400 boys and the same number of girls in turn, were given the chance of a week of great adventure in the schools' camp at Abergele. For most it was the chance for their first ride on a train and their first wondrous sight of the sea.

The camp consisted of a huge marquee and something like 25 bell tents, all of which were hired. A field close to the beach was rented each year from a local farmer and the camp was laid out in a huge rectangle, with a playing area in the centre for football and cricket.

Although the cost for some was probably more, I remember the struggle my parents had to find the 6s 6d (35p), charged at our school for the week's holiday.

They then had the extra anxiety of having to provide me with an enamel mug and plate, a knife, fork and spoon, even pyjamas got a mention, as well as extra clothing and boots. My dad's old service kitbag was ideal for packing all this in.

Not only were such things needed, but pocket money too, and I remember how we were encouraged to save our pennies from the beginning of the school year. Thrift was very much more of a virtue than it is today.

On arrival, we would all would be lined up in order of school, each school being allocated its own tent. A hot meal would be waiting, cooked by some of the 25 men and 25 women teachers who had voluntarily given up a couple of weeks of their own summer holiday to help with the camp activities.

Camp rules would be read out, and one of the more important ones concerned swimming in the sea. We were told that any boy who attempted to go swimming unaccompanied by a teacher would be packed off home to Derby on the next train. As far as I know, nobody ever was, and that went for the rest of the rules. Those days, even on holiday, discipline was accepted as the normal way of things.

There was a camp bank and camp shop, and we were persuaded to put our pocket money into the bank from which withdrawals could be made after each meal.

The boys of each tent were required to do orderly duty. This meant being awakened one early morning and going along in the chill of the dawn to assist the cook in preparing breakfast for 200. It was no easy job to keep a 'dixie' full of porridge stirred, so I remember how we worked in relays, a team of three to each dixie.

I can never remember homesickness as being much of

a problem, though many were away from their parents for the first time.

The conditions a lot of us had left behind, dark slums and real poverty, could not come near to competing with the fresh air, good food, the sea, the shingle beaches, the funfair at nearby Rhyl, and the games and country walks organised by caring teachers.

On a carefully-chosen day, without mist or rain, an expedition into the mountains near to Abergele was one of the highlights of the week.

Each boy or girl carried a paper bag containing beef and cheese sandwiches, a tomato, a banana, a piece of separately-wrapped fruit cake and lemonade powder to make drinks from mountain streams. Then, in the charge of experienced leaders, we would set off in a long line.

After all the years, I can still recall the singing, the high-spirited jostling and laughter, the steep climb and the banquet of sandwiches on reaching the summit – nor has that glow of achievement altogether faded with time that took so much of the weariness out of the slower return to camp.

Friday was the day of departure and the camp had to be left spick and span for the next arrivals. That meant a busy Thursday afternoon. We were formed up side by side across the camp site, and at the blow of a whistle we all moved forward across that vast field. Every scrap of litter was collected to be put into bags, and every pan and stove scrubbed until they were shining.

There would be a camp concert and a sing-song on that last night.

During an interval a prize of a shilling was handed out to each member of the best kept tent, the best orderlies and winners of the football and other competitions.

It all ended when the Second World War began. Abergele camp lives on only in the memories of those who get fewer each year… soon to be gone forever, like those dedicated teachers and all who made it so successful and delightful a project.

Those who can look back on this brief but so bright an interlude in a long-ago childhood must surely experience a glow of nostalgia whenever the name of Abergele is mentioned.

Shirley caught napping at 'Firsy' school

MY earliest memory concerning Firs Estate School is of my sister and our friend, Joan, who lived across the road, running up the street, hiding round the corner and shouting to me to fetch my coat and they would take me to school. Of course they didn't wait for me, I was too young.

by Shirley Hitchcock, Weavers Green, Mickleover

I remember my first day at nursery, it would be about 1942. I would be three. I was shown my coat peg in the cloakroom, this was just inside the doorway of the nursery – the left-hand side of the building approached from Raven Street.

A very stern-looking headmistress approached and I was led to a very small chair. I didn't know her importance then, but she looked like a very old 'Victorian' lady. She wore a high-necked dress in black with a long skirt which finished just above her black boots. Her hair was scraped back into a bun, she wore small glasses and I never remember her smiling.

In the afternoons, camp beds would be arranged in rows, and we were given a grey blanket and told to go to sleep! I was very disappointed as I wanted the blanket with the cat embroidered on it in red wool – I had to make do with a blanket sporting an embroidered car or lorry.

The first activity I remember was of sharing a seesaw: it was boat-shaped, a metal-framed apparatus. I must have bounced too much as the other girl tumbled out. Being in the playground it must have hurt her, I don't know how badly, but I do remember her screams. She later became my friend, her name was Sonia.

My favourite lesson/activity in those early days was music and movement. The teacher would turn on the radio and we were instructed to do various activities. We wore our vest and pants and danced barefoot. I remember playing with small beanbags, we had to gracefully throw them in the air, twirl round and catch them. Sometimes were were chosen to 'do a solo', like a budding Isadora Duncan!

The afternoon naps must have continued for some time as I remember being asked to take a girl home, because she had been sick in her bed. The teacher whispered to me that she lived in Dean Street; I can't believe I was allowed to escort her home, but I did.

I had one very horrid day when in the infant school. All the children were sitting cross-legged in the hall ready for assembly. We sang a couple of hymns and the head mistress gave a few notices. Suddenly I heard my name – I was instructed to go to the platform and was ridiculed in front of the whole school.

Apparently, a girl had been given money by her grandmother, who lived close to my house, to buy bread for her on the way home from school. The shop was on the corner of Leman Street and Boyer Street, and the lady had two very vicious Pekinese dogs. Anyway, I was supposed to have taken her bread money and spent it! It was untrue but I never forgot that dreadful humiliation, I cried for the rest of the day. I never spoke to the girl again, her name was Jean.

Alongside the nursery classes was a small garden. We were encouraged to keep a piece to dig and put worms in jars!

I loved to sing and dance and play in the band. The first hymn I remember learning and singing was Glad That I Live Am I.

Shirley Hitchcock's first school photograph in the 1940s.

Times must have been hard for families during the war. I remember a lovely young lady teacher in the infants department who would bring double lunch so that some of us could share with her. We had to pay tuppence ha'penny per week for our milk but it always seemed to be ice cold. Sometimes you could have two bottles if a child was away. We would take it in turns to be milk monitors. I loved having responsibilities.

Before I left the infants school I remember two landmarks in my education. Number one was the pride in learning to tie my shoe laces, this wonderful accomplishment was followed by learning to 'tipple-up' or handstand against the school wall.

Rite of passage and I moved to the junior school.

We entered school via Percy Street, and the cloakroom was in front of the entrance door and the headmistress' office was next to this. The first classroom on the left was my first year room and I remember making and embroidering a Radio Times cover. It was pale green cotton, the pattern was unusually modern, not my usual design, and my mother didn't like it, particularly (although I think the charge of 2s 6d for materials was more the reason), so the teacher bought it for her home.

I loved art, music, English, history and PE. Miss Brown, the deputy head was very encouraging, and she entered one of my paintings in the children's art exhibition at Derby Museum. I don't remember if it came anywhere – compliments and prizes weren't a priority in those days.

I remember a new PE kit being introduced – the bottoms were navy or green knickers and the tops were in red, blue, green and yellow and were shaped like a triangle tied at the back and a drawstring round the neck. We were allowed to take these wonderful articles home for washing. I remember going for tea at a friend's house in Moss Street. After tea, June and I did a 'demo' for her

mum and dad – budding acrobats! We had a new vaulting horse in the hall and I was always willing to demonstrate new exercises. I aimed for the handles on one occasion, slipped and ended up underneath the horse. The class thought it highly amusing, but I was told off.

At Christmas time, each class would present a play to the school. One year I was chosen for a part and had a new cream-coloured skirt and top bought. I remember hating the fact that the other girls in the play could wear dresses but my mother thought a woollen outfit would be more suitable for winter. Another 'starring role' I had was to mime to a story read by the teacher. I don't remember receiving an Oscar for the performance, but it was great fun, anyway.

My claim to fame was that I always stayed in the A stream throughout the school. Some pupils would be moved up and down the scale – A to C, I think at the end of the term. I loved lessons and worked well, but must admit I did have a mind of my own and would take punishment with a stiff upper lip if I deserved it. Sometimes I objected most vociferously if I thought decisions were wrong.

Punishments for most misdemeanours would be to stand under the clock in the hall, about where the dividing doors are, with your hands on your head. Woe betide any pupil who relaxed their hands before their time was up. Miss Pattison would appear at the end of the hall to check the hands were still in position. On one occasion I was summoned to the head's office, and I was made to stand facing the wall. I don't know if Miss Pattison was of Roman Catholic faith but she was taking a service for several Irish pupils whom I assume must have had a separate service for a different religion. Anyway, she was a heavy smoker and would have piles of cigarettes on her desk – in red boxes with a black cat on them. Craven A, I think they were. I hated the smoke. Miss Pattison always wore a hat, usually brown or navy blue.

If you didn't heed your warning a more serious punishment would ensue. For some reason caning took place in the art room. This room was at the top of the hall where the cookery department stands today. A male teacher always administered the cane, and sometimes it would be the wooden ruler. Girls as well as boys were caned. Once I moved my hand and the cane fell on the teacher's knee. New rules were later enforced, and the teacher held your hand in position.

A very positive memory of Firsy is of the music and singing. I really enjoyed daily assembly. Each class would march into the hall to the strains of Miss Pattison's piano playing. The first hymn I remember hearing was Praise My Soul The King of Heaven – but I could never understand what the word 'heels' had to do with praise, but I sang merrily.

When I progressed to the fourth year, the classroom was next to where the head's office is now on Faire Street. I was dared to do a prank at the end of term. The dare was to do a little flourish as we entered our classroom after the assembly. Each class would stand at command and march in a crocodile to the final music which was always The British Grenadiers. I was to leave the crocodile, and sing and dance the last lines 'with a to ro ro ro ro ro to the British Grenadiers'. The whole class collapsed in laughter, but needless to say the music stopped and once again I was summoned to the head's office. I clearly remember the look of horror on the head's face when she asked if I would like to do a solo for the whole school seeing as I was such a good entertainer. I replied: "Yes please" – no further comment!

Another happy memory is of watching films in the 'dark room'. This was where the present head's office now stands. I don't know the original purpose for this room but black blinds blocked out the light permanently. Slide shows were given once a week (if you were well behaved).

I remember being 'madly in love' with a boy named Robert, and in the dark room promised to give him a sixpence if he would say he loved me. He did. I gave him my sixpence, and the next week he said he didn't love me if I hadn't any money – my first lesson in love!

We had student teachers as we do in schools today. Ours were known as 'Practising Teachers', presumably from the Practising College – Bishop Lonsdale on Uttoxeter Road. I can picture the supervisor who would sit in on the students' last teaching practice. I think her name was Miss Sims, she was small, dark-haired with sharp features, and she always explained everything in great detail.

I can't leave my memories of Firsy without mentioning a couple of good friends, Anne and Joan. We all had a similar sense of humour and would pool our ideas for plays and sketches usually involving plots to push 'pompous' fellow pupils off their pedestals. We would dissolve in laughter at the thought of their demise.

I was never happy about the fact that a few pupils – myself, Anne and Joan included – were seen as failures at not passing the 11-plus examination and were prevented from attending the Grammar School. However, we left Firs Estate in 1950 and the 'Secret Three' progressed to Abbey School for Girls.

Memories stirred by the smell of Horlicks

MY first and lasting moment from schoolday years was the smell of the warm Horlicks drinks that the teachers enjoyed at playtime at the Brighton Road Infants School where I first attended school in 1929. The children had cold milk, and how we enjoyed drinking the cream from the top of the bottle through the straws. The milk, of course, was free. When the newly-built Wyndham Street schools opened we moved there and thought it was wonderful to have a large playing field and new books and desks and an opportunity to go to the swimming baths.

by Dorothy Wright (née Godson), Farningham Close, Spondon

It was in Mr Simpson's class that I received my one and only stroke of the cane for talking – it hurt, and I didn't talk quite so much after that.

At 11 years old, in 1935, I went back to the Brighton Road Senior Girls School where we wore red knitted jumpers, navy pleated tunics, black stockings and black shoes. I enjoyed my days there and continued with my swimming and life-saving and ran for the school in the school sports at the Municipal Sports Ground. The head teacher, Miss Sherwin, was very strict and was held in great awe by the pupils, and we had great respect for all the teachers. After our cookery lesson we would all stand in a line in front of Miss Sherwin in the hall and she would inspect the fruits of our labour. If it was cakes, she would try one, but we didn't part with our lentil soup which was carried home in a jug.

The school had an annual outing by train from the then LMS railway station in Midland Road and I remember going to the Port Sunlight Soap Factory and to Windsor Castle where we also enjoyed a boat trip on the River Thames. We saved weekly to go on the trip and it cost us about 3d a week. These school trips were one of the highlights of our year as not many people were able to afford a holiday away from home.

I went to Sunday school in the Star Room at Alvaston, now a greengrocer's shop I think, and then went on to Bible Class in St Mary's Church, Boulton Lane.

We were all dismayed to find that Miss Sherwin, our school head teacher, was our bible class teacher on Sundays, and she gave us a rota for pumping the organ which she played for our hymn singing. We learnt our Catechism in a private house with the intention of being confirmed. I particularly remember one Sunday school outing when we went from Derby station to Little Eaton station and were allowed to play in a wood at Little Eaton and gather bluebells to take home with us. It was a very short journey but seemed a long way to us children.

On Saturdays, after our dinner of sausage and tinned

tomatoes, my sister and friend Jean went to the Alvaston Picture House matinee, costing 2d each, and very occasionally we were given 4d which enabled us to climb the carpeted stairs and to sit in the balcony. How we waited longingly through the week to see the next episode of Flash Gordon or the Mystery Riders. The cinema was crowded with children, and there was a great deal of shouting and stamping at the exciting parts of the films. When the Gaumont Cinema at The Spot opened we then transferred our affections to the wonder of colour films and entered the world of movie stars like Errol Flynn, Clarke Gable, Spencer Tracey, Marlene Dietrich, Claudette Colbert and others.

In the summertime if the weather was good we were allowed to miss Sunday school and the whole family and our friend Jean would catch the Castle Donington bus, alight at Aston-on-Trent lane end and walk all the way to Weston-on-Trent and then down the lane to Kingsmills where we had our picnic by the River Trent.

We were allowed to splash around in the pool at the bottom of the waterfall but it was too dangerous for us to swim in the fast-flowing and dangerous River Trent. There was a swing fastened to a tall tree, and I still have a photograph of us swinging out over the water. After a tiring but happy day we all walked back to Shardlow Road to catch the bus for Alvaston.

Other picnics were taken with school friends to Anchor Church just beyond Swarkestone, and we walked all the way there and back, enjoying the walk along the canal side at Shelton Lock. We played in the old ruin, paddled in the River Trent and gathered bluebells at Ingleby woods. We had no money for bus fares but just enough to share a bottle of lemonade. I wonder if the girls who went along remember this – Ethel Hobson, Doris Cheetham, Joan Brown, Margaret Sutton and Jean Watson. We had no money in those days but made our own pleasures and vivid memories remain.

During the Easter and summer school holidays, three weeks and four weeks respectively, my mother would put my sister and I on the Yorkshire Traction bus from Derby to Huddersfield and we stayed with our grandparents for the whole holiday. My grandmother was very strict but we enjoyed ourselves. We walked a long way every week to a Co-op shop and carried flour and yeast for her bread-making and all the other groceries. I do remember my grandfather listening to his crystal set and putting the headphones to my ears – it was magic.

We spent happy days at Easter gathering violets from the hedgerows and early nettles that my grandma would boil. I remember playing 'make believe' by a stream that ran at the back of their house. Sometimes we would go by tram to Lindley Moor and grandad once took us in his lorry to Manchester to pick up some building materials. These outings I am sure were the start of my love for the hills and moors and their memories are ever with me.

At the age of 14 I was to leave school. This was a sad time as I had to face the world and look for work. I was already competent at shorthand and typing as we were taught shorthand in the fourth year at school, and I had received private lessons from a Mr Howell at Alvaston, and this stood me in good stead when seeking my first job.

Rumblings of a war were in the air and my school days were coming to an end. They had been happy days. We didn't have much money to spend, but found pleasures in other simple ways and I knew that my parents did their best to give us as much as they could and for this I have always been grateful.

Sealed into the claustrophobia of air raid shelter

MR COCKERSOLE, the head of Springfield School, beating a drum that signalled we must evacuate the classroom and go to the air raid shelters dug underground behind the school. Sitting on long forms with our feet on wooden duckboards squelching in mud as the submarine-type roof closure was locked into place. The feeling of claustrophobia and the smell of wet concrete.

That wonderful and greatly respected headmaster of Spondon House School, 'Gaffer' Walton, who tried to make us all into concert singers, often failing dismally as the grunters were identified. Who always managed to keep all children under control despite half the teaching staff having been called up and most children coming from one-parent families for the same reason.

Keeping rabbits at the school and taking some of them to shows. Others, I now realise, were destined for the pot in the school canteen to eke out the meagre meat ration.

The gas mask fights between pupils. The trendy cases of rexine and linen far outdoing the ordinary square cardboard boxes in which they were issued.

The wonderful sense of team spirit created at the school by competing for your own house, Raleigh, Drake, Scott and Shackleton.

by Margaret Hill, Queen's Park, Bournemouth

The good all-round education despite the lack of teachers, and above all, the happy atmosphere created during a desperately difficult time.

Derby at War

Playing away from home

FOR a kid of 10, the late 1940s were an opportunity to create your own Disneyland on every street corner.

The war had not long been over and life was one adventure after another. Every game had to do with the Army or the Navy or the Air Force, unless of course it was to do with being a cowboy.

I was a kid growing up right across the road from Normanton Barracks, the home of the Sherwood Foresters. The war was over and I could sit in my backyard and listen to the rat-tat-tat of gunfire coming from the rifle range at the furthest part of the barracks.

Here was evidence that our soldiers were being taught their fatal skills in case of any future conflict.

I felt secure in the knowledge that the Foresters were just across the road.

At the top of the street was a static water tank, still full of water that stank in the summer and froze in the winter. Although it was fenced off, we kids still managed to float boats of scrap bits of wood on the dangerously deep water. We even risked 'skating' on the ice in the cold winters.

There was also an air raid shelter made from red brick buried beneath the ground.

It had steps leading down into the dark, smelly bowels that only a few short years ago were clean and serviceable and offering people sanctuary from the German bombs.

We kids were able to play almost anywhere that we wanted to without fear of harm coming to us, unless it was through our own boisterous behaviour.

I lived in Hampden Street, a street with two sides.

On our side, the houses were red brick terraces with entry ways spaced at intervals to allow us to reach our tiny back gardens.

The other side of the street were all semi-detached houses with not only back gardens but front gardens as well!

Whichever side of the street you lived on the six-week school holidays meant that we kids were all as one in a fantasy world of our own creation.

by Barry Fox, White Moss, Blackley, Manchester

Most of the time we went around in a gang of between six and ten, the ages ranged from around ten to 14 or 15. The older ones would take care of the younger ones and more often than not our parents would let us 'nippers' go if "so-and-so is going".

The pecking order was clear. Us youngsters were the 'servants' of the older ones. We had to carry everything and do any tasks put to us, "because your mam said I was in charge."

We would carry the ball or the coats, and woe betide anyone of us that dropped anything.

My favourite adventure was going to Barrow-on-Trent for a day out.

Barrow was a sleepy village that, to us, could have been Africa, it seemed so far away.

The journey was a thrill in itself. No-one had even a bike in those days. Bikes were adult transport. Dads went to work on them and mums did their shopping on them. Hardly anyone owned a car so the bike was essential. As a result we kids walked everywhere.

Going to Barrow needed to be planned. We had to organise bottles of tap water and Spanish root for the trip. Maybe we could take pop bottles back to the shop and buy a loaf of bread with the money.

Barrow was about five miles away from our house but to us it represented setting off on safari. Preparation was vital.

We would set off early in the morning, walking down Sinfin Lane, past the Richardson's tannery, then International Combustion. We may have paused there to see if there were any misshapes on the tip at the Zubes Factory. Then on past the Army arsenal and on to the end of the bus route. When we reached the terminus we knew that we were entering the 'countryside'. No houses, not much traffic and now we would smell that mixture of cow dung and stables that was known as fresh air.

On the way, I remember that we would call into a tiny chapel at the side of the road. The chapel only had about 20 or 30 seats and the old pews were all rotting from the rain that teemed in through the slateless roof. It did have an organ that needed to be pumped by a pedal, although not many of the keys worked.

I always thought that it was a strange place to have a chapel, right at the side of the road with fields all around it.

Normanton Barracks, the scene of much military activity in the late 1940s as soldiers honed their skills for any future conflict.

As the years went by the place just gave up the ghost and fell down. This was our first stop for refreshments and the water bottle was passed around as we rested.

Eventually, we would reach the canal. The tow path was narrow and we had to walk in single file, the eldest at the front.

As we walked at the side of the water we passed old stone bridges that gave access from the road to the fields.

On the still water we may see a moorhen and her chicks swimming in two lines and forming a glistening 'V' on the water as they swam.

We would pass fishermen sitting among the bullrushes. If one of them caught a fish we would run and stand with morbid interest as he removed the hook from the flopping fish before dropping it into his keep net.

Then it was on to Barrow!

This tiny little village had little to commend it. A few shops, a church and the odd farm.

It did, however, have a secret, known to all of us town kids. If you walked over a couple of fields of cows and daisies, you would discover the River Trent.

After our long sweaty walk, the luxury of throwing off your clothes and paddling through the thick mixture of black mud and cow dung, to reach the cool water, was divine.

We would swim until we shivered uncontrollably before leaving the water and lying amongst the buttercups in our underwear whilst we dried off enough to get dressed and get ready for the long trek home.

I recently tried to retrace this journey by car. There was no static water tank, no Normanton Barracks with its soldiers. No country chapel, in fact no country lanes any more. Just lots of little boxes made to look like houses. I had a heavy heart thinking of all of those sweet innocent days that we had together, playing away from home.

Aussie ex-pat remembers her evacuation

Kathleen Hollick (née Mordey), Morley, Perth, West Australia

I LIVED in Derby from when I was two years old until I migrated to West Australia in 1967 with my husband and two sons.

We lived at number 1 Hill Brow, off Forrester Street, from when I was two years old. My memories are vivid of the day I was evacuated at the outbreak of the Second World War.

I went to Gerard Street School and we all got on a bus with our gas masks in a square cardboard box hanging around our necks. One of my brothers went to Belper and I went to Wingerworth, near Chesterfield. It seemed like the other side of the world then!

After a couple of months or so, mum decided if we were going to be bombed, she wanted us all together so we came home to Derby. I went back to Gerard Street School until I went to Homelands School for the rest of my education.

We had a big cellar, which was reinforced with wood all around and the escape hatch to the outside was up the grate where the coal was delivered. Mum put a double bed in there, a wireless, and electric lights were fitted, also several large torches, so instead of upstairs to bed we went down the cellar every night whether the siren went off or not.

In Babington Lane, there was a big barrage balloon and an ack-ack gun which rocked our house when a raid was on, and the barrage balloon used to hover over our house each time it was put up or brought down. It was like a huge silver whale.

One day, a lone German plane flew over our house at about 7am – it was looking for Rolls-Royce. It dropped bombs on Victory Road, part of Rolls-Royce and the LMS station.

My dad took us out in the backyard to see it with a big iron cross on its side – my mum kept calling to dad to bring us back inside, but I'll never forget seeing it. I also remember VE Day. We had a big street party in Forrester Street, every window upstairs and down had Union Jacks and bunting, and we were all very happy that the war had ended.

Houses and side streets like this one were ablaze with bunting and flags on VE Day, May 8, 1945.

A little darkness lifted for us all on VE Day

ALMOST a year after D-Day, June 6, 1944, the nation celebrated VE Day – Victory in Europe Day.

How can I convey the depth of feeling people expressed that day? The outstanding emotion was joy – joy that a tremendous load had been lifted from our shoulders. No more air raids, no more soldiers being killed, for thousands of mothers, wives, sweethearts, prayers had been answered. How to express that joy? Well this is how I saw people celebrate their first fear-free day after four long years of privation, shortages of all kinds and in many instances fear and suffering.

First and foremost it was a national holiday. I remember going outside and hearing the church bells ringing merrily for the first time in years, people without exception looking happy and cheerful. Most of the ladies were planning and preparing to celebrate with a great tea party for the children. The men were busy with flags and bunting to decorate the street. Radios were blaring. In one street a piano, an old one, was being trundled out ready for the singing and dancing which would be enjoyed later in the day. Children were excitedly running about helping and no doubt hindering. They were in for a lovely unforgettable day.

by Tom Bird, Churchside Walk, Parliament Street, Derby

These activities were going on in nearly every street, and the result was a lovely colourful sight all over the town.

Shortly after 2pm, I went down the town. The Market Place was absolutely full. I have never seen so many happy, cheerful people congregated together, the atmosphere was electric. People were singing, dancing and thoroughly enjoying themselves.

One little incident stuck in my mind. A young lady was in the telephone booth talking to someone. One reveller opened the telephone door and began singing "All alone by the telephone". Immediately the song was taken up by the crowd. The young lady, embarrassed at first, entered into the spirit of the moment and thoroughly enjoyed the novelty of it. One jolly reveller appointed himself unofficial compere. He was good, too. He soon had the big crowd laughing at his jokes and joining enthusiastically in the singing and revelry. I don't know where he got his mike from but one appeared magically. I left the Market Place with the strains of the war song 'We're going to hang out the washing on the Siegfried Line' ringing in my ears.

When I got back home to Harrison Street a transformation had taken place. Tables had been placed in the street, the ladies had put nice tablecloths on them and cups, saucers and plates had appeared. Chairs had been provided for the children who were scampering around trying to decide where to sit. But the biggest mystery of all was where all the goodies came from. Considering that we had had four years of strict rationing

Celebrating VE Day at a street party in Cummings Street, Derby.

Locals gather for a party in Harrington Street, Derby.

of butter, sugar, lard, fruit, all kinds of meat, ham, eggs and many other household foodstuffs: It was truly remarkable how these things appeared on the tables.

Many ladies must have raided their hidden stores of fruit and other goods painstakingly saved for that special occasion that may come along some day. The result was that a jolly good time was had by all. The children, and I suspect many of the grown-ups, had a share as well.

Later that day, at night time, it was the grown-ups' turn to celebrate. They had a good old sing-along and dancing which lasted well into the night. Then they went home tired but very happy. No need to bother about the 'blackout', no air raid warnings tonight. Good luck and good nights were exchanged, thus ended VE day for most of the people in England.

One of the highlights of the day was a broadcast by Winston Churchill to the nation. It was Churchill's tribute to the nation.

The lights went out and the bombs came down, but every man, woman and child in the country had no thought of quitting the struggle… London can take it.

So we came back after long months from the jaws of death and the mouth of hell, while all the world wondered. When shall the reputation and faith of this generation of Englishmen and women fail? I'd say that in all the long years to come, not only will the people of this island, but of the world – wherever the Bird of Freedom chirps in human hearts – look back to what we have done and they will say, do not despair, do not yield to violence and tyranny, march straight forward and die if need be – unconquered.

Now we have emerged from a deadly struggle a terrible foe has been cast on the ground and awaits our judgment and mercy.

A truly fitting end to a perfect day – May 18, 1945 – VE Day.

Dad's wartime wireless proved our saviour

by Peter Saunders, Manor Road, Hoylake, Wirral

THE wireless provided much of our home entertainment. Dad built our set. He had worked at Batterby and Hefford, a radio retailer in Derby. I recall Hitler's ranting speeches coming over the radio, and the worried expression on dad's face as he talked to our neighbour, Mr Beck, across the hedge at the time of the Munich crisis. My father had been in the trenches in the First World War and knew about the iron fist of the German military machine.

When the Government issued Anderson air raid shelters, named after the Home Secretary, dad had to excavate a large pit at the end of the garden. The floor was concreted and curved sheets of corrugated iron were bolted in place, then covered in soil. Bunks were fitted inside and a piece of sacking screened the entrance. When the air raid siren sounded, my brother Derek, who died

The former chapel dating from 1846 which later became the Coliseum cinema. On the corner of Traffic Street and London Road, The Coliseum pub and Carpet World now stand on its site.

in childhood, my sister Brenda and I were wrapped in blankets and led down the garden path to the gloomy, dank, candlelit shelter.

Mum kept a large pre-rationing tin of Nuttall's Mintoes in the shelter as a comforter for broken nights, and she would tell us stories of her own childhood as searchlights stabbed the skies. There was a searchlight unit in Normanton Park, and an anti-aircraft gun during the early stages of the war. The Parker family, across the road, had a different kind of air raid shelter in the form of a large steel table, with strong mesh sides; it was kept in the dining room and used for meals as well as providing a degree of protection from all but a direct hit. We used it as a den when playing with David Parker.

Dad became an ARP (Air Raid Precautions) warden and spent many nights in uniform at what he called 'the post' (his sector HQ), or patrolling the streets, shouting: "Put that light out" whenever gaps in curtains might have attracted the might of the Luftwaffe to rain bombs on Derby. Dad's radio became even more important as a medium of family entertainment during the war years; Saturday Night Theatre, Monday Night at Eight, Workers' Playtime and Tommy Handley's ITMA were compulsive listening.

Carlton Road Congregational Church was at the top of the avenue. It dated from 1930 when a town centre church relocated here. Its former building in London Road, with its classical Greek-style columns, became the Coliseum Cinema, where later I spent many happy hours. I was sent to Carlton Road Sunday School, and the Saunders children were in the Cub, Scouts, Brownies and Guides based at the church. During the war years, the church served an important social, as well as religious, function. An amateur dramatic society was formed, and performances of popular plays like Quiet Weekend and Quiet Wedding attracted capacity audiences in the church hall.

Skip Webster was the Scout master of the 93rd Derby (Carlton Road Congregational) troop. He was a First World War veteran and served in the Home Guard in the Second World War, receiving a commendation for his bravery during two potentially fatal incidents on a grenade-throwing range.

There was a little too much emphasis on drill for my liking, but I enjoyed playing in the Scout band, progressing from triangle to side drum soloist. The band led a march around the block after monthly church parades. There were enjoyable Scout camps at Brailsford and Turnditch, and I liked healthy open air days and nights at Drum Hill, the Derby Scouts' camp site at Little Eaton. My father volunteered to cook at Scout camps – his plum duff achieved some notoriety – and later became Scout master himself.

During the build-up to D-Day, convoys of military vehicles roared along Derby's ring road, known to us as 'the arty' (short for arterial road). A group of us were standing on the grass verge in Warwick Avenue one day, watching a US army convoy of trucks, when packs of K-rations were flung out of the cabs, landing at our feet.

Perhaps the Yanks thought we Limey kids were at the verge of starvation. Those waxed cardboard containers held basic field rations, including chewing gum, lemonade powder and toilet paper. What a treasure trove. There was great excitement as we squabbled over the share-out.

Wartime whispers of young love

by Harold Richardson, Trowels Lane, Derby

MONDAY, January 1st, 1940: This first day began for Betty and me alone at the corner of her street. She had her arms under my jacket and mine were under her coat. There was warmth in our closeness and though her feet must have been as cold as mine, it didn't seem to matter then.

The church bells had finished their lovely welcome to the New Year and we had given our own whispered greetings to each other when she suddenly pulled more tightly on to me and placed her head on my chest. "This time next year," I heard her say, as if talking to herself, "My love, where shall we be?"

Touched by the sadness in her voice, I didn't know what to say, then thought of something I had once heard at the pictures. "It's going to take more than a war to part us." I told her, and squeezed more to show I meant it.

I felt her head move and she was looking into my face again. "Do you think then…?" But she didn't say anymore, only kissed me on the cheek.

When I began my walk home the incomplete moon had given up. While the stars did what they could for the deserted, blacked-out streets and me, I had to keep an arm outstretched for lamp-posts as dark and cold as the night. And with only a blur of white paint to show their sharp corners, I had to grope a way around frost-lined bricks of surface air raid shelters. Even more hazardous were the emergency water supplies, tanks of unimaginable gallons of slimy water standing by for the fire raids we have been promised, but whose only contribution to the war effort so far is a mounting toll of drowned cats. And above all the madness, I imagined the grotesque barrage balloons, swaying and awaiting a war that has never had the courage to get started.

The door was unbolted, as always, when I reached home and all was in darkness with not even a glow from the fireplace.

I didn't mind that nor the freezing chill that was no better than the streets outside. I wanted no glimmer of light that might reveal the cause of the faint scuffling along the tin hearthplate. In dread of what my shoes might step upon, and scalp prickling, I felt my way past the pantry door towards the opening where the stair began…

Everything was iced over when I cycled to work. Not keeping my mind on what I was doing, I came a cropper. My front wheel just slid away as I was coming down Chaddesden Hill and I ended up in the gutter with a damaged knee and bent pride. Fortunately, my bike was all right and I was able to get to work by eight o'clock as usual. There, the boss met me with my 'cards' in his hand. On top of all other upsets he said there was just no work available.

Went home again to drop off my tools and get my knee bandaged. Then to the Labour Exchange to sign on. Was offered a job at Qualcast, so on my bike again.

When I got there I couldn't find anybody willing to take an interest in me, despite the 'green card' in my hand. I was eventually led to a hellish place of heat and gritty air with rising smoke all but obscuring the roof high above. Underfoot was black sand, and overhead, clanking cranes. Above the din, it was explained to me in shouts that I would be labouring for the moulders, even introduced to my very own wheel-barrow and shovel. I can't remember what it was, I said in reply, but my guide's face suddenly showed displeasure. I turned and bolted for the patch of daylight where we had come in.

Have spent a most boring day at home, and with the coming of night I could not stir myself, even to seek my pals. I am finishing this in my bedroom, the time is now 9.30pm – I think I will get into bed.

Thursday January 4th: Still have no job to go to and no chance of getting one. I've walked around, calling on different firms but no-one gave me any hope.

I suppose it is understandable in this wintry weather with nothing but cold winds and ice, and on top of it all nobody knowing what might happen with the war being on. But then, except for the newspapers reporting daily losses of our ships, you'd hardly guess there was a war, but for the strips of brown paper stuck on windows. This, we are told, will minimise the danger of flying glass in the event of an air raid. I notice no mention has been made of flying bricks, I mean, how do you stop that?

Then again, everybody you see has this cardboard box slung over their shoulders, inside which is a gas mask – or should be, but with nothing ever happening, if they are anything like mine that box is stuffed with all sorts of things. It is more or less compulsory to carry it around with you because without it you wouldn't be allowed into cinemas or dance halls. At the skating rink, old man Clarke checks at the pay box to see if that bit of string is over your shoulder with the box dangling close to your backside. He at first insisted on having them bouncing on us while on the rink and would make periodic raids among the skaters to pull off the floor any who had invaded his scrutiny at the entrance. He had to drop that lark though because of near fights over his habit of pulling girls off balance and clutching them around the chest.

Markeaton Park is now a vast Army camp and the streets themselves are filling with uniforms, mostly Army, but Air Force as well from the barrage balloon sites around the town. Navy too, mostly those on leave I should think. Then air raid wardens, auxiliary firemen and the new special police.

In another year or so, after my 19th birthday, I shall be called up for the Army, unless I volunteer before then for the Air Force or Navy. Arthur is keen on us joining the Navy but Albert reckons it's the Air Force for him. But what's the use of bothering now?

Mam lit a fire for me in our room this afternoon. We choked with smoke at first. In fact we couldn't get near the room for it and had to open the front door to let some of it out. It's years since we had a fire in that grate because we rarely use the room, It is too damp and musty. What wallpaper there used to be has long since fallen off, bringing lumps of plaster with it and much of the rest has crumbled into little sand hills against the rotting skirting board. There is an old easy chair in there and a sofa that used to be black and shiny but now has a greenish look to it. Then there is the table. Almost incidentally showing off carved legs while its once polished top has scaled into old age. It's amazing with its size how it got there in the first place. Even mam can't remember and seems to think it was there when they moved in more than 20 years ago.

Whatever was blocking the chimney must have crawled out or melted because the smoke got less going out of the door and more through the chimney pot. But not before Liza Fenwick from across the street at number five had noticed and shuffled over in unlaced boots to poke her nose in.

"Eh, God 'elp us, Elsie'" she said to mam, all breathless and clutching a shawl of sacking to her shoulders. "All that smoke, right turned me over, it has. Ah shouted to our Ted, 'Ted!' ah shouted, 'look!' ah sezs to him, an' ah just run over, thought you was out at the back, ah did, Elsie. Thank God it were nowt" she flopped into a chair at our living room table. "Ah'm fair done up," she went on, mopping her face with her sack shawl. 'An' in me rush ah've forgot me fags." Mam gave her a Woodbine, then took one herself before giving me the rest of the packet. I went back into the front room, closing the door behind me.

I brushed the easy chair with my hand and pulled it up to the fire. Mam had left an old bucket half filled with coal. I knew there wasn't that much to spare but she had understood my need to be on my own. All afternoon I kept to that shabby old chair smoking mam's cigarettes, my gloom deepening with the fading daylight.

For the most part, it was Betty occupying my thoughts. I tried sorting out my feelings towards her. 'She isn't all that important to me,' I kidded myself. 'Especially when she gets so jealous of my pals. But it's not that: if I live to be a hundred, I can never be good enough. I have seen Betty home; its gables and bay windows and the tall trees surrounding it.

Streets…No! worlds away from my place where I was sitting. She even speaks differently to me most of the time, although I have noticed how, now and again, she repeats some of my own rough words.

Why should she care for me? What have I got? Nothing! And what's more, never likely to have anything.

Yet she does care. I know it in the way we secretly touch hands when others are there, and then there is that earnest way she has of looking at me those times I am so thoughtless, even unkind to her, mocking her because she knows about books and people I've never heard of. And all the while when I am so proud of her good looks, I fill with a strange ache because I know she could do much better than go out with me.

I left my seat to the darkness; and the dying fire to its last struggles with the returning chill. In our living room-cum-kitchen, mam had my tea ready, with water simmering in a saucepan on the fire hob. She ironed my shirt while I ate, then went to the corner shop to get me another packet of cigarettes while I washed at the sink. Dad had not been in all day although he, too, is not working and my sister, Kath, 15 only last week, was not then home from the mill.

I left the house at 6.30pm to call for Albert. We have been friends since the early days and with Arthur, who lives next door to me, make an inseparable trio. He lives in the next street in a house much like ours, two rooms up and two down. He is the eldest of seven, including three infants, making nine of them to share the one liveable room. Nothing out of the ordinary by West End standards.

They never open the front door so I had to use both hands to feel my way down a pitch-black entry to knock at the back. One of his sisters let me into a dimly-lit room whose floor seemed to be waving up and down with crawling children in various stages of nakedness. I was met with the usual smell of drying pee and the fire range was bedecked with squares of cloth, ragged nightgowns and dark blue knickers. A space leading to one of the three chairs in the room was cleared for me.

On the other two kitchen chairs sat Albert's mam and dad, one each side of a dullish yet smoky fire. His mam, rather fat, scraggly-haired and dressed in a kind of grey-black from head to foot, sat sternly upright with folded arms. I had to step over infants, a cat, and a scraggy dog who looked too miserable even to raise its head. A semi-circle of wide-eyed and wet-nosed children formed around my chair.

"He ain't in," said the tallest, removing a pink-sucked thumb.

"Shush!" said Albert's mam. "Speak when yo' spoke to. He ain't in," she repeated.

"He never bloody is" Albert's dad lifted his head out of his hands and blew irritably into his droopy moustache. He was wearing a cap and a grey-looking muffler. Tallish and thin, his long, morose face looked remarkably like the dog's, who just then roused itself to scratch half-heartedly behind its ear. "Dos he know about yo' coming?" he went on, not looking at me but searching with finger and thumb each waistcoat pocket, as if trying for a cigarette end. Finding nothing, he spat into the fire before leaning forward in his wooden chair, elbows on his knees and head down again to his hands. You could tell by the lines on his face, the way they crossed his cheeks with never a smiling bend to skirt his mouth, you could tell Albert's dad had never, in his whole life, been pleasantly surprised. "Forever bloody gallivanting, that he is."

"He's not back from work yet, our dad," spoke out the bold, tall one again. "It's his late night. Yo' know Thursday's his late night."

"Shush, ah said!" Albert's mam unfolded an arm. "Ah

shan't tell yo' agen. Yo'll feel this next time." She let her threat sink in, then said: "It's his late night, Thursday's his late night."

The semi-circle around my chair began to widen as far as space would allow. "I'd better meet him at the skating rink then, eh? I reckon that'll be the best," I said to Albert's mam.

"Ah'll tell him where yo'll be, he shouldna be all that long, and knowing him he won't bother with his tea. Hey, and when yo' do see him, yo' tell him another thing. I want him back here afore ten, yo' tell him that, the door'll be bolted else."

"I'll be off then," I said, feeling awkward inside.

The tall thin one rushed to open the door for me, and as I stepped outside she leaned forward into the darkness. "I'm going to marry you," she said.

Saturday, January 6th: No moon again tonight and if it had not been for a sky alive with stars it would have been quite dark by the time I reached the low cemetery wall. There was no-one waiting for me, no sound and no movement except for that which I fancied took place among the graves on the other side of the wall.

I've never understood Betty favouring this creepy meeting place. Even in daylight it is a shadowy place of dismal trees unwilling to let in the sun, where a mouldy dampness never seems to leave the chilled earth and flowers die quickly in their glass jars.

I whistled to keep myself company, ashamed the stirring of the trees should bring on the jitters and send cold shivers down my back. Betty, nervous about so many other things, has never had these fears and laughs at me when I try to explain them. I can never forget the time she took me into the cemetery and led me to an unmarked grave, "This is where my mother is," she had said, kneeling on the damp ground. "She's here."

I heard her footsteps first, then from out of the darkness I saw her pink coat, and nearer still, her silhouetted hair against the stars. "Hello love, am I late?"

Quickly and breathlessly, she kissed me on the cheek. "I'm so sorry for keeping you waiting in the cold." It was then she put her arms around my shoulders and kissed my lips. "There!" she said.

How I look forward to Saturday nights, with just enough money in my pocket to get us into the best seats, the one and nines at the Popular. Maybe a packet of cigarettes, although Betty doesn't smoke, and sometimes an ice cream at the interval.

As always on a Saturday night, the Pop was full despite the film not being up to much. 'Spies of the Air' with Barry K Barnes and Roger Liversay. But neither Betty nor me gave full attention to what was on the screen. With the lights down and close together in a double seat on the back row, I had my arm around her and she rested her head against mine.

How I sometimes wish we could stay in there for ever.

Our cold walk back in the blackout was made more cheerful through streets busy with the emptying of the pubs. There was quite a bit of singing – of a sort. The favourite seemed to be 'There'll always be an England', and then, 'We're gonna hang out the washing on the Seigfried Line'. The way they yawped away you could have thought the war was as good as won.

We stayed a while under our friendly tree close to Betty's home, and after our goodnight kiss, I began my long walk home.

Father's diary recalled executions

by Mrs D. Brodie, Bethulie Road, Derby

MY FATHER, Ernest Blackshaw, was born in the tiny village of Thulston, near Elvaston, in 1885. He was one of six boys and four girls. His grandfather was coachman to the Earl of Harrington and his father was a bricklayer on the estate. They lived in a cottage next to the Old Chapel House, with a stream running through the garden where the children used to play – and fall in. Today, there is a large Georgian type house where the cottage stood on the left of the main road through Thulston. How they all crammed in the cottage I don't know, but they had a very happy childhood.

Many years later, the youngest boy, Charlie, told me how he used to set off very early with his mother when he was seven, walk all the way to Derby, help carry the shopping, and to use his own words 'felt he was in Heaven' to have a ha'penny bag of boiled sweets from the Market Hall to suck on the way home.

All the family were keen, regular churchgoers, so much so that when their father's work meant they had to move to a cottage at Lockington, three or four miles away, the Vicar, the Rev. Charles Prodgers, couldn't bear to see this tribe walking there and back twice every Sunday, and rather than lose them he provided them with a pony and trap. They all enjoyed this, especially the younger ones, and in later years told us many amusing stories about Tommy the pony, whom they kept in the field at the back of their Lockington cottage. Their cottage is still there today, I think, and has a little porch over the front door, and is opposite Lockington Hall gardens.

I realised why. In it were the names, numbers and particulars of two men of the 18th West Yorks whose execution he had to attend as a member of the military police.

Three hundred and fifty one men were shot at dawn during the Great War, many of them by their own men, and for many years even their relatives weren't told, and their names were omitted from the war memorials, such was the secrecy surrounding them.

On September 5, 1916, the date these two men were executed, my father had drawn in his diary a religious cross, proof of where his sympathies lay, even though he was in the military police. I think his old Vicar, Mr Prodgers, would have been proud of him.

All four of the Blackshaw brothers returned safely – quite rare I should think for that to happen. My father, Jack and Charlie rejoined the Corporation Tramways as conductors, and my dad worked his way up to be chief inspector by the time he retired in 1950. He played in the Tramways Football

Corporal Ernest Blackshaw in the mounted police in 1918.

(Back from left to right) Charles, Jack and Frank, and (front from left) Ernie, Harry and Ted, taken in about 1950.

Altogether it was a very happy and peaceful life. Little did they think in those days that their lives would change so much or ever imagine the horrors they would experience in the Great War of 1914-18. Four of the boys volunteered, Harry, Ernest, Frank and Charlie, the youngest, who was only 17 but said he was 18. When a fifth brother, Jack, decided to join up, and he wasn't as fit as the others, the vicar suggested he stayed at home and help his mother.

My father, Ernest, decided on the Cavalry, and joined the 17th Lancers, the Death or Glory boys, with the Skull and Crossbones badge. However, when he was fully qualified in horsemanship he transferred to the Military Mounted Police and set sail on the Nitonian in December, 1915, for foreign parts. Fortunately, he had been sent a diary for 1915-16, the only one he ever kept, and what a gem, for 1916 was the year of the Battle of the Somme. First of all, the day after they set sail his horse died and was thrown overboard – very sad for him.

In all the years since 1918 he never showed us his diary and it wasn't until after he died in 1962 that I read it, and

team on their ground at the back of the old "Welcome" Temperance Hotel on Brighton Road at Alvaston, and as children my brother and I used to help him mark out the pitch with sawdust. My mother also played her part off the pitch – she used to wash a dozen sets of kit, and with no

Corporal Ernest Blackshaw (front left) in the military mounted police.

washing or drying facilities other than the old dolly tub, the smell of embrocation lingered somewhat.

My Dad also was a keen and regular Rams supporter, as was I, and when I was lucky enough to win two tickets to Wembley in 1946, when Derby won the FA Cup, I never regretted giving them to him. He took his brother Frank and they reminisced for years about it.

It must have seemed quite a short space of time to the ex-servicemen, after experiencing the horrors of the "War to end all Wars" to be plunged into yet another in 1939. Not quite fair – just 20 years of peace – just long enough to bring a son up and see him off to war.

We drank cocoa while planes droned overhead

I WAS born in the Nightingale Home in London Road in 1935, and my sister, Margaret, was born two years later. We spent our formative years including most of the 1940s, living in one of the many rows of terraced, brick-built houses which lined the streets of Derby in those days and, in fact, in many cases still do. This was at 14 Society Place, just off Normanton Road.

by Lon Houlston, Pritchett Drive, Littleover

They were comfortable buildings for those days, even though lacking in common amenities and bitterly cold in winter. Still, what did that matter? We knew no better and thought ourselves very fortunate to have such a roof over our heads. Downstairs consisted of a hallway from the street leading on to the bottom of the stairs. The front room was on the left and was very rarely used, but on special occasions – such as Christmas, or when relatives were visiting – a fire would be lit in the grate. On the right was the living room where we spent most of our time and where a coal fire would usually blaze away. The window overlooked a small lean-to conservatory which housed my father's canaries. The kitchen was off the living room and included a huge iron range which my mother seemed to spend a lot of her time and energy polishing with black lead. A large square sink sat under the window. Upstairs were three bedrooms.

There was no such thing as central heating. This was many decades away and together with everybody else, we depended on smoky coal, paraffin heaters and hot water bottles (as the war years went by, we learned that even rubber bottles perished and would not be renewed – these would be replaced either with pot ones or by a brick warmed in the oven and wrapped in a towel).

At one end of the small garden was the outside lavatory and at the other end was a shed in which stood the brick copper which again was heated by a coal fire and where every Monday our mother laboured amidst clouds of steam and much activity with the dolly pegs and the blue bag. The tin bath hung on a nail on the whitewashed wall and beneath was the old cast iron mangle, each growing ever rustier with use.

We were comfortable and set for the duration of the war.

There were now certain preparations we all had to make first, however, which included fixing sticky tape to all the windows to prevent the dispersal of glass shards when broken by bomb blast, putting up blackout curtains made of some obnoxious material, so we didn't 'show a light', and making up beds in the cellar ready for the air raids.

A concrete slab on brick legs was laid over the cellar grating in order to stop the entrance hall being blocked once the bombs started falling and a pile of sand and a stirrup pump stood ready to put out any incendiary bombs. We were all issued with a gas mask in a cardboard box which we were expected to carry with us everywhere. It smelled horrible and was claustrophobic but I cannot remember actually having to wear it. Ration books and identity cards soon followed.

Communal air raid shelters were erected every couple of streets or so as were concrete sectioned static water tanks.

On both sides of the street were rows of metal drums which caused a lot of head scratching as folk puzzled and wondered on their purpose. Once they were lit and clouds of black oil fumes poured out it was pretty obvious what they were – smoke screens to confound low flying aircraft. As I remember, there were also metal dustbins which people filled with scraps and which were collected regularly to feed the pigs. It surprises me now on reflection that there were any scraps of food left at all, never mind enough to feed the pigs.

When I think back to those days, the thing that stands out the most is the fact that there was literally no traffic at all. The only people I knew who had a motor vehicle were the milkman, who lived next door, and the doctor who only came to see you if you were really ill. This left the roads clear for the games that kids delighted in at all times, such as football, whip and top, marbles, cigarette cards, tick, and hop-scotch. We did have to be careful to keep out of the way of the steamrollers which were then responsible for most road repairs. We kids were fascinated by the gruntings and hissings of these mechanical monsters which provided a great side show.

The iron railings which surrounded the little gardens around Chestnut Avenue were torched out and went together with the old pots and pans, to make Spitfires.

We all had a little corner shop in those days from which we obtained most of our needs and, if things were a little tight sometimes, a slate was available for a limited time. Ours stood on the corner of Society Place and Silver Hill Road, and after food rationing came into operation in January, 1940, was the place where you bought a whip and top, a pea-shooter or a utility set of snobs. I can't recall what the owner was called but I do know that the lady worked a very long day and I am sure that she was on her own.

Higher up Co-operative Street was the most important shop in the vicinity – the chip shop. This was always well patronised and provided a cheap and nourishing meal. I remember my sister and I going with a basin and getting it filled with peas and chips and hurrying home before it went cold. There was always a queue of people waiting and I can still remember the lovely smell of fish cooking away in the bucket as the chipman turned the handle of his mechanical peeler.

We soon got used to the wail of the air raid sirens and we all – my mother, my sister and myself – spent many a night on the wooden pallets in the cellar drinking cocoa and listening to the drone of the aircraft, both British and German, as they passed overhead. As the war continued we sometimes took a chance – particularly if it was a cold night – and stayed in the living room dressed in our pyjamas and dressing gowns. We were all prolific readers and were quite happy to use this form of escapism. My father, by the way, was employed as a tool-maker by Rolls-Royce, invariably working on nights and travelling to and from work – as everybody else did – on a bicycle that had seen better days. No need for garages then and any traffic congestion was due to nothing else but bicycles going backwards and forwards to work.

Funny thing, despite all the shortages and the rationing, I cannot remember ever feeling hungry and I think it is a fact that our wartime diet finally proved to be very healthy simply because we could not get the unhealthy foodstuffs. I did not manage to lay my hands on a banana until after the war and our meat content mainly consisted of rabbit, liver, some beef when we could get it, corned beef, spam and a chicken once a year at Christmas time.

The war may have rattled on around us but life was all right for us kids. We had no feelings of deprivation as these were the only conditions we knew and were to be regarded as nothing but normal. We took it all in our stride. There would be more difficulty in later years in trying to adapt to the traumas caused by the peace.

In the late 1940s, my parents moved up the road to take over my grandfather's business on Normanton Road. But that's another story…

The day the Luftwaffe paid a visit to Derby

by Leslie John Wormsley, Lawn Heads Avenue, Littleover, Derby

UNTIL August, 1940, the people of Derby had become accustomed to regular air raid alerts lasting most of the night, listening to German aircraft drone overhead on their way to targets, mainly on Merseyside, and thankful that the only explosions were that of our own ack-ack guns.

The inevitable thoughts in people's minds were: "When will the bombs fall on Derby and who will be the unlucky ones?"

Only the pilot of that single German aircraft on the night of August 19 would know why he released 12 bombs at that time, but to the residents of Regent Street, it was a decision which brought home to them the harsh realities of war.

Six bombs screamed down on to the 85 neat, terraced houses in the street, destroying 14 and damaging many more.

The other six fell close by, hitting the Queen's Hall, Haselhurst's the ironmonger, four houses in Litchurch Street, High Street and two fell between Reginald Street

School and Derby High School for Girls.

I lived in the middle of Regent Street and was sheltering in the cellar at the time and the memories of that day are still vivid in my mind.

I remember the scream from my mother as the whine of the bombs became louder and louder. The upheaval of the floor and sudden darkness as the lights went out. The period of utter quietness which followed owing to temporary deafness. The sparkle of the coal dust in the air when my father lit a candle.

The sounds outside of the rescue services arriving. The caution we took as we climbed out of the cellar to view the damage. The tears in my mother's eyes as she saw her brand new curtains cut to pieces.

I remember the compulsion to watch them dig out an elderly couple across the road, who survived with hardly a scratch. They had crawled under a strong table in the front room and the whole floor had sunk into the cellar.

The shock of seeing my friend Cyril Davison's house destroyed and the relief when I found him, safely protected by an Anderson shelter.

The precarious climb of a rescue worker, who retrieved a coat containing all Cyril's father's money

Salvaging goods from a house severely damaged during an air raid in Regent Street, Derby, on August 20, 1940.

from a wardrobe balancing on a ledge, which used to be their bedroom.

The sorrow felt for an old lady whose house was destroyed, standing watching while men searched for a tin trunk that contained her 'treasures'.

When it was found and opened, a few eyes moistened, for laying on the top was a large Union Jack. This was quickly hoisted to a high roof beam over the wreckage.

The tragic figure of Mr Bentley, our street chief air-raid warden and manager of the London Road Co-op store, who was roaming around with a bandaged head. His wife and only daughter had been killed.

The laugh we had when another of my friends, Alan Eley, showed me his outside toilet. In the space where it used to be was a crater resembling an ornamental pond with a fountain of water right in the middle. We said the bomb must have gone right down the pan.

The look on my mother's face when, on answering a knock at the back door, found herself face-to-face with the Mayor of Derby. She moaned to him about the curtains and he gave her £5 out of a relief fund.

I remember the soldiers with fixed bayonets guarding each end of the street, keeping out anyone but residents and the feeling of being a celebrity as I was allowed through the guard and crowds of sightseers to fetch buckets of water.

The water mains had received a direct hit, and residents were paying threepence for a bucket of water, which to me was good business, paying much better than my paper round.

The all-clear sounded about five hours after the bombs had dropped, but we had already been out doing what we thought we had to, completely oblivious that the alert was still on.

'Clothing made some poor kids look like Norman Wisdom'

I LIVED near the centre of Derby from the beginning of the Second World War until 1963.

Wilmot Street, near The Spot, was my home from 1940 until 1963.

First recollections were of nursery school, which was situated at the top end of Wilmot Street, namely Christ Church. My two elder sisters were in classes. One sister was nine and the other was six – I was three, and I recall they took me to nursery at 9am and picked me up around 3.30pm.

I remember this period because the teacher always seemed to try and and make us sleep on rubber mats most of the day. We were slapped on the legs if we did not comply.

At the age of five, I moved up to Grade I. I loved this – no more induced sleeping.

I think after the war children between the ages of five and 14 grew up very fast. I think this was due to very large families and each family unit had a full day to survive reasonably. I was one of six, varying in ages from three to 18. I was a middle child having a younger sister and brother, and two older sisters and one brother.

My elder sisters had their work cut out to help my mother cope. Dad seemed always to be at work.

We must have been living from week to week, because pawn shops were abundant and all of us hated the idea of taking items of clothing and shoes to pawn on Monday and retrieve them on Friday. My mother was paid a sum

by W. J. Doyle, Derby Road, Chellaston

of money on Friday night and after paying rent for the house and food over the weekend she seemed to struggle all week to make ends meet. I think that's why in later life I lived Fridays and Saturdays being worry free!

So, Mondays were black, especially in the winter, because clothes and shoes were in short supply. I remember one period, I must have been about seven, mum bought me a pair of clogs from Woolworth's for 1s 6d. I wore them only once, because the ribbing I got from others was horrendous.

Because I had two older sisters I rarely received hand-me-down clothes, but one day I do remember my mother forced me to wear what today would be the equivalent of tights! Most children at Christ Church School turned up in some ridiculous wear at some time. Some looked like Norman Wisdom in obviously tight clothing – while others looked as though they had lost a couple of stone overnight – but we all realised survival was most important.

Out-of-school activities for me was earning a few pence by various means. I would go to Morledge market and scrounge orange boxes, then bring them home and chop them up into small fingers of wood and bind them with string or chicken wire. I would take these bundles in a sack and sell them to houses in posher areas like Mill Hill Lane, Charnwood Street, and the upper part of Burton Road. These homes were classed as luxury residences – owned by doctors, lawyers and the upper echelons of society. I had a surefire way of earning a few bob. On a good day I made about 3s 3d a bundle.

I gave Mum half of the cash – because she helped to chop up and bundle the wood into a saleable commodity.

With my small fortune, I went regularly to the flicks. I

idolised the stars in the hundreds of films I must have seen. The Coliseum and the Picture House were very close to Wilmot Street. I have a soft spot for both places in my memory.

When I was not at the pictures, I played street games with friends. There were no cars, buses or taxis in Wilmot Street, so it was safe to play.

The games I remember most were marbles, hop-scotch, bluebrick, lurky lurky 1-2-3, conkers, whip and top, milk bottle tops, dishcloth fights, and football with a tennis ball using a front door or a terraced home for a goal.

At the age of 11, I left Christ Church School and attended Rykneld School, then a new building, which unfortunately has since been demolished. I was there for a few years.

From my Wilmot Street home I would set off at 8.15am and arrived for 9am if I was lucky – I say lucky because from 7am each day I did a paper round, and sometimes the papers were late from the wholesalers and this sometimes made me late for school. No excuses were tolerated – you still got the cane!

In the evening, I had another paper round and got a telling off from the newsagent for being late. I sometimes wonder how I made it at all. I delivered papers for the duration of my schooling at Rykneld Secondary Modern.

I earned 7s 6d a week, of which 3s went to my mum. With the rest I bought a bike on the weekly for 1s 6d. The rest of my wages were spent at the cinema.

On leaving school I was fortunate to gain an apprenticeship with Carriage and Wagon Works, which lasted six years. I later worked for Rolls-Royce and Swissair. Looking back at those early years I am convinced that the harder it was to survive the better it was for the masses.

Armistice Day tears

by Ron Parnell, Brooklyn, Burnie, Tasmania

D URING the early 1920s at Brighton Road School (now Southgate Infants) the school Armistice Day ceremony was held indoors due to rain. As we were singing the closing hymn, Abide With Me, I noticed the Class 4 teacher suddenly move behind a blackboard on an easel, crying uncontrollable tears. This was the first time I'd ever seen an adult cry. That scene has stayed with me all these years. Perhaps the solemnity of the occasion or the words and music of the hymn broke the wall of sorrow she had so successfully kept in check. The headmaster told us that her husband had been killed in the last month of the First World War.

Well fed and clothed, a comfortable home, love, care and attention awaited me on my return from school. I learned one day that this was not the same for all boys. A boy allocated to share a desk with me had no coat, no socks or shoes, even though it was winter. He had to wait until someone came home to let him in. That day he showed me his lunch. Two hacked slices of bread thickly smeared with lard. His drink, water from the school tap. I told my mother who wanted to help him, but the boy never returned.

Young girl's impressions of a city at war

by Dorothy Wright, Farningham Close, Spondon

I T SEEMS only like yesterday when war was declared and I was 15-and-a-half. Throughout the years that have flown by I find that memories of the war years have remained the most intense in my life. The military data is well recorded and I just want to tell you about the little things that happened during those eventful years and made an impression on a young girl.

The first winter was bitterly cold and we had soldiers from Scotland billeted in Alvaston. We made up a small party from our avenue and plodded through the snow to Alvaston lake which was solidly frozen and there were people skating on it. I took a very heavy pair of skates that had belonged to my grandad when he used to skate on the frozen River Derwent, and although they were too big for me the soldiers took it in turn to skate on the lake.

Shortly after that the soldiers left for the south. I was working for Nutt Horne and Co and the young men in the office were called up to serve in the RAF or the Army. Each evening, the girls in the office had to carry the ledgers – very large and heavy – down flights of stairs into 'Jimmies' yard and then down into the cellars where the beers and wines were stored. Then each morning we carried them back up again.

When the boys were on leave they came to see us – one a marine, one a pilot and another in the Army. My friend in the office, Marjorie, was married in the cathedral and I was a bridesmaid. Very sadly, after the wedding both he and his best man were killed in the Battle of El Alamein.

We had the excitement of a barrage balloon based down Curzon Lane, and one once broke loose and landed on the roofs of houses in our avenue. There were stirrup pumps in the front gardens ready to be used in case incendiary bombs were dropped. ARP, Civil Defence and Home Guard arm bands were worn and our Anderson shelters were being dug.

Our two neighbours shared with us, which made it quite a squeeze for seven of us in the shelter. We always went down to the shelter when the sirens went off, and it was a long sit on some of those nights. Our neighbour was deaf and he would sit with his ear trumpet outside the door curtain to listen if it was 'one of ours or one of theirs' passing over! Eventually, when it seemed we were in no danger, two of us would sleep under our dining table after first covering the top with cushions.

I remember sometimes being out with a friend, and when the sirens went we would go to the ARP shelter which was in the culvert under Harvey Road. The benches were very hard and it was cold down there. After the 'all-clear' we would quickly run home.

I went to work at the Royal Ordnance Depot in Sinfin Lane in 1940, and worked in the correspondence section as a shorthand typist. We worked one month on days and one month on nights, working alongside the military, and all of us doing our best for the war effort. Those ATS girls were bricks, and marched in all weathers from Normanton Barracks down Sinfin Lane to the depot and back again at the end of a long shift. I made particular friends of two ATS girls and they would come to my home for a sit around a fire which they really missed. One girl's father was a baker at Wath-on-Dearne and he made my 21st birthday cake for me – no icing, but it did have fruit in it!

When we were on nights we came from Alvaston to catch the special buses from Northcliffe House. There were no lights to see where you were and all the bus windows were painted blue. You were spot searched at the depot gates going in and out – security was utmost.

I particularly enjoyed working on nights and it was my job as a fast shorthand writer to go to the canteen, some distance away, and to sit by the radio and take down in shorthand the midnight news bulletin. It was no easy job as the broadcaster spoke quickly. I then ran back to my section and typed five copies of the news and this was picked up by sergeants from various departments and pinned up for 1am on the mess room, NAAFI and canteen noticeboards, for all to see what was happening on the war fronts. I had to make myself familiar with the war areas, and names of rivers and towns in many countries and I found the names on the Russian front the most difficult.

If someone in our section had a birthday we would meet at the Norman Arms to celebrate before going on our night shift. We didn't meet in the town as it became full of Yanks and got very lively. They all had much more money to spend than our soldiers.

On a Saturday, if we could stay awake, we would go to one of the many cinemas and had plenty of choice and sometimes would have a simple tea in either the Gaumont, Odeon or Picture House cafes. There were occasional orchestral concerts at the Grand Theatre, Babington Lane or in the Central Hall.

My mum would queue for cigarettes for my dad and also for anything else that might be going to vary our diet. We had simple and plain meals, a balanced diet, and I was never hungry, but for my mum the problem of feeding five of us and making sandwiches must have been a headache.

We had few coupons to clothe ourselves and I made my own dresses on my grandmother's sewing machine. Underwear was made from parachute silk if you could get it and I once made a coat from one of my grandmother's best woollen blankets. We could sometimes get drawings from a drawing office and when boiled they softened up into lovely handkerchief material! I did not spend my coupons on stockings but painted my legs, both winter and summer, with Henry Miners Liquid Leg Lotion. Mind you, I had chilblains in the cold winters without stockings.

I stayed at the Ordnance Depot until after the end of the war and on my 21st birthday I took my friends to the Gaumont cinema as a celebration. It is as clear in my mind as if it was yesterday.

The night the captain descended on No.3 section

by J LeC Smith, Croft Close, Ockbrook

ONE evening our Captain Fenn was on a surprise round of post inspections and so far had not been displeased with the results. Such defects as he had seen were of no great military consequence and there had been a rewarding eagerness by those who erred to accept correction. His newly-bestowed authority was sitting warm inside and repelled the night's chill. His last call was at our post, No.3 Section, hidden among the hospital outbuildings. He chose a silent and circuitous route to reach his objective with the object of eluding a badly placed or unobservant sentry. Gaining the door without a challenge, however, he turned back and patiently combed the surrounding paths. He now stamped his feet and noisily cleared his throat and indeed only just refrained from breaking into a whistle. There was no reward, all else remained silent. He could only assume now that the post sentry was at the hospital gate a quarter-of-a-mile away. As he retraced his steps he started to compose his homily and decided for himself what would be the best strategic position for the post's guard.

As he jauntily approached the door he pictured the immediate scene. The sudden and expectant hush, his decisive and staccato bark, a most frantic scuffle and within an instant the whole confused assembly orientating itself into a rigid line before him, fearfully awaiting his judgment. Then his faint, but warming, smile, a little straight talking and a positive chorus of 'yes sir'. Alas for our dreams!

The general light inside was poor enough, but the lamp itself, a single, unshielded, yellow-painted bulb, quite captured the eye of the entrant and made all else indiscernible. The captain stood between the parted blanket covering the door and gazed at it as if spellbound, blinking furiously. He imagined, rather than saw, a ring of hostile eyes amid the surrounding gloom. He suddenly felt spot-lighted and naked, the warm confidence of superior rank deserted him, he was just one against many and, as was his misfortune under such circumstances, he stuttered.

His defensive, aggressive "Www …" however produced no derisive jeer, in fact it produced nothing. In spite of the yellow spotlight and his vocal struggles his entry had so far passed unobserved. Far from being the fox in the henhouse of his previous expectations or the Daniel in the lion's den of his present imaginings, it soon became apparent that he was making no impression whatever.

As the lamp released its hold on his eyes and he surroundings became clearer, he saw that the members of No.3 Section were going about the various businesses without regard for his awful presence. One bed-making individual back-sided into him with arms full of paliasse and gave but the most off-hand of apologies, while another heavily tapped him on his newly be-pipped shoulder and thumbing the blanketed door behind said: "You've left the blackout caught up, mate." In spite of himself and with credit to his training he paused in his "Www …"s and adjusted the offending shield, but realisation of the indignity caused a sharp rise in his already upward trending temper.

The consonants are not efficient clarions, and had his pent-up vocal organs not have exploded into their first vowel the might have stood there unregarded all night. As it was, the whole delayed query burst forth with a considerable bang.

"Where's the guard?" Everyone, with the exception of the elderly gentleman in the far corner, looked at the explosive visitor with mild surprise. Each decided that the provision of an answer to the ill-understood, albeit thunderous, question was not his special responsibility and after the briefest and most uncomplimentary pauses each resumed the task in hand. Only the owner of the shirt on which the captain had unwittingly placed his foot spoke at all, and he with gentle sarcasm "Do you mind?"

The captain went over the top. "Do you know who I am?" The query was charged with outrage and threat. The shirt owner, having recovered his property, kept silent. It had been a heavy day, he was out of fags and this turn of duty had meant him missing a darts match. He was certainly in no mood for midnight guessing games with staff strangers and none of his compatriots offered to stand in.

The captain decided that he was attacking on too broad a front and that the section leader alone should bear the brunt. Unfortunately, this wise decision coincided with another attack of stutters and for some seconds his "Hhh …" was no more successful than his "www"s had been.

This slight delay did not perturb his phlegmatic enemy, but brought captain's temperature up to boiling point, so that his eventual "Who's in charge here?" was almost falsetto.

As such it touched a kindly soul who had some experience with an hysterical wife and he ambled across the floor. The captain surveyed the tousled hair, unshaved chin and frayed braces with distaste.

"Are you the section leader?"

"No, it's Archie. I'm in th' corner," said the self-appointed emissary, indicating the elderly gentleman aforementioned, who lay on his pack, pillows propped behind, nodding gently as if in agreement with the suggestions which an invisible Morpheus was whispering in his ear.

"But I shouldn't wake 'im now, 'e 'as trouble getting off."

But Fenn hadn't heard the plea, he was already across the room and prodding the poor old white-haired form with his little cane.

Archie awoke with a start and a grunt, mumbled incoherently, dropped his eyes to the cane and in his chest, and slowly followed it out and up with narrowing eyes to the purple face of Captain Fenn.

"Are you the section commander?" said Fenn.

Archie turned to the occupant of the next bunk, who was sitting thereon cleaning his boots.

"What's he say Arthur?"

"Wants to know if you're the section commander," bellowed Arthur in his ear.

"Yes, he is" he went on in normal tones addressing the captain, "deaf, you know, is Harch. Put on your 'earing haid, Harch." The bellow was back for Harch's benefit.

The captain burned with impatience as Archie leisurely sought his apparatus among the paraphernalia. He hopped from one foot to the other, looked at his watch three or four times, tapped his cane in his palm and scowled at the rest of the section, who at last had been made collectively aware of his presence. He looked yet again at his watch, its message not having been appreciated before. Three long minutes since he entered, it told him, and the only man on his feet himself.

He burned again, "Hurry up man!" Archie had the gear assembled, but seemed to detect a technical hitch. He clicked his fingers in the microphone and turned the little white knob.

"What's up, Harch?" bellowed Arthur, "battery gone flat again?"

"Aye," said Archie, "damned thing."

He fiddled for a little while longer than included his right ear towards the captain, "You'll just have to shout mate," he said.

To shout was just about the only thing the good man was able to excel in at the particular time, and the invitation was quite superfluous, except that it unlocked the vocal impediment, but it did nothing for his coherence. In the ensuing five minutes he broke every rule in the Army manual which he so much admired, which was his bedside companion, and of which he imagined himself to be the most devoted disciple.

His strictures, commands and questions cascaded in such overwhelming rapidity that even they had followed in a rational sequence, had they been delivered at high noon and had they been directed at a body of super-trained commandos, they would have caused not a little confusion. Jumbled as they were, and jumbled in the small hours, and received by a jumble of ancients and raw part-timers, they eliminated each other like a falling row of standing dominoes and left just nothing.

No even in Fenn. He was drained. He looked at his watch, tapped his palm with his cane, turned, blundered into the wrong side of the door blanket, searched for the door handle which wasn't there, turned back again to face his innocent tormentors, forlorn and spent. The kindly sole ambled forward yet again, opened the door and Fenn departed into the night. The section readjusted itself for rest.

"Funny b....r," said someone.

Working Days

How I became a theatreholic

by Anne Scales (née Brodie), Pentyrch, Cardiff

I WAS born Anne Brodie, in September 1948, the only child of a carpenter/joiner who fortunately worked for British Railways in Derby, so the family could all travel free by train. My parents, who both enjoyed theatre, periodically took me to London to see the latest West End comedy. I even have a London programme of Noddy in Toyland! There were also works outings to pantomimes at Derby Hippodrome; and we were the first family in the street to have television.

I acted myself, at Pear Tree Junior School, and later at Parkfield Cedars, including playing Jessica in The Merchant of Venice. In 1967 I left Derby, to study for my degrees; but I often came home, with free rail passes, until the summer of 1971, when I married an ex-Bemrose graduate, Michael Scales. Since then we have lived in south Wales, where I carry out freelance genealogical research.

My first recorded trip to Derby Playhouse (then of course in Sacheveral Street) was on May Day, 1962. I soon became a theatreholic: I have 99 Playhouse programmes from 1962-71!

I first went to the Playhouse with St Thomas' Road Methodist Church Youth Club, but at other times I went alone or with schoolfriends, or with boys from Bemrose or Derby School.

At some stage I joined Derby Playhouse Young Playgoers' Club, and in 1966-67 was its secretary. My first Playhouse programme states that Young Playgoers could 'obtain very attractive price concessions, and take part in interesting social and cultural activities'. Membership cost 2s 6d in August 1964, and probably hadn't risen by the autumn of 1967, from around which time I have an undated pink membership application form stating 'Membership of the Young Playgoers Club is limited to anyone between the ages of 13 and 21 and to FULL-TIME students of any age. Membership entitles you to:

(1) Book seats at half-price for all performances, except on Saturdays at 8pm, on Bank Holidays and during pantomimes. Seats cannot be booked earlier than half an hour before the performance;

(2) Take part in all activities organised for members, such as coffee mornings, special entertainments and outings to other theatres;

(3) Receive advance notice of such activities and of programmes of plays.'

By October 1965, in addition to offering discounts and trips, the assistant producer, John Innes, was hoping to initiate YP sessions in improvisation etc; though at that time no premises were available. But from Autumn 1966, the theatre had a large rehearsal room (accessed from Sitwell Street up a fire escape I think!) and we met there weekly on Wednesday evenings. We had a talk by Peter Cheeseman, and sessions on stage make-up, theatre design, etc; as well as playreadings and mime workshops. Sometimes we met the cast of the Playhouse show: I remember meeting Marius Goring, the guest star of The Bells. In 1966-7, 18 of Parkfields' Upper Sixth were members! Peter Kenvyn ran the YP then, having arrived in the autumn of 1965 as an assistant stage manager, and quickly risen to stage manager, then assistant producer. In 1967-8, the Playhouse received Arts Council funding to extend its youth work. Chris(tine) Denmead took over as PRO/Youth Officer from September 1967 to the summer of 1968, and was replaced by Jeff(rey) Dowson from the autumn of 1968.

Although I suppose I was too young to understand everything, I did enjoy almost all the plays I saw – I only remember actively disliking two or three. Of course, many of today's plays, involving nudity, swear words, simulated drug-taking, etc, are very different from those of my teens – stage censorship was not abolished until 1968!

In 1969 Derby Playhouse celebrated its 21st birthday, and in its souvenir brochure the chairman, Major Malin, told how it began in Becket Street in 1948, with twice-nightly weekly rep to a club audience, 'with a great deal of amateur assistance'. The theatre moved to Sacheveral Street from 1952 'with an all-professional acting company, still very much helped by voluntary assistance both front of house and backstage'. The fire in 1956 caused a 13-month closure, but led to 'an improved theatre' and 'better productions'.

In 1960, Derby Playhouse became the first repertory theatre to change from weekly to fortnightly (better prepared) productions; the same core company members appearing in a succession of plays, acting in one each evening (twice on Saturdays) while rehearsing the next each day. A new play opened on the Monday after the previous one closed on the Saturday, with the stage crew busily demolishing and building sets over the weekend, between playing small acting roles. Only a few plays ran for three weeks, though Christmas shows ran for a month (with two shows a day during the school holiday fortnight). From February 1965, openings were deferred until Tuesdays. From Autumn 1966, more guest actors were introduced, but memorable company regulars from my early days were Mary Lainè (for 11 years from 1956-67), Michael Hall (for eight years to the summer of 1966), Carolyn Moody and Gareth Gwenlan. And in 1964-65 I had a particular crush on the dishy Bernard Holley.

The Playhouse also played host to the Derby Shakespeare Society, which each spring performed two plays successively for a week each, from Monday to Saturday. (This perhaps also served to give the regulars a couple of weeks of welcome break before rehearsing their next show).

In May and June 1971 a programme explained why that summer the theatre would close for 11 weeks ('better summers' having resulted in audiences being poorer in May, June and July of the previous few years); and why, that autumn, a regular three-weekly production cycle would be introduced, allowing more time for rehearsal, with shows opening on a Thursday and lasting two-and-a-half weeks, with a 40-week season including 'no more than 12 productions by the Playhouse company'. By then, fund-raising was well in hand for the Playhouse's new building in the Eagle Centre, to which it would move in autumn 1973, and where it achieves continuing success today.

Full-price tickets in spring 1962 ranged from 2s 6d to 6s 6d, with no mention of reductions other than for YP and Theatre Club members; the latter paying 5s a year to join, entitling them to half-price seats on first nights. Tickets must have been good value, because in the 21st anniversary brochure, box office staff of the 1960s remembered with great affection one little old lady in a pink hat who used to book the same seat, Q3 in the rear stalls, about three times a week – it was by a radiator, and cheaper than heating her home!

Playhouse programmes have improved massively since

The fire in 1956 caused a 13-month closure, but led to 'an improved theatre' and 'better productions'.

The old Derby Playhouse building in Sacheveral Street in 1977.

current productions at other 'local' theatres (up to about 13, from Sheffield to Northampton) for which bookings could be made at the Playhouse through the Midlands Inter-Booking Scheme.

In the 1967-68 season, some programmes said: "This theatre operates a Student Trainee Scheme in co-operation with the Manchester College of Art & Design". For 1968-69 this is replaced by "Northern School of Drama, Manchester." In December, 1968, one such student mentioned was Elizabeth Estensen.

the early 1960s. There was, of course, a list of cast and crew, and a synopsis of scenes. This was followed by 'Members of the audience are requested not to smoke except during the intervals. Ladies are requested to remove their hats.' Not until September 1967 did that paragraph change to 'Members of the audience are requested not to smoke in the auditorium at any time'. There was also an informative paragraph about the next show, and a list of other forthcoming productions, as well as details of seat prices, and acknowledgments; and advertisements for local shops and services. Until May, 1968, there was no article about the production, the play, the author, the director, nor the issues involved; and there was not even a biography of any of the actors, never mind a photograph of each. From that date there was occasionally a photograph and biography of a guest star, a biography of a guest director, or some background information about a play; but it seems to have been March 1969 before photographs of more than one actor appeared in the same programme, and this was far from regular practice even then.

A nice touch in my early days was that when someone new joined the company, he or she might be introduced to us in a special paragraph in the programme. This was the case in 1962, with Frederick Pyne, who at 25 had just made his stage debut at the Playhouse in Simple Spymen, having joined the company early in April as assistant stage manager, straight from RADA, where he had won 'one of RADA's highest prizes'. Freddie Pyne, of course, later became a regular in Emmerdale.

Another nice touch from September, 1970 was a list of

My 1960s Playhouse visits fostered a lifelong enjoyment of watching familiar (not necessarily famous) performers take on the challenge of different roles. Nowadays, in Cardiff, I am minutes secretary of the Friends of Welsh College of Music and Drama, and for the last decade I have loved watching drama students develop over their years at college, and of course am delighted when I later see 'my' boys and girls acting professionally on stage or screen.

My 24-year-old son Peter shares my interest, and was a keen member of Cardiff's Sherman Youth Theatre (and its first magazine editor), and of the National Youth Theatre of Wales, before studying for a BA in Drama, and an MA in Theatre Film & Television Studies, at Aberystwyth; where he has appeared in many plays and musicals, and obtained his Equity card. He has been DJ at the Welsh BAFTA Awards Ceremony in 1998 and 1999, and last year was Front of House Manager for the Welsh International Film Festival.

I haven't acted since leaving school, but here in Cardiff I have stage-managed several successful plays for the Sherman Adult Drama Group, and Peter and I help with Everyman Open Air Theatre Festivals. I have also edited several Lesley Ross plays, and helped run his Ripley Theatre (not Derbyshire's Ripley), spending five successive summers with them at the Edinburgh Fringe.

Half a lifetime of interest and support has been honoured by my having been selected for the 1998-99 TMA/Barclays Theatre Awards Panel.

In 1998 I was thrilled to attend the Derby Playhouse Gala Evening of Blues in the Night, complete with champagne buffet, and with a super post-show cabaret by the cast. It was a very poignant evening for me. Thanks to nurturing by Derby Playhouse during the 1960s, I had enjoyed 36 stimulating years of theatre-going. I hope to enjoy at least 36 more.

The man from the Prudential

IT WAS a complete change from being a tradesman doing as asked, to persuading the public to buy insurance and pay their dues. I met some lovely people and also some with some very odd habits.

Two of my clients, a mother and daughter lived about six houses from each other. One washday I saw them pushing a big mangle between their two homes. A neighbour indicated that this was a regular occurrence.

One lady had a mania for house cleanliness. I called on Fridays, about midday. From the outside door, through the kitchen and dining room and beyond, newspapers were laid to be walked on. The table, sideboard and piano legs were wrapped in newspaper.

Another widowed lady never failed to have her money on time. I was told she worked long hours at any sort of job, however menial during those depression years, to pay the instalments on a secondhand piano for her daughter.

A tall, red-haired, well-built woman, bare arms folded across her ample chest, shouted to me as I crossed the road to her. "Where the b….. h… have you been?" She was one of my more difficult customers but, that day, was all charm. Astounding. She invited me in for a cup of tea. I was hesitant. Her husband was due home soon and I wasn't too sure of the cleanliness. It was clean, and he did come home. A tough-looking man, an outside worker,

*by Ron Parnell
Brooklyn
Burnie
Tasmania*

corduroy trousers held up by brass buckled belt, bowyangs at the knees. Despite an outward appearance of toughness he showed another side, a love of budgerigars. I was taken to see his 100 or so in his garden aviary. He must have forgotten I was there as he talked to them almost like a mother to a newborn babe. A lesson in humility to me?

I had a very difficult case. My client, a woman of about 25 and her husband whom I'd never seen. If I wasn't at their door on Friday between 5.30pm and 6pm there was no chance of collecting any money. The moment hubby arrived home, within minutes they'd be off to the pub. So I decided to make a visit on a Saturday morning just after 9am. However hard I knocked on the back door there was no reply. I did something I didn't normally do, I looked through the window of what would be the dining room. What a sight. The room was a pigsty. The fire burnt out, the hearth mostly covered in greasy papers holding cold chips and bits of fish seemingly flung into the ashes. A table covered by more greasy newspaper, unwashed glasses, empty bottles and stale chips plus the remnants of a loaf of bread. Kneeling on the table in the mess trying to cut the bread was a child probably no more than four. His only clothing a short, dirty vest, his little backside bare to the world. I knocked and knocked without success (I can't remember what action I took).

An insurance collector learned a lot about the way people lived!

Pay demands paid off

IN JULY 1937, aged 14, I left Reginald Street School on the Friday, and began my working life at F.W. Hampshire's in Sinfin Lane, Derby, the following Monday.

It wasn't a lot different from school. We had to wear a uniform, a khaki overall, white muslin cap with khaki trim, and were not allowed to talk but had to get on with the work.

When we needed to go to the lavatory we had to ask the white-uniformed forewoman for the key which she kept in her pocket. Hard luck if someone was already using it, you had to wait until the key was returned.

I recall vividly one little newcomer too terrified to ask for the key sat with a slowly growing puddle collecting around the legs of the stool she was sat on.

Our pay rate was two and a half pence an hour in old money. After deductions my first week's wage was eight shillings and ten and a half

*by Ivy Ryalls,
Strathmore
Avenue,
Alvaston*

pence for the 48-hour week. Saturday mornings were a normal part of the working week in those days.

It was an incredibly clean place. Every Friday afternoon at about three o'clock all production stopped, and we all had to get down on our knees and scrub everything with hot water and bar soap. The floors were all wooden, the corridors too, and they all were scrubbed, and also the lavatories.

There were on-the-spot searches of employees as they left the factory. It was to make sure none of the products were concealed about a person.

In those days an employee was moved around the different departments wherever extra hands were needed, and in that way many skills were acquired. I enjoyed working where the fruity brown sauce was made because I could nibble the dates, and when we packed fruit jellies the flavours were wonderful. I wasn't at all keen to work in the custard powder room, because your clothes, hair, shoes, everything was dusty with custard powder. You wouldn't dare go out in the rain or you would turn into a blancmange.

I dreaded having to work in the room where the powder shampoos were put into sachets. My eyes and nose streamed the moment I started work.

Ivy Ryalls outside her parents' home in Porter Road in 1941.

Making the fish glue to cover the sticky fly papers wasn't too bad. I had to dig the brown noxious gunge out of a wooden barrel. Up to my elbows I plunged, it was soothing to the skin, and I always got a seat to myself on the bus going home. PHEW!

When I was about 17, I was 'promoted' to work in the stores upstairs. Requisitions from every department came there for me to gather together the ingredients for whatever that department was producing. I loved getting the orders from the face powder, lipstick, face cream, and rouge departments. The concentrated perfumes for these toiletries were kept in a separate little room. There was row upon row of labelled bottles, the smell was wonderful. My fiance was serving aboard the aircraft carrier HMS Illustrious in the Pacific, so one day I just dabbed the cork of one of the bottles on to one of the sheets of a letter I had written to him. I thought that it made a rather greasy mark but I sent it off.

About two weeks later I received a frantic appeal from him not to put any more perfume on my letters as all the ship's mail was enclosed in mail-bags, and the whole lot was impregnated with the smell from the letter addressed to him… ah well! The thought was there.

Although the firm did manufacture ointments etc for the Armed Forces, I didn't feel that it was actually war work, and so I left the firm (I did return many years later). I went to work at International Combustion exactly opposite F.W. Hampshire's.

I was put in the training school with other women. We were taught to read engineering drawings, to work drilling machines, lathes, and borers. How to use all the tools of the trade, files, scrapers, depth gauges, feelers, micrometers etc. And then introduced to the big workshop to start working on components for the torpedoes for the Admiralty's submarines.

It was so cold in that workshop especially during the night shift, and in the winter. My workbench was close to the huge doors that opened to let in the railway engine… and the rain, snow, sleet and fog.

Women's wages were abysmal for the amount of hours worked and the type of work they were expected to do. We learned that women in other workplaces were on a higher wage than we were, so a small posse of us bearded the boss in his den one day, and eventually got a two shillings and sixpence a week increase in the women's wages. We learned later that the boss had said he was terrified at being confronted with a number of women in his office. Women standing up for themselves had never been known before. I bet he wasn't half as scared as we were.

When the war ended many of the women returned to their home towns. A few of us were transferred into inspection in the machine shop were we worked on components for power stations. I stayed there until Easter 1947, and as I rode home on my pushbike the snow was still piled high at the side of the roads.

In September of that year I gave birth to our first child, a son. A daughter followed in 1950, and for the next ten years I was a full-time homemaker.

Towards the end of 1960 I heard that toffee-packers were needed at 'Fancygoods', a little factory at the foot of the bridge that crossed the canal on Boulton Lane, Allenton. The work was only for a few weeks leading up to Christmas. What an experience!

A very good year

by Keith Webb, Nottingham Road, Spondon

NINETEEN hundred and 38 (1938) was a very good year. It was the year I was born. Mum's midwives were two neighbours (Mrs Gadsby and Mrs Oldknow) both later chosen as my godparents. I was born at home on Saturday, October 15 at 6.10am. Home births were the norm, with neighbours and relations playing a major support role at the birth and at many times after. Preparations were made weeks in advance for adequate clean linen and basic needs to be stored in the well polished dressing table drawer in readiness for the approaching big event. My father was a weaver at British Celanese Spondon and my mother struggled on his inadequate wage of on-off employment to bring up five of us. We were poor, but always well looked after, with a sense of cleanliness and pride. Times were hard in those far-off days, meals were meagre and 'housewife ingenuity' in creating meal out of 'scrag ends and yesterdays leftovers was an absolute necessity of the period . . . Uneaten portions from someone a little too finicky were highly sought after by a sister or brother with a more voracious appetite.

With many adults out of work, homegrown produce was a priority and the smallest of gardens sustained a range of well-maintained vegetable plots. Often menfolk would rise early in the morning to complete a sortie into the countryside on a poaching forage or snare fishing. Seasonal fruits and vegetables growing wild were also sought, their locations would be meticulously memorised and the poachers would go to great trouble to cover their tracks from others of the same mind. Any excess which wouldn't keep could easily be sold for a few bob or swapped for a bartered gain. Chicken coops adorned many backyards and in some cases there was the occasional duck or even a pig or two. I can remember the excitement in our house when mum won a young hog in a local raffle. However, nobody fancied killing a young male pig or even finding sufficient scraps to feed it up, so she sold it to a local farmer for ten bob (a relative windfall for mum at that time).

The tension in Europe was rising and on Monday, September 4, 1939, the unmistakable voice of Neville Chamberlain in an historic radio message to the nation proclaimed the country to be at war with Germany. My mum recalled how the household fell silent as the severity of his voice resonated around the small room.

Broadcast announcements, giving advice and other information and emergency procedures were bought into operation. There was the stark realisation of the outbreak of the Second World War, affecting every house in the land in one way or another: gas masks, identity cards, ration books, food on a graded points value system. Anderson shelters, air raid wardens, Home Guard units, and rocket sites and the big ack ack anti aircraft gun emplacements. Nissen huts and barrage balloons with their long thick steel hauser cables anchoring them firmly to the ground – well most of the time anyway. All this was soon to become part of a very different daily life.

Dad was already in the Territorial Army at the Drill Hall in Becket Street and being retained he had all his kit at home. With only a few hours' notice he was called to service with the Sherwood Foresters at Normanton Barracks. My mother recalled the sense of inadequacy that they felt on their last night together, each knowing the reality of him fighting on foreign soil. He trying to reassure her that it wouldn't be for long and he would be back before she knew it.

Many a brave face hid a host of fears at this dreadful time. After a fitful, near sleepless night, the autumn dawn came all too soon and they rose early in readiness, for their last long walk together. It was a family affair, my mother pushing my pram with me tucked snugly up inside and my sister Brenda perched on the pram apron between the handles. Jean and Muriel either side of the pram and Frank striding along in front of my Dad with an old brush handle over his shoulder as a pretend rifle. Osmaston Park Road was teeming with many such families as they and their menfolk all headed to the Barracks to enlist.

Those tall heavy iron gates and massive brick gate pillars surmounted with the imposing dark grey stone copings and the individual pitched roof timber sentry boxes just inside were to be imprinted on everyone's mind that day as lingering farewells were abruptly interrupted by the bellowing voices of the Senior NCOs marshalling the somewhat-bewildered men into long silent lines on the barrack square. Gone was the brave camaraderie; replaced now with thumping hearts as minds tried to come to terms with the awesome reality: this was it, . . . this was really it . . . the start of the impending war . . . training was beginning with surreal earnest . . .

The families stood around in nervous groups outside the barrack gates before breaking away to make the journey back home in subdued silence. The loss within such families was immeasurable. Days seemed longer as wives fought back their almost continual tears, their sense of despair and vulnerability as they cleaned and recleaned and polished their homes or gathered to talk over each others' fences to console or boost each others' confidence. Lines were full of washing, washed and rewashed again, anything to make the hours fill up before the weariness of the night's broken sleep.

It was a time of situations never experienced before, a time when neighbour comforted neighbour, where bonds of friendship were forged to tie people on both sides of a street with a togetherness and understanding of each other's helplessness and devastation through the duration of the war and, for many, many years beyond.

Keith Webb more than 50 years ago.

Each rallying to help the other, their true emotions hidden from their children's inquiring faces. Yet, despite the inner turmoil of their hearts, neighbours, friends and relatives formed the backbone of the British Back Home. Women took on men's jobs, learnt new skills in engineering, munitions work, farming and jobs which were all strictly men-only before the war.

They achieved a standard in their work which can only be attributed to guts, determination, patience, hidden talents and their dexterity. Many, of course, were also mothers still lavishing love and care on their 'orphans of war'. Feeding their faces as best they could. Borrow a cup of sugar here, swap ration coupons for something else, have essentials on tick at the corner shop and promising to pay the coalman the next time around. I can still recall our coalmen, the Holmes family from near Ripley. They

delivered to our family from before the war right through into the 1980s. During the tough times of the war years they helped many a family in our road with coal on 'strap' and probably many others around and about the area too. I wasn't old enough to take all of this in at that time, although much of it was in evidence as I grew older, but in later years, mum and I spent many hours discussing those somewhat tragic times. She recalled the day of the War Office official notification where the words leapt from the page: '…Sergeant Frank James Webb
MISSING PRESUMED DEAD….'

The numbness sweeping through her body, her hand shaking, reaching out subconsciously to steady the chair against the kitchen table as lifeless legs drained support. Stricken with the enormity of grief and fear and the woolley greyness of the future. a panic situation searing every corner of the mind, unable to think any clear thought. My own helplessness in the feeling of not being able to do anything effectively to help someone you love, than to cling to her frail wrought sobbing body in a gesture of comfort. A time where fears and tears took over all of us many times together and also in our moments alone. Where happiness dissolved and puffy eyes absorbed the enormity of the emotions. I can remember the desperation of her careworn face cupped in workworn hands. These were situations I relived many times through my early life of those dark and nervous war-torn days.

The haunting sound of the air raid warning siren heralding another night in the Anderson shelter at the bottom of our garden, half buried in the ground with the top half covered in concrete and mounds of earth. The blast sheet of corrugated high tensile steel set up across the entrance and shrouded with another wall of sand bags. Some 'shelters' were cold and wet and dank. We were lucky – ours was dry, and our neighbours: Ted Oldknow from 107 and Cess Fearn from 111 (whose families shared the shelter with us), had made extra seats, bunk beds and bookshelves. Lighting was by hurricane lamp or candles in saucers of water, plus of course the obligatory blackout blanket at the entrance.

We came close to being bombed on two separate occasions. Firstly, that fateful evening of January 15, 1941, bombs were jettisoned on Derby a matter of a mile or so away from where we lived. The more daring stood outside the shelter in the pitch black of the night as the lone bomber circled. Some said the pilot was lost and his hits were just lucky, caused by him frantically loading his bombs as he was picked out in the criss cross of the search lights from Osmaston Park Road recreation ground. Or was he the target marker plane? Whatever the true facts, the Midland Station and the local area around was badly damaged. The following German aircraft filled the black night sky above us, shadowy silhouettes of around 40 to 50 enemy planes, the sharp distinctive lines of the tracer bullets and the exploding anti aircraft shells from our local defence units now erupted as frenzied efforts were made to repel the marauding Heinkels and Dornier bombers. There were soon reports amongst the neighbours of Derby Train Sidings being damaged, with the surrounding houses being blasted and set on fire and many people killed.

The second incident of an even closer bombing was on the morning of July 27, 1942, as we were having breakfast just before 8am when the droning noise of an aircraft flying very low drew us all outside. The image is still very graphic in my mind as it approached the Rolls-Royce factory some 100 yards away and, flying only a matter of some 20 to 30 feet above the surrounding roof tops. The menacing black image with the large German cross clearly on the side of the plane and then the bombs being released. The impact noise was deafening. No-one thought to run for the shelter, the sirens had not sounded and there had not been any ground fire at the aircraft. Someone shouted to get down on to the floor as the blast rattled the windows but did not cause any damage. All the neighbours were in the back gardens shouting to check if other families were all right. Reports soon reached us about the damage at Royces and the devastation of the houses in Hawthorn Street. The death toll and injuries were also severe as it was from other parts of Derby as the lone attacker proceeded unhindered bombing and strafing the suburbs and centre of Derby.

Like most other houses we had black-out blinds or black-out blankets up at all the windows in the house and one inch wide brown sticky paper stuck across the small Georgian style panes of glass on the inside of each window to help stop injuries from flying shards of glass in the event of bomb blast.

My memory is also of a pre-war friend of my father's, who was in Dad's platoon, calling to see my Mum with the first actual news of Dad's death. He had himself been badly injured and sent back to Blighty to recuperate. He related to Mum how they had been pinned down in the trenches in France for nearly a week by German heavy artillery and snipers. The conditions were horrendous, meals were meagre, bully beef, hard biscuits, and hard, very hard chocolate on very sparse occasions if you were 'lucky' with supplies. The torrential rain was incessant, forming ponds in the thick heavy clay of the trenches as they crouched down, their rubberised ground sheets doubling as capes draped around their aching shoulders and lower limbs. The rain drumming on their wide-brimmed tin helmets as if they were under a tin roof. Soldiers with sodden boots and puttees, their feet soggy, cold bloodless white crinkled skin peeling away on its

own with continually being immersed in sodden wool socks. Waiting, waiting, waiting for the command to advance.

Finally it had come, and rain-soaked aching limbs seemingly devoid of energy scrambling out of trenches up behind the excavated mounds of earth, piled up in front, as the only safety barrier between them and the enemy. He recalled my father leading the platoon forward and the image of the moment of bodily destruction as a snipers' bullet struck dad's ammunition pouch. He tried to comfort mum, saying that dad wouldn't have known anything about it, as it happened so fast. Even though I was so young, the incredibility of my imagination as I conjured up this very poignant scene in my mind, still sticks vividly with me, even to this day.

I cried because my mother was crying, and the soldier was crying too. Yet I didn't fully understand the implication of this first-hand account of death. Death not just of someone, but the death of my father . . . I had no image of him, except from my mother's treasured photographs. I was too young to remember him. I was just 18 months old when he went to France, never to return. We never knew his true final resting place, as like many other families didn't of their loved ones.

Notwithstanding all the turmoil which must have constantly enveloped my mother's life in these traumatic times, the love and affection she gave to us all is something I have treasured deep within my soul and which will remain with me forever. It is hard to understand how mum had so much resilience to cope with those hard times in raising five of us together with the tremendous loss of dad. Above all of this sadness was surmounted in her a dry sense of humour, a sense of goodness, respectability, the pride of doing a good job and a level of care and protection to us which I feel together with the depth of her love and beliefs guided our early formative years.

Despite the hand-me-down clothes and the friends' and neighbours' pass-ons, mum always ensured they were pressed and clean. Washing in those days was generally by the use of the galvanised tub and ponch with a washboard and mangle, plus a good lathering of green Fairy block soap or red carbolic. Water was invariably heated by the coal heated brick copper which we had to fill by bucket and then ladle or empty the hot water out in the same way. The fireplace for us was a cast iron range in the kitchen consisting of a combination hot water boiler and cooking ovens which were coal fired. When chopped sticks were not available one of my jobs in the evenings was to make paper sticks out of old newspapers cut up into lengths about nine inches long and then rolled tightly and twisted into half a reef knot which enabled them to burn slowly enough to get the small coals alight, then the large sheet of newspaper (very versatile this commodity) placed across the front grill of the fire to form a draw screen to get a good draft through the bottom of the fire to ignite the coals well – before banking up the fire with bigger coal lumps.

Chimneys always needed to be swept regularly and cost either sixpence or a shilling dependent on how thick the soot was in the main chimney. Our local chimney sweep was Mr Hunt who lived with his family at number 103. As the youngest of our family I was always despatched outside to watch for the sweep's brush to appear out of the chimney pot, then rush back in doors to tell the sweep – who by then knew before me by the amount of soot that had come crashing down into the hearth dislodged by the hard coal tar deposits from the inside of the chimney pot.

A major family chore of those days was to black lead the cast iron grate and to wire wool clean the stainless steel trims and also clean out the intricate system of the range's pre-formed flues. When the fire was made in the morning we used to put house bricks in the range warming oven until they were nearly too hot to handle, then wrap them in towels and take them to bed with us at night as hot water bottles.

With all the love and attention bestowed on us, life, apart from the obvious, was generally a very happy time for me; until my first day at primary school. How memorable that day is. Like a lamb to the slaughter, I held my mother's hand and clutching my lunch box, cheerfully made the short journey to the Nightingale Road Infants School along with the other unsuspecting kids. We were led into the large school hall and made to sit cross-legged on the polished wood block floor. It seemed a good game, we were enjoying ourselves all chattering away and shouting to each other…. Then Miss Prince, the headmistress appeared. She looked about 8ft tall and 3ft wide and had a loud booming voice that scared the pants off you as you sat. She read out a list of rules and regulations, which didn't make any sense to me at all and then we were ushered into classrooms to sit on small, low, round-backed chairs at little diddy desks. Miss Marfleet, the class teacher, read us a story and then gave us some paper and crayons to draw and colour with. What a great time I thought. The school monitors appeared with the milk. Third of a pint glass bottles with waxed cardboard lids (from Hadfield's Dairy) with a small press-in section to put the straw through. What a treat: cool fresh milk and extras if you wanted it. This was OK, I thought. Then the school bell and everyone filed out of class into the playground. I was so excited with my first day at school I ran all the way home to tell my mum all about it. "What are you doing back here," she said. "It's only 11am. Now come along back to school." …."I didn't want to go back.

I've been once – No-one had said I had to go all day…"

I struggled but to no avail. With a tight grip on my wrist and that determined glint in her eye which said an unspoken: 'No Messing', mum frogmarched me back to the school office. There I was met by that same formidable figure of Miss Prince. Ah, Mrs Webb, the Wanderer returns. "Come along Keith," she said taking an even firmer grip on my other wrist. "Come inside to the classroom and play with the lovely wooden blocks." "NO. NO!" I wailed, "I don't want to play with your horrible bloody wooden blocks."

"Keith!" exclaimed my mother. "Don't use that word." I'd heard bloody on the streets with the big kids, but it was the first time I had ventured to use it. Obviously, I had chosen the wrong time, I thought, as I felt the smack of my mother's hand on my bare leg as she was much quicker than the recoil I tried to make in anticipation. My leg smarted and started to glow a deepening red. I fought back the tears as I heard Miss Prince saying: "Don't worry Mrs Webb, Keith will be fine with me and we will see you at 3pm this afternoon," as she led me firmly away.

Somewhat subdued now, I reluctantly accepted my new daily routine. Funnily enough after that first week I settled well to school life. Many thanks here to the great dedication of teachers, Miss Marfleet, Miss Draper, Mr Turner, Miss Frawley. Mr Bissel the French teacher, Mr Norton and the respective heads, Miss Prince (Primary) and Mr Stevenson (Juniors). They were strict, caring, informative and interesting teachers of the old three 'three Rs' regime.

As war progressed to its final stages, the highlights of our after-school hours was to go on to Osmaston Park recreation ground with my two best mates George and Ray Jeffreys where we would visit the Army detachment who would let us sit on the ack-ack guns and the large search lights. They would then operate the turning and elevation mechanism for us and we would pretend to be the Army in action.

The War was continuing in Europe with the Allied troops and long-range bombing sorties gradually making more and more progress against the badly hit lines of German defence as they fell into panic, retreating on several fronts until an unconditional surrender on Monday, May 7, 1945.

VE DAY … VICTORY IN EUROPE

Plans in our road had been bubbling along for over a month as families guessing that the war was rapidly drawing to a close started to get together to co-ordinate our celebration street party.

On the morning of Tuesday, May 8, the houses were abuzz with activity. Two hand car loads of trestle tables arrived outside our house about 10am and were erected down the centre of the road, they started outside our house and stretched end to end right up to Mrs Thorley's at No 116 a distance of some 60 yards. Homemade coloured bunting and flags criss-crossed the road from house to house. By afternoon crisp starched white sheets appeared as if by magic from the various houses to act as tablecloths and then from the houses up and down the block materialised trays and bowls of prepared food, chairs, stools, beakers, plates, dishes, sandwiches, trifles and jellies and tins of Carnation cream. Kids were milling about getting in everybody's way, everyone was laughing and joking and music was playing from gramophones and radios. Adults and kids alike were acting the fool until it was time to sit down to eat. There was no mad scramble despite all the excitement. Kids were lined up behind the chairs provided by their own family (that way you got to take your own back home afterwards). After the vicar from Saint Bartholomew's, our local church, gave a blessing and we all said the Lord's Prayer and grace, we were then seated and tucking in under the eagle-eyed supervision of our respective parents. The hubbub of noise at the tables was tremendous and afterwards we helped to clear away, and the adults organised games and competitions. I can remember it all going on late into the night as I watched from the upstairs front bedroom window as neighbours and friends and other visitors joined in with the dancing and others stood watching and drinking and joking together.

The next morning when I went outside the front gate, people were already busy cleaning up the road and carting away the trestle tables. This period was a turning point for many families as their loved ones started to come home. The spirit and laughter was now noticeably more to the fore in people. Jobs became more available, particularly in the clearing up operations in the aftermath of those suppressing war years.

With the war ended, we used to stand by the park gates at the top of Nightingale Road as the American convoys drove up Osmaston Park Road from Allenton towards Normanton Barracks. If we waved and cheered loud enough they would throw us boxes of sweets, bars of chocolate, tins of cigarettes, peanut butter, boxes of dried egg powder, packets of biscuits and tins of fruit. The dried egg tasted amazingly nice when cooked.

Up until then, the only time we had fruit in the house was if someone was ill, or if it was a birthday party, and at Christmas of course. Because Mum never had any money during these war years for presents our Christmas stockings consisted of a freshly-washed, well-laddered nylon stocking part-filled with crunched-up old newspaper balls, leaving just enough space for two or three apples, a couple of oranges, probably a pair of socks and a new handkerchief and a variety of nuts or a mixed bag of sweets.

Yet we had a great time. My first really proper toy was when I was seven and that was a homemade cut-out plywood kangaroo, whose legs moved forwards and backwards, together with a flat board about 36ins long and eight wide. You put the kangaroo on to the board, lifted up one end and the kangaroo would 'walk' down the board. Not like the hi-tech presents kids enjoy today, but we had fun as a family and despite the poverty, we were happy.

I can recall those long summer days newt fishing in the old pond at the rear of the Corporation bus depot on Ascot Drive. Pushing our trolleys to the old gas works at Deadman's Lane, Wilmorton, to fetch hundredweights of furnace coke, long walks to Robin Wood and Calvery Wood and all-day fishing excursions to Swarkestone Lock, camping at Anchor Church, night fishing on the Trent and Mersey Canal, lurky, hopscotch, cricket against the lamp-post outside Mrs Lloyd Jones' at number 112, climbing in the Broadway Cinema lav window to watch the films without paying in the days before we earned pocket money, then hiding under the seats so the usherettes couldn't find us until we could find an empty seat of our own. Playing on the old Teapot Lid and cone-shaped roundabout and those high steel frames and thick heavy duty chains which we used to climb to sit on the top bar of the swings on Osmaston Park Road recreation ground. The large static water tank there, a massive concrete retaining structure some 70 yards long and about 30 or 40 yards wide. It had been built as a reservoir of water for fire-fighting purposes, but at the end of the war after a number of tragic instances of young children being drowned, it was finally drained and broken up. Afterwards it became known locally as The Hollows and we used to slide down its steep slopes on old tin sheets. By the time you got to the bottom, some thirty or forty feet, the tin would be well warm but the exhilaration of the sheer speed and danger was well worth the struggle to climb back up the hill to be able to have another go.

Recycling isn't something new. The Hollows was used as a tip by the Derby Borough Council Parks Department and also the locals. Many is the lad who has built himself a pride and joy of a cycle or trolley from parts reclaimed from this dump. We used to strip them down and scrape and wire-brush all the rust off before repainting the frame in a variety of scrounged, left-over colours, and getting some flash-looking transfers from Kings bike shop at Allenton. Pram wheels were well sought after for the trolleys.

The Rec, as it was affectionately known locally, used to then have a large area of well-tended rhododendron bushes which when all the different-coloured blooms were in flower was a beautiful sight. Wintertime would see us sleighing down the big slope to the entrance gates, where there would be a look-out, and if there was no traffic on 'Ossy' Park Road we would then shoot across the junction into Nightingale Road and carry on down to its junction with Marlborough Road. On a good winter's day when it was really icy there could be as many as 60 or 70 sledgers of all ages whizzing down the slopes or pulling their sledges back up for another fast run.

We had a great time in the winter of 1946-47 when our gang built an igloo outside our house in Marlborough Road, it was nearly 15ft across and nearly 6ft high, almost blocking the whole of the road. Not that it mattered though, because the snow everywhere was 4ft deep with snowdrifts up to 8ft in some places. We used to spend hours in the igloo as our headquarters or den. Heat was provided by 'Winter Warmers' – Tate and Lyle treacle tins into which we used to put smouldering tinder, then swirl the can round and round on the string handles so it created red embers which gave off sufficient heat without too many obnoxious fumes.

In the school holidays we used to wait for the Co-op bakery van to arrive freshly filled up with gold-coloured crusty bread still burning hot from the bakehouse ovens. We would carve a thick slice off the loaves and spread it sometimes with real butter, or home made dripping and eat it still warm …mmmmm …I can taste the memory.

Then there was old Bill Fletcher who used to come down the road shouting in his gruff base voice: "Bring out your rags, bring out your rags, a day-old chick for your rags." He'd be pushing a big old-fashioned pram with enormously large wheels. On the undercarriage shelf under the actual pram body would be a long wooden box crammed full with baby chicks. He always had a wind-up gramophone on top of the pram with one or two 16 inch diameter bakelite hard-type records which every so far he would play and give an impromptu dance in the middle of the road. He was like a Pied Piper, the kids joining in were fascinated with his comical routine.

Shops I can remember were Mr and Mrs Jackson's general provisions: super people, at the corner of our block with Nightingale Road; Godlington's newsagents opposite the park gates on Osmaston Park Road; Miss Bradley next door to them used to sell haberdashery. Allsebrooks, general provisions, was at the corner of Arkwright Street and Marlborough Road. In Nightingale Road was Fellows general provisions at its junction with Addison Road; further down Nightingale Road was Ledbeter's chemist, then 'Slasher' Martin the local barber: he charged a shilling for a 'bolsh' which was your side hair shaved off up to your crown line and left about one inch high on top of your head, and it always stuck up like a carrot top no matter how you tried to comb it!

Further down was Goodere's newsagent: Alf and Dorothy (Dot) Goodere were smashing people. Later on

when I was 14 I was a paper lad with them, delivering evening and morning rounds, a Saturday evening Football Special round (nowadays The Sporting Green), a Sunday morning delivery round and later on a Sunday morning money collection round. Alf was a great humourist, great to work for and paid well over the local rate. There was always a waiting list to work there. Alf was also a father figure to me, he was someone who I had a great respect for and morally and mentally he did a lot to develop my character at that age. He worked tremendously hard both in the business and for his family and always was there for others with his enthusiasm and help and advice.

He was to my mind probably the first investor in people without any thought of a return for himself.

Our house was a three-bedroomed council semi with good-sized gardens to the front and rear. Distemper was the wall coating of the day, subtle greens, browns, yellows and blues, with complementary homemade stipple patterns providing the forerunner to the dado rail and to be followed by thick-course wallpaper which had joint seams about half-an-inch wide. You had the choice of cutting the joint seams off with scissors (a very slow, boring and laborious job on rolls 32 feet long) or, having a wallpapered wall giving the impression of vertical broad lines every 20 inches or so all the way around the room. Progress then bought the 'knock-off' salvage edge/joint seam which in turn progressed to the ready-trimmed edge as we know wallpaper today.

I used to make my pocket money at ten or 11 years of age by getting up early to go mushroom picking, collecting water cress or potato picking, wood cutting in The Hollows to provide logs, or chopping sticks (sixpence a 3ft tin bath full), depending on the seasons. I also used to sell young white mice. I started off with two and finished up with 166 in rows of cages. However, I solved my rising problem by selling them off for a shilling each, creating a roaring trade, but was always conscious of ensuring continuous adequate stock and, of course, a good source of steady income. The stall in the Market Hall pet section was always a good fall-back to pass on excess stock at albeit a slightly-reduced profit margin, as also was the little pet shop in Bradshaw Street, now long since demolished with the creation of the Derby city inner ring road/Bradshaw Way.

In the school holidays and at weekends, I used to get up early to go with the milk lady, Zena Hutchinson, who lived at No.105, to fetch the milk from the Crows Nest Dairy, near Melbourne. We had to be there for 6am start, load up the van and then come back and deliver the glass bottles of rich creamy milk in and around Marlborough Road. All these services provided pocket money for the Saturday trip to the flicks, either the Regal, ABC, the

Coliseum or the Broadway. Three great venues and usually packed out – John Wayne in Wake of the Red Witch, Gene Autrey, Roy Rogers, Lassie – and many, many more classics of the day, plus other treats.

So much time has elapsed, yet to this day I can still recall every family's name and their house number in our block during the war (and of some in the adjacent blocks as well), so close was the camaraderie and friendship of all those years, although I left there nearly 40 years ago.

An old lady came up behind me with a knife...

**by Ron Parnell
Brooklyn,
Burnie,
Tasmania**

I WAS engaged as a journeyman carpenter for Browning Brothers Speculative Housing Estate at threepence an hour, less than the going rate because custom decreed that having just finished my time, I must possess less skill and knowledge. One could say it was a minor form of cheap labour. The first job was, with a young fellow of my own age, laying and nailing floor boards in a new house. We worked well together, and as fun held a competition to see how many nails we could hold in our left hand and nail continuously until they had all been used. It was possibly 50 and this knack sped the job along. Apparently, we were happily hammering away and hadn't noticed someone watching us, but my first pay day, the clerk of the works said they'd decided to pay me full rate. I learned afterwards, a company director had seen us merrily banging away and was impressed.

After two years I decided a change was needed, so joined an old established firm. One interesting job was making, for a client, replicas of what he thought the three boxes used by Portia in the Merchant of Venice would look like. He was a Shakespearian fan, and had a small theatre in his garden. I was sent to fix a stair handrail and repair the back door lock in a poor quarter of Derby. The tenants were elderly and while screwing the door lock back I felt a presence behind me. Turning, I found the old lady, her lips muttering unintelligible words and waving, a rather large carving knife. I moved quickly out of the way, and called to her husband who disarmed her.

A short cut down memory lane

**by Ken Baines,
Hillcrest Road,
Chaddesden**

WAITING my turn in the barber's chair, I picked up a copy of "Derbyshire Now", and the mention of Buxton took my mind back several years to when my wife and I, (a ventriloquial speciality variety act) were working on the Tom O'Connor Show at Buxton Opera House. Even now I smile as I think of our last appearance there, filming as extras in a television drama, for even solemn moments can have a funny side.

The scene opened with a gathering of relatives at a funeral, and I was chosen to drive the lead car. (Cynics might call this a dead-end job so I was careful to keep a dead-pan expression on my face!)

The script called for the cars to be driving away from the house, which was situated just opposite Buxton ambulance station. As everyone appreciates, television producers re-take scenes time and again until everything is recorded perfectly – and so it was on this particular day. Filming in the morning, we all moved off down the road, (preceded by the hearse) when alarm bells started ringing and an ambulance roared out of the station with sirens blaring!

Production assistants jumped into the road, earphones all askew, frantically shouting – "Cut – go round again!"

We were travelling down a long semi-circular avenue so had to follow our planned route along a main road, passing a park on our left, then turning up a hill to return to our original position. This took around 25 minutes to get back to location. "Quiet!" – "stand by!" – "cameras rolling!" came the shouted instructions, and we were on our way again.

Would you believe it? The same thing happened again – and again. In all, we did this run six times before the producer was satisfied!

As we drove, passers-by stopped and raised their hats in deference as the procession passed by. This was so nice – but some were still there the next time we passed, and again paid their respects. Since this happened half-a-dozen times, I can't help thinking that if any were tourists they might have got the wrong impression of Buxton. After all, you don't often see so many funerals all at once in the same place!

Ken Baines and Peggy and their characters.

Memories of such amusing incidents are now flowing back. The entertainment scene has changed greatly over the past few years. Older readers will remember when every village in our lovely countryside had its own Miners' Welfare or Social Club, and most of our small towns had their own theatre. This encouraged real variety as we knew it. Sadly nowadays it seems essential for an entertainer to possess a horrifically-loud amplifier, (with possibly a twangy guitar as a necessary addition), and perform to a backing track through massive speakers!

In those days, of perhaps 50 years ago, variety meant comedians, magicians, speciality acts (like ventriloquists), and singers who didn't need a microphone to reach an audience. Gone are the days when the chairman of such venues as the Alfreton Miners' Welfare or the Heanor Labour Club had only to stand up to announce the turn (as they used to call them), to command immediate silence and attention.

We artistes learnt our trade in such places – sometimes with hilarious effects!…. I was an up-and-coming solo ventriloquist at the time. Later, my wife also became a ventriloquist, and we formed a double speciality act using around 12 cheeky boy, girl, and animal figures in all. This was to become quite a unique speciality, having two 'vents' in one act.

To show that funny things can and really do happen I ought to use the heading: How not to make an exit! On this occasion, the evening's entertainment at a Miners' Welfare Club comprised of a girl singer; a double comedy act (friends of mine), with myself as speciality ventriloquist.

The show went quite well until the comedy duo's second spot, when lethargic and indifferent applause showed the audience didn't rate them as star material. In fact they 'died a death' as we say in show business. Now, don't get me wrong – the vast majority of acts occasionally finds an audience is not always on their wave-length, but on this particular show, if they didn't actually 'die' then it could be said they were 'seriously ill!' However, this night's unconscious humour was a classic.

They were too embarrassed to walk through the packed club, so they opted to jump out of the dressing-room window at the back, asking me to pick them up in my car later.

They threw open the window and jumped over the window sill into the darkness (it was after 10.30pm). A rush of cold air swept into the room – followed by two voices swearing loudly outside in the dark! I looked out but could see nothing but dark oblivion. I turned to the entertainment secretary, who stood grinning and said: "I can't see them at all". "You won't," he replied, "They'll have slid down the quarry" ... "The quarry?" I gasped. He laughed and said: "Oh yes, the ground slopes away steeply just outside the window..." I leant out of the window and shouted: "Where are you?" and a strangled voice came back: "Stuck in some flaming bushes – we both are!" The secretary said: "There's a footpath further along, you'll get back on the road from there."

Having packed my equipment away, I drove my car down the street slowly. Fifty yards along the road they stood on the kerb waiting for me – a somewhat dishevelled double act by this time.

Their clothes were muddy and torn in places, and bits of greenery stuck to them. They would have gone down well in an Underneath the Arches sketch, but I don't think they were in the mood for it!

Bombed shop had cosy neighbour

by H. E. Rhodes, Bramfield Avenue, Derby

I WAS employed by General Electric Services, as a Radio Engineer in 1936. This firm was owned by Arthur K. Haslehurst, later known as Col A K Haslehurst.

The Cosy cinema in London Road had projection equipment by Hallee system, music was played to films by 12 inch records and synchronised to the film of the week, this produced some unusual programmes. Later it was one of the first cinemas to have real talkies installed. The Cosy was owned by Mr Kinder Haslehurst the owner of Haslehurst Hardware next to the Cosy, but in 1940 it had a bomb dropped on it which destroyed the shop and butcher's shop next to it (Mr Milward's). No-one was hurt. Myself and other staff started to sort out the damage.

Mr Haslehurst also owned the shop on the corner of London Road and Canal Street known as Small Profits and Quick Returns it was also a pawn shop. These premises were cleared out and Haslehurst Hardware was established.

The Cosy remained closed for a short while, as inspections were made, for bomb damage. In November 1940 I was called up as a radio mechanic to the RA... and that's another story.

A city and an industry that have grown up together

by F.W. Coles, Reginald Road South, Chaddesden

PRIOR to the coming of the railways, Derby's population had increased steadily since the year 1800 mainly due to the silk workers. The merging of the railways, however, had a profound effect and the population increased from 11,000 in 1800 to 44,000 by 1860.

The built-up area of Derby was contained to the south and west of the River Derwent and stretched from Nuns Green (King's Mead ward) in the west to the Midland Road area travelling in a southerly direction.

One had to walk through hedge-lined lanes to get to the areas now known as Normanton, Chaddesden, Markeaton and Rowditch.

In 1877, the Borough of Derby extended its boundaries by acquiring the village of Litchurch. This undoubtedly was due to the building of the Carriage and Wagon Works in 1875.

During this period of time the Markeaton Brook was spanned by about ten bridges within the borough boundary and remained a continual source of flooding.

Derby was regarded as a better place to live than some of the surrounding towns and an indication of the standard of living is portrayed in old copies of the Derby Mercury, now kept in Derby's libraries. The Midland Railway Company was a regular advertiser and appeared mainly on the front page advertising its daily trips, such as Leicester 2s, Manchester 3s 6d and Grimsby 3s return. W. Scott's, of 16 Irongate, advertised 'Gents' business trousers and suits', trousers being 8s 6d a pair and suits from 25s. A piano could be purchased for £18 18s or on terms at 10s 6d per month. A gents' gold watch would cost £5. Present household names such as Barlow and Taylor, Thurman and Malin, and Andrews Little Liver Pills were regular supporters of the Mercury's advertising columns.

The better-off population were found to be living in Friar Gate and St Mary's Gate. A railway worker's wage was 29s per week and remained very stable over the next few years.

The working day of the Carriage and Wagoner started very early in the morning, and breakfast was eaten in one of the three canteens provided in the works. The building which we know as Litchurch Lane canteen, housed two separate canteens. The one at the log road end of the building was referred to as the Preachers' Room, since the local clergy used to run breakfast-time services on four mornings a week.

During this early period of the Carriage and Wagon Works the 'body builders' worked to a full set of drawings which numbered only about six per vehicle. These drawings contained all the necessary dimensions, and one can only admire their skills in building carriages of high quality without detailed drawings.

By 1898 the works were well established and a passage recorded from the Institution of Mechanical Engineers Proceedings July 1898, read as follows:

"The carriage stock of the Midland Railway consists of 4,786 vehicles and the wagons amount to 116,331. The number of persons employed in these works is 3,450 men and about 150 women. Eight passenger train vehicles and 180 wagons are built per week. The superintendent is Thomas G. Clayton and he, besides being responsible for organising the building of the Carriage and Wagon Works, was also responsible for designing new types of carriages, as he had included in his plans of the works a new drawing office sited on London Road adjacent to the then staff offices."

By 1910 the works was complete and was one of the largest and most modern carriage and wagon building centres in Europe. It had taken about 34 years to complete and it incorporated all the necessary services for the flow line production and repair of carriages and wagons. This had been achieved during a period when design and techniques were beginning to advance rapidly.

The two large railway centres, the Carriage and Wagon and the Locomotive Works had a profound effect on the town of Derby and all three developed hand in hand.

New industries were attracted to the town and the population grew at a far greater rate than at any other time in the town's history, increasing from 44,000 in the late 1870s to approximately 230,000 today.

Housing estates sprung up and those built near the works attracted the railway workers and their families. Houses in Rosehill Street were of a generous design, adjoining the open spaces of the Arboretum and a number of the staff became resident in this area.

Several fine houses were to be found close to the works, such as Litchurch Lodge, set in its own grounds opposite St Andrew's Church. Ivy Lodge occupied the whole of the area which is now known as Ivy Square, and alongside it The Hollies. Large houses such as Wood Villa, Grove Villa and The Gardens flanked Osmaston Road, each having splendid open landscaped gardens. Even the China Works, which was formerly the Workhouse, was similarly blessed.

Bateman Street contained the entrance to a large goods depot, which was sited on the opposite side of the Derby-Birmingham line to the signal and telegraph buildings, now the Apprentice Training School.

On the opposite side of the works, the Longbridge was constructed in 1900 and this gave a route joining Osmaston Road to Ascot Drive where it passed along the edge of the old Osmaston Manor and St James' Church. Part of this church's vicarage is still standing on the corner of Longbridge Lane and Ascot Drive.

During the latter part of the 19th century the town centre was dominated by the Cockpit Wharf. Its existence as a canal barge centre was being threatened, however, by the increase in rail traffic.

Another form of public transport, the trams, was fast developing and stretched out on most of the main roads in town.

At the south end of the works, opposite Deadman's Lane, the Horses Infirmary, that is the stables, was constructed to provide medical care and training for railway horses. On the adjoining paddock, local churches, principally St Osmond's and Osmaston Road Wesleyans, would organise their Whitsuntide Sunday school treats, hiring the railway horses and carts draped for the occasion. The processions from church to paddock were accompanied by local brass bands.

St James' Church, on Dairy House Road, was considered to be the popular place of worship for the "Waggoners", while St Andrew's, known as the railway church, became the haven of worshippers from the Loco Works.

Victorian schools were built to educate the expanding population, Wilmorton (1892) being among them. Some of the others were Pear Tree, Orchard Street, Nuns Street, St Anne's, Gerard Street and Ashbourne Road.

Railway workers carved their names in these schools and also provided the Midland Institute, the first in the town provided by a works, for educational and recreational facilities of its employees and also by building the Railway's Servants Orphanage on Ashbourne Road, originally for the orphans of railway workers, but now used more often to help during temporary periods of difficulty.

The "Waggoners" have always been prominent at times of national crisis, none more so than those who served in the forces during the 1914-18 and 1939-45 wars, while those who were kept back in the works found themselves working long hours, often seven days a week, on a great variety of "war work".

During the Second World War, battalions of Home Guards were formed and most of the "Waggoners" volunteered or were recruited into the "Second Front", fire-fighting, ambulance driving and other activities.

Throughout its history the Carriage Works, along with other railway centres, has been prominent in fostering

The Carriage and Wagon Works sheet metal workers' social club dinner held at the newly-opened Co-op restaurant in Albion Street in the 1960s.

first aid and ambulance work. As a voluntary organisation it has developed into a successful, efficient and competitive force, conscientiously fulfilling a vital task.

The "Waggoners" have established over the years a reputation of producing first-class tradesmen, so much so, that an apprentice certificate issued by the works has become a "passport" to every outside industry. Its value has now been greatly enhanced by the creation of its own works training school in 1951 and the new modular system of training and although faced by the dramatic shortening of time still upholds our great tradition with increased national value.

Much of the success of the works is due to our forefathers who were responsible for its design and building and its continual development and modernisation have enabled it to remain a modern and competitive supplier of rolling stock throughout the world.

Every conceivable type of carriage and wagon built at Derby has been built in workshops of the original construction and it is only now, 100 years later, that major alterations have become necessary to accommodate the building of the new breed of 75ft carriages.

It can be said that Derby and the Carriage and Wagon Works have grown up together.

Derby is a railway city.

The special

DERBY'S annual Railway Works shutdown was on. For the family man a week's unpaid respite from daily toil. These holders of one free railway pass a year could travel to any point of the compass within the rail system of Great Britain if they so desired, even if it meant going over the lines of other companies.

Extra trains were provided for the more popular seaside resorts like Blackpool, Skegness and Yarmouth. One train of these earned the nickname locally of "The Kidney Bean Express".

In the station entrance hall dour ticket collectors carefully scrutinised the passes before allowing anyone to penetrate the portals they so jealously guarded.

Beyond those portals it was gloom, clamour, dirt and smoke, but high amid the cast iron roof framing, rays of sunshine mined the soot-encrusted glass to fall and scintillate on the bright empty rails of Platform One. One or two rays even strayed to sparkle on the polished picture windows of the gleamingly clean Glasgow to London Express, which in its livery of crimson with gold leaf, has deigned to stop its two mighty locomotives at platform two.

Blue-clad figures darted like butterflies in and out under its carriages. With long-handled hammers they tapped out a ringing symphony from the burnished steel

by Ron Parnell
Brooklyn
Burnie
Tasmania

tyres of the wheels. Flames from the roaring inferno in one of the engine's fireboxes illuminated the coaldust-streaked face of a fireman as his brawny arms fed the fire's greedy guts with a black meal to develop latent power for the 120-mile non-stop journey to London. Meanwhile, the drivers lovingly wiped, with clean cotton waste, unseen specks from the shining brass controls of those monsters.

Platform one was a mass of colour, movement and noise. Crowds of human beings stood amidst pyramids of luggage. Among the pyramids were bags and baskets openly exposing to the world the odd butcher-wrapped package or a white-faced cauliflower surrounded by a sea of green kidney beans. This spawning of nature's generosity from tiny back gardens or hired land of allotments would feed the hungry railway families during their enforced seven days leave. For the men, freedom. For the women, merely a change of kitchens.

Seaside holidays for the masses were only financially possible because of a strange system that had evolved. Accommodation in private homes. The host landlady would quite happily, for a fee of course, give bed, dining facility and use of kitchen as and when required, hence the bursting bags and baskets. The only other expense to the users was "The Cruet" (provision of salt, pepper and vinegar) usually a shilling a week (an hour or more's wage).

The adults stood by their luggage, looking around them or trying to converse above the noise. Shy and frightened children clung to their parents' hands while fearless others were everywhere, running, jumping, screaming, bawling or just plain fighting.

The great hands of the station clock jerked their way to the appointed hour and a strident tannoy voice warned of the approaching Special. A cathedral hush fell over the soon-to-be travellers. In the quietness that followed, the crowd seemed to take a deep breath. Seconds later, a tremendous cheer rang out, echoing under the cavernous roof as around the curved line at the station entrance and through a self-inflicted shroud of smoke and steam, the twin engines of the special clanked 16 coaches alongside the excited crowd.

The awaiting horde grasped the brass handles of the carriage doors, jerking them open. Seconds later the platform was empty, but for visitors and the usual tail-end charlies, scrambling from one crowded compartment to another. On this special there was no gold leafed insignia, no white antimacassars on seat backs, no toilets at the end of the carriages. No brightly-lit dining car, no curtained picture windows framing damask clothed tables with a lamp, shining glass and gleaming silver, no stewards patrolling the corridor with his call: "Anyone for the next sitting".

The carriages of the "Kidney Bean Special" had been written off years ago. For 49 weeks of the year they had laid hidden, rotting in out-of-the-way sidings. On the 50th week they were trundled into the workshops, given odd repairs, a splash of paint, a cat's lick of cleaning.

What matters? Who cares? Once a year they are Cinderella's coach with all its magic, to seven glorious days of freedom and change, however small.

Jack mixed with the world's greatest loco designers

by J. LeC Smith, Croft Close, Ockbrook

WHEN 17-year-old Jack went from the cloistered calm of an art school in London to the clattering, shattering steam locomotive building and repair works of the mighty London Midland & Scottish Railway in Derby, he found low-browed, bowler-hatted, beer-bellied foremen with greasy waistcoats ruling the roosts. These overlords strutted about their domains all day, barking their orders and marking their boundaries by precisely directed jets of chewed tobacco expectorant.

However, he quickly found out that they had no interest whatsoever in such foreign irrelevances as he, whether they were skulking around as Engineering Apprentices until they were 21 or thereafter as 'erectors'. Thus, during his five years in the works he did not learn what it was like to be subjected to the shadow of a 'boss'. But when he was transferred to the chief mechanical engineer's main drawing office in London Road, the realm of a real supremo, one Tommy Coleman, he experienced the awe and sometimes terror which could be inspired by a big man over his minions.

Weather-wise Tommy was rather like a beetling thunder-cloud; one which threatened, but never actually broke into, a storm. His oppressive and glowering presence was sufficient in itself to make even the most frigid underling sweat. He made daily excursions from his sanctum into the locomotive office, where three rows of long drawing benches stretched into the distance. The visits were pre-signalled by some sort of bush telegraph, so that when he actually appeared every head was down and every pencil poised or being pushed. He always trailed a little band of acolytes, who, when he came to a stand at a board, would split into two, to flank him either side, there arranging themselves in strict seniority. Dexter would be his chief sidesman, little Owen, the office manager, whose bald head complemented Tommy's own, but as he was right and proper, at a much lower level, and his sinister assistant Ernie Durnford, whose hairy one nodded like that of a Front Bench politician at Prime Minister's Question Time when the television cameras are running, whenever his mentor opinionated. Owen was a Robertson Hare-like character, just asking to be sat on, while Durnford buzzed around like a blue-tailed fly waiting to be swatted. Tommy rarely failed to oblige them. Meanwhile, the owner of the board had slunk round to the far side opposite the big man so that when questioned he had to explain his design upside down, so to speak.

On joining the drawing office Jack was allocated to Frank Pepper's Experimental Section and as a result quite a large portion of his activities were carried out away from the introspective company of those inside. The out-of-pocket expenses allowed were quite generous for someone as undemanding as he, so that helped to augment his pittance of a wage. For three years he was, along with a handful of others, the lowest of the low, a temporary draughtsman, and it was not until 1940 that he was elevated to the permanent staff as a junior draughtsman. This great honour was somewhat tarnished by a drop in his take-home pay and he was by then newly-married, so that the flogging of expenses became even more urgent. These were the early days of the war and his travels enabled Jack to scour the shops in far away places

A locomotive fitted for testing waiting to leave St. Pancras.

for fleeting supplies of non-rationed foodstuffs, such as strawberries in season. One day he came with a 3lb jar of real marmalade, which was quite an improvement on that currently being made by Barbara with carrots, bless her.

Bread and butter trips out meant either pre-arranged visits to the Motive Power Depots to see how experimental fittings of locomotives in service were faring, or flying visits to inspect locomotives themselves which had broken down, perhaps causing traffic delays. For the latter Jack went out under his title of Inspector of Casualties. As such he covered the Midland Division of the LMSR, which was the area of most of the pre-amalgamation Midland Railway and he would always be accompanied by a representative of the Motive Power Department, to ensure fair play in reporting the cause of the breakdown.

Much more exciting outside work was assisting the Locomotive Testing section, particularly in recording cylinder steam chest pressures. The locomotive under test would be fitted with Crosby indicators which produced a paper record of the required data, while it was hauling a normal service train. The paper records were examined later in the office and the effects of various valve settings established. The indicators had of necessity to be located close to the cylinders and to enable the test team to

operate them a special protective screen was erected around the front end of the locomotive. Two members of the team, one either side, squeezed between the screen and the hot smokebox flank, had to take recordings on receiving a bell signal from a third, riding in the loco cab, who recorded the milepost position, speed, valve setting, regulator opening and such. If the smokebox door was not perfectly sealed and air was drawn through, the heat for the front-end testers became excessive and areas of the smokebox glowed red on occasion.

Most of the testing was carried out between Euston and Carlisle, where the necessary prolonged high speeds were possible. Only when standing over the front buffers of a 50ft locomotive running at 90mph is it realised to the full that the transition around a curve is far from smooth. The 100 tons of hot steel behind is just longing to continue in a straight line, while below the little flanges of four bogie wheels fight to persuade it otherwise. The resultant conflict produces a series of violent lurches, making shuttles of the testers, and making their taking of recordings an exacting task. But all in all it was very enjoyable work, although not without a few unfortunate incidents, in one of which Jack thought his end had come. This was on a Derby to St Pancras run and the train was just leaving Leicester station where the line immediately enters a short tunnel. The rails were greasy and having put the front end of his locomotive with its human hangers-on well and truly into the tunnel mouth, the driver opened the throttle wide, but found that he could get no grip on the rails. As a result the wheels spun round at about 1,000mph and the noxious fumes from the chimney shot out in a continuous roar. Within seconds the tunnel mouth was completely devoid of air and full of hot exhaust smoke and gasses, and the trapped testers were quietly going under. Had they actually perished and been sent down below, they would have scarcely noticed the transition. Suffice it to say that a few grains of sand deposited beneath the whirling wheels saved the day, and they not only survived but carried on testing.

Back in the office there was much lampooning of the management and senior staff by the janitors, particularly on the occasion of the annual fuddle which took place on the afternoon of the last day before the Christmas break, when a lunchtime pint or two had provided the necessary lubrication and courage. Poor old Ernie Durnford was a sitting duck and got far more than his fair share, although, of course, no names were mentioned.

Throughout the year they enjoyed some deadly serious fun too. Beside each board there was a large flat area of bench used for the laying out of drawings relative to the work in hand, and one or two of these became fine pitches for the playing of shove-halfpenny football, especially when dusted with a modicum of French chalk. The field of play was defined, dare it be said, by lines scratched on the polished wood, and the goals were made from the wire of paper clips straightened out and then suitably bent so that their ends could be inserted on holes in the bench top. A halfpenny with its underside smoothed was the football and each of the two players had a penny which he struck with a pencil held flat on the surface. They took alternate strikes, the object being to work their penny and the 'ball' into a shooting position. If the opposing player failed to spoil the set-up with his next strike then the first would take aim and try to cannon the 'ball' into goal. It was not permitted to cannon the opponent's penny; an infringement resulted in the injured party being allowed two successive strikes. Each game was played in two halves and strictly timed, and considerable skill and cunning was developed by some. Lunch hour and after-hours matches were arranged and there were league tables, cup ties and a cup. Some years later somebody invented Subbuteo and made a fortune.

The management didn't choose to do much about excesses at Christmas parties and seemed to turn a blind eye to the 'football', but they did have serious objections to the pinning of unofficial notices on the official board.

An outsider scores the winning goal against the League Champion in the 1938 FA Cup Final.

Rightly so, Jack supposes, but some of them were a good laugh. One ran thus:-

NOTICE TO THE STAFF

It has come to the notice of the management that employees are dying on the job and either refusing or neglecting to fall over. This practice must cease forthwith. Any employee found dead on the job in an upright position will be given instant dismissal. In future if a Section Leader notices that any employee has made no movement for a period of more than two hours it will be his duty to investigate, as it is difficult to distinguish between death and natural movement of some employees. Holding a pay packet in front of the suspected corpse is considered a possible test. There have been cases however, when natural instincts have been so deeply ingrained that the hand of a corpse has made a spasmodic clutch, even after rigor mortis has set in.

When war threatened in 1939 long air-raid shelters were dug just outside the drawing office and the draughtsmen plus associated clerical staff were called upon to practice evacuation there too. But no drainage had been incorporated in the construction and so daily hand pumping of water accumulations had to be carried out. By whom? Who better than the horny-handed experimental and testing juniors, especially as their normal work was being tapered off. The practice evacuations proved to be the only time the shelters were used, for the expected big daytime air-raids on Derby never came. During that time Jack and his colleagues made abortive attempts to get into the services but the successful running of the railway system and the use of its vast workshops for the manufacture of armaments and repair of aircraft became a top Government priority and

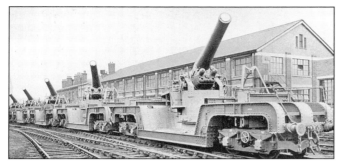

Railway mounted guns standing alongside the Locomotive Drawing Office.

no releases of designated staff were permitted. By 1942 Jack was spending all his time in the office undertaking such hazardous tasks as making drawings and illustrations and writing texts for instruction manuals. These accompanied British locomotives, modified to burn oil instead of coal, on their way through the Mediterranean to Egypt, Turkey and Iran. Some of these are still lying on the sea bed.

In all he spent nearly five years ostensibly 'on the boards' but had done very little actual draughting. So much for his Matriculation 'Excellent' in art which had been partially responsible for him coming to Derby in the first place. Nevertheless, by rubbing shoulders with some of the finest steam locomotive designers in the world he acquired a great admiration for the clever men who, by simply drawing pencil lines on paper, could immaculately conceive a self-contained, self-propelled, 100-ton monster, which, having been fed and watered, would propel huge loads at 100mph day after day, year in and year out, across the length and breadth of the country. These experiences taught him too to admire other great products of Derby and its shire; Whitehurst with his superb timepieces, powered by gravity, Arkwright's mills, powered by the rushing water of the river Derwent, Rolls-Royce with its outstanding motor car engines, culminating in Whittle and his jets, powered by petrol vapour. A real centre of excellence.

---

by Mrs Frances Cooper, Mackworth

The lady with the lamp

IT was 58 years ago when I joined British Rail working for the Outdoor Machinery Department which later became Plant & Machinery.

I worked for them from 1941-1976 and my wage when I began as a battery attendant at Derby St. Mary's Wharf was £2 5s 0d. One of my jobs as a battery attendant was to fetch a carboy of acid, (which was used to top up the batteries for the electric cars which pulled the drays), from the Power Station in the Locomotive Works on Siddals Road to Derby St Mary's Wharf. I had to drag this on my own all the way. I sometimes wonder how I ever managed.

I was later transferred to the job of electrician's mate and moved to Derby Midland Station and then to the job of electric lamp attendant. I was then the only woman working with 102 men, and in all the years I worked with them I never heard one of them say a word out of place. No swear words were ever uttered within my hearing. Whilst working as electric lamp attendant I had to go round all the railway offices and clean the lights. I also cleaned the station lights. I was known as the Lady with the Lamp. One of the many places I had to go was Chaddesden Sidings and I had to walk carrying a 6ft ladder, spare lamps and a bucket. There was no transport to take us from site to site; life was tough, we had to walk carrying our equipment.

I had to work because I was widowed in 1958 and was left with a nine-year-old daughter and there was no pension from my late husband, only a widow's pension.

One Friday I was working in St Andrew's Wharf where the railway car park now stands. This was a big distribution centre for the railway and I was going up to the top floor on the lift when the lift broke down and I was stuck between floors. I was there for hours when one

Staff from the outdoor machinery department of British Rail: George Shackleford (left) and Jack Parsloe.

Staff from the outdoor machinery department of British Rail: (from left) foreman George Shackleford, Frances Cooper and foreman Jimmy Hicklin.

of my colleagues, Tommy McCandless came looking for me. If it hadn't been for him hearing me call out, I would have been there all weekend.

We worked 12 hours a day, seven days a week during the war and we did not get paid for holidays, only Christmas Day.

It was not until 1952 that we had a house of our own when we were presented, by the Mayor of Derby, on August 4, 1952 with the 10,000th Corporation House on the Mackworth Estate. The *Derby Evening Telegraph* was present for the ceremony.

Sadness as four-legged friends were carted off to France

MY GRANDFATHER, Percy Wakefield, worked at St Mary's Wharf, Chester Green, all his working life. These pictures are from the annual presentation of the depot's safe driving awards (we have the medals) for road transport drivers in 1947-48-49 (interesting to rail enthusiasts as the 'LMS' lettering on the lorries in the early pictures gives way to 'British Rail' after the 1948 nationalisation). The awards were made by the railway top brass, probably area managers, and all the vehicles were bulled up and polished for the day – too bad if you were expecting an urgent delivery!

The photographs were probably taken by the *Derby Evening Telegraph*, but I have never seen a copy of the issue they may have appeared in.

Percy Wakefield was born in 1891. In 1910 he moved to Derby and got a job working with the horses at the Midland Railway Depot, St Mary's

Percy Wakefield (left) meets the Mayor in 1948.

by Iain Wakefield, Sedgefield Road, Branston, Burton

Wharf, Chester Green. He became a drayman for the railway and delivered goods in and around Derby.

At the outbreak of the First World War, he volunteered to enlist but was rejected by the Army, again, as unfit. He was reported to have a 'weak heart'. Frustrated at being rejected again, he volunteered to become a railway ambulance man. His duties included unloading the wounded off the specially-built ambulance trains that arrived at Derby station. These trains arrived at night so as not to draw attention to the dreadful carnage they contained. He transported these poor souls to hospitals and nursing homes around the county. He was very moved by the suffering he saw and became grateful to the medical board that had declared him 'unfit'.

He also had recollections of the Army

Percy Wakefield (centre left) receives his Safe Driving Medal during the mess room presentation at St Mary's goods yard.

A line-up of LMS vans at St Mary's goods yard. Percy Wakefield is second from the right.

Percy Wakefield is pictured fourth from left during a presentation at St Mary's Goods Yard.

The Midland Railway Tranship Shed, now the Derwent Business Centre in Clark Street, Derby.

coming to St Mary's on several occasions and requisitioning horses. The draymen complained that they were left with the 'old nags' whilst all the strong, fit animals went to France. There was always sadness when their fine horses were being loaded up and taken away, as the horse would become a good 'mate'.

In 1917 he married Beatrice Brimley, a Burton girl, and

moved to Manchester Street, Derby, and their son Harold was born in 1921.

Between the wars motor transport started to replace the horse-drawn drays and Percy was taught to drive a lorry and moved over to motor transport to become a motor driver. He spent his career delivering tobacco that was stored in the bonded warehouse in Clarke Street

Winner Percy Wakefield (second from left) at St Mary's in 1948.

(now the Derwent Business Centre). These deliveries were to wholesalers and tobacconists in Loughborough, Burton, Ashby and the surrounding districts. He could remember just about every vehicle he drove. His favourites were the ex-Army Dodges acquired by the railway just after the Second World War.

Percy retired from the railway in 1963 and had an active retirement enjoying his garden and reading just about anything he could get his hands on. He lived in the same house and remained fit and strong until his death at the age of 95 in 1986 – he just wore out – so much for his weak heart!

The mahogany tree

IT'S 1927, and in the tropical jungle's green light, amid a cacophony of sound from chattering monkeys, unseen birds and guttural calls of black skinned foresters, a 150ft-high mahogany tree squeaks in agony as it breaks and crashes to the forest floor. Its green foliaged limbs are cut off and left to rot while its body, now a log, starts a long and hazardous journey by elephant power and narrow gauge railway to the coast and finally as shipboard deck cargo to join others of its ilk in the huge timber yard of the London Midland and Scottish Railway Company's

by Ron Parnell, Brooklyn, Burnie, Tasmania

Derby storage yard. There it rests in fog, frost, snow and cool summer heat so vastly different to its home temperature. It took nearly two years for the vagaries of the English climate to drive out most of the log's natural sap.

It's 1929, and during the last two years the log has been checked for splitting and pronged with instruments to measure its sap loss. Now its time has come and huge steel pincers lift it on to a table. Held in tight embrace by hydraulic claws, the table moves towards a band of shark toothed steel travelling at high speed which slices the log into thin boards.

Eagle-eyed inspectors scrutinise every inch of the timber. If it passes the test it is then stacked on top of others with a spacer between to allow air to circulate across both surfaces while it rests for months in the semi-darkness of a huge seasoning shed.

It's 1931, and the now-seasoned boards travel again into the sawmill where they are cut to length and width, some finishing as large as 30ft long by 3ft wide. A high-speed planing machine reduces them to three eights of an inch thick. The best side is chosen and this is sanded smooth ready to receive the many coats of paint and varnish yet to come. It is this last operation that highlights the beautiful deep red colour, grain and texture of mahogany.

Laid flat on felt-covered trestles the backs of the boards are painted with hot Scotch glue. A length of hessian, steaming hot from soaking in the same solution is quickly spread and stretched tight over the glued surface. Workers using their bare hands in a circular scrubbing motion smooth out any air bubbles formed under the hessian. This action unites the glue on the panel with that in the hessian, creating a creamy white froth which when dry securely seals the two together.

When cured and required the boards were moved to an area and cut to an accurate size ready to be fixed to the already assembled railway carriage framing. They will then form the weather resistant panels of the outer skin. At this point the purpose of the hessian becomes apparent. It prevents the thin panels from splitting as the coach builders carefully glue and nail them to the cambered surface of the carriage wall framing.

As the vehicle progresses through the various stages of assembly the panels receive up to fifteen or more coats of paint and varnish. This number, carefully worked out and tested in the railway laboratories, was designed to enable the timber to withstand not only climatic changes but chemical attack from tunnel smoke and fall-out while in the highly industrialised areas of the day.

When the carriage left the assembly line to go into service the beautiful wavy bands of grain and the rich red colour have gone. In their place is a mirror surface of crimson embellished with lines of gold leaf and the company's coloured insignia.

It's 1933, and the milling crowd on the station platform hushed its chatter and stared with anticipation. Parting the curtain of lashing rain and winter gloom, two giant locomotives, hallowed by exhaust steam and cascading water from the roofs of the train's sleek carriages glide to a stop. The end of a 600-mile journey.

Porters cried 'All change', door locks clicked and passengers disgorge in streams like ants from a damaged nest. Not one in the crowd spared a backward look at the inventiveness, the expertise, the care and skill that had gone into the design and construction of the vehicles that had carried them. The acme of coach-building art had carried those passengers in comfort, speed and safety throughout that winter's day.

Certainly, no thought was given, even if they knew, to that tropical giant which had crashed to the forest floor six years before.

Can we have our toilet back?

by Ken Baines, Hillcrest Road, Chaddesden

'DON'T WORK with animals or children' is an old showbiz maxim.

Heading a variety bill at Halifax Civic Theatre during their school holidays programme, a supporting act was a troupe of performing dogs. Their star was a huge mastiff-type dog who literally foamed at the mouth when he heard music. He went barmy! As our dressing room was close to the stage we were asked if he could be fastened to our toilet until it was time for his entrance.

He was so fierce we daren't stay in the same room. Then – calamity! – during one afternoon matinee there was a loud crash, and he suddenly bounded on stage with the chain still around his neck – towing our broken toilet behind him! He stopped the show – it was hilarious! I wish we could get laughs like that. Incidentally we didn't get to use our toilet for the rest of the week!

Taken live off a TV screen while Ken Baines was representing Derby in BBC TV's Top Town series in the early 1950s.

Ranby's department store in Victoria Street, Derby, now Debenham's. The picture was taken before the demolition in 1961 of the Queen's Head on the left of Ranby's and the congregational church on the right.

Mrs Betty Ottey (née Oldknow), Inglewood Avenue, Mickleover

Of boys and Brylcreem

IN 1943 at the tender age of 14, I started work at Ranby's in Victoria Street. I was employed as a cashier at a cash desk which was no more than a pen with a door on it. The overhead pulleys contained cups which travelled from counter to cashier and back (if I pulled hard enough). I was so small I had to stand on a box to reach. My first cash desk was in the hardware department in 1943. Everything was in short supply, and we had very little to sell. I remember the queue right along Victoria Street when we had a supply of Pyrex dishes, priced at 1s 6d (7½p) for a basin and up to 7s 6d (37½p) for a large casserole dish. We had sold out by lunchtime and my arms ached that day.

My next desk was gents' outfitting on the corner of

Green Lane in two shops divided by a small arcade. The days were so boring as we had no stock to sell. I

Betty Ottey wearing a homemade blouse.

remember we had some red sleeveless pullovers that nobody wanted, so every night we had to put mouse traps in the big drawers so they wouldn't get eaten. One of the young male assistants sent me a mouse in the cash cup one morning. I think my screams were heard at the top of Green Lane.

Ranby's had a chemist's department which was kept going during shortages by making leg tan which sold like hot cakes at 1s (5p) a bottle. The girls who made it were orange from top to toe that day.

We young girls were very popular with the boys if we could get them a 1s 6d (7½p) jar of Brylcreem when Ranby's' quota came in.

When the drapery department had a quota of material we young girls would dash down to see if we could get a yard of something to make a blouse, for 1s 11d (9½p) and three clothing coupons. We all used the same Butterick paper pattern, but tried to get different colours. My best friend Mary Hames was a wizard on the sewing machine.

Money was very short, and we only started on 12s 6d (62½p) working from nine to six five-and-a-half days a week. I had risen to only £1 7s 6d when I left at 17½ years.

After handling thousands of pounds, we were a happy crowd, going to the drapers' ball in borrowed gowns and setting our hair with sugar and water.

Working life begins at 14

by Ron Parnell
Brooklyn,
Burnie,
Tasmania

FATHER'S excellent record with the company enabled me to take a seven-year apprenticeship in January, 1927 as a railway coach builder at the LMS, Derby Carriage and Wagon Works. I had hoped to be a draughtsman, but the world recession killed this.

The first year was to be spent as an office boy in the blacksmiths and spring-makers workshop. It was January 6, 1927, and I was a 14-year-old innocent straight from school. Fires blazed and roared. Horizontal bars of light moved slowly between ghostly shapes to fall and vanish in clouds of steam. Above the sound of machines at work, rhythmic notes rang out, bang-tap, bang-tap, accompanied by floor-shaking thuds and showers of sparks.

No-one had prepared me for what I would see, hear or do. Eyes becoming accustomed to the gloom, I saw ordered chaos in a workshop split in two sections.

One half contained 30 brick-built blacksmiths' fires. The other, a row of gas-fed furnaces, flames belching from the sides of closed doors, and in this section's centre a sunken water trough surrounded by metal tables. Between the two halves of the workshop several machines spat noise and fumes.

The thuds, the impact of small steam hammers, pounding lumps of red hot metal into the desired shape. The incandescent bars of light were lengths of thick spring steel plate, five inches wide, dragged out of a furnace by men using long tongs. The semi-molten plates were carried to the tables, bent into the desired shape, then immersed it in the large trough, creating the clouds of steam.

A wooden structure comprising an office, a store, and above, a foreman's control centre. Inside the office was a Dickensian desk, with sunken inkwells, grooves for pens, a shallow drawer, and high stools for three clerks. The office boy and a female clerk shared a table.

Harold Patter, age 40, head of the office, a bachelor, always smartly dressed. Tall and slender, pebbled pince-nez on his nose. A long, narrow face sporting a black moustache, the ends heavily pomaded and twisted to two inch-long points. Long-fingered hands that each Sunday played beautiful music in Derby's Roman Catholic cathedral.

Other staff was Ethel, a shapely 26-year-old blonde, Jim a married man of 30, and Florrie, who shared the table with me. Two years my senior but light years ahead in worldly wisdom. Harold ran a happy office and all quickly made me feel I was one of the team.

My duties, a general dogsbody to all, including a whisky-faced, droopy-moustached, bowler-hatted foreman. I attended to their every whim, making the tea, buying cigarettes, newspapers, Harold's moustache pomade, sweets and lunches. I was paid to remove and replace 200 clock cards every day, checking for absentees and late comers. I became very adept at flipping them into the racks. It was during this operation that I used the only technological device in the office – a rubber date stamp.

Thursday mornings saw me weaving between fires and furnaces with a flat board 30 inches long by 18 inches wide, held in front of me, tray wise, the outer edge supported by a strap around my neck. In each of the 200 slots in the board rested a copper elliptical token, its face stamped with the pay number of an employee. It was my job to see every man received the right token. My first week, I had to hand out, not only the token, but envelopes containing dismissal notices to 50 men as production was being cut. A week's notice and no redundancy pay.

The Derby Carriage and Wagon Works staff outing to the Peak District in the 1950s.

Another Derby Carriage and Wagon Works staff outing in the 1950s.

to find the right ones. I fear my carelessness found one truck in the north of the country and another in the south when they should have been vice-versa. Mr Potter was not amused, he had to take the rap.

The main gates opened on to Lichfield Lane. During lunch hour on pay days this became a scene of noise and colour.

To me straight from school, the office work was interesting and with night school three times a week plus lots of homework, the year was quickly over. The Christmas week brought with it a curious custom in that every office boy made a list of the men he had handed pay tokens to. On the morning of the break-up, he would go to each man and ask for a tip, marking the amount on his list.

During tip gathering I vaguely noticed a lot more crib bags around than usual. By 3.30pm the reason became apparent. All fires were extinguished, machines cleaned and oiled, areas tidied up and the foreman discreetly missing. The men gathered in groups, each to their own friends. Christmas party time was on and I was invited to the blacksmiths'. The springmakers had their own, the other end of the workshop.

A steel table had been washed and covered with newspaper, on which rested plates of mince pies, sausage rolls, Christmas cake and other goodies. Mr Potter gave me permission to join them for a while on condition I didn't touch the drink.

By 4 o'clock the alcohol was working and as many were returned soldiers, old battles were fought and war songs sung.

The office party was a little tame and sad after that. I was to start my trade apprenticeship proper in January. Custom decreed that no-one clocked off on the last day and passing the card racks I instinctively noted the cards' virgin blankness awaiting the fumbling fingers of the next nervous schoolboy.

As general dogsbody, the lack of internal phones meant I delivered and collected messages from other offices. This meant meeting other staff, including offices boys. I was unaware that the birds and bees did anything else but fly. I was quickly enlightened.

Keenly interested in everything around me, this freedom of message carrying allowed me to poke my nose into all sorts of places.

One of my duties was to fix labels to railway wagons full of different types of scrap metal. These wagons were in long lines awaiting dispatch and often it was difficult

---

Dental clinic visit prompted a change of career

Dorothy A Robinson (née Kingston), Darwin Road, Mickleover

ON leaving Queen Elizabeth's Grammar School, Ashbourne, aged 16-and-a-half, I went to start my training at Derby City General Hospital. In those days this was the hospital for people who lived in the Borough of Derby.

I went to the City Hospital as a trainee nurse. One of my duties as a sub probationer was to work in the dispensary with a lovely lady called Miss Holford, who was head dispenser. Every Thursday afternoon I had to go down to the dental clinic to help as part of my training.

Eventually I kept thinking about my days in the dental department and decided this is what I wanted to do. This was much to the disappointment of my parents, as my sister was a staff nurse/acting sister on Ward 7 and they wanted me to be like her. But I left nursing and became a trainee dental nurse at Mill Hill Clinic.

The senior dental officer was a Mr Arthur Stafford, a man every one held in awe, but I liked him and respected him for his strict but kind discipline. Sadly he died many years ago and Mr Freddy Grossman took his place, once again a very nice man, and a little easier to work for.

My days at the City Hospital were not lost, however. Every Thursday afternoon I went to the dental department to treat staff and expectant mothers who needed treatment and once a month I went to the Derwent Hospital to treat the TB patients.

They were good and happy years. My dental officer was a Miss Rigby (née Sweeney) a Scottish lady. She was lovely, and so kind to the nervous children who came for treatment. I worked with her until I married and eventually left to have my first baby. I was there 12 years in all.

We visited schools and referred children for treatment for both conservation ('the dreaded fillings') and extractions. As you can imagine we were not the most favourite visit to the children, but the staff were most kind and always made us welcome.

Extraction sessions were held every morning in the big main surgery. There were three dental nurses, a dentist and an anaesthetist. Conservation and orthodontics took place in the other two smaller surgeries with a dentist and dental nurse in each surgery.

We also had sub probationers from Derwent Hospital in the recovery room. Although I was delighted about my happy forthcoming event, I was very sad to leave my friends and, of course, all the children who came regularly for treatment.

Follow the Rams

The start of problems with visiting fans

by Alf Parry, Highfields Close, Ashby-de-la-Zouch

I BECAME a regular Rams supporter in 1946 during the first, full, post-War season, after hostilities ended and after my release from Army service. I looked forward to a profitable partnership between Raich Carter and Peter Doherty, two of the game's all-time legends. In reality it proved to be a fleeting spell, with Doherty leaving around Christmas, and not being allowed to take over licensed premises in the town, whilst remaining a player.

Other living legends of that period were: Stanley

Rams players Dave Mackay (centre) and Roy McFarland leap for the ball during the game against Chelsea on February 12, 1970.

Charlie George scores the Rams' sixth goal from the penalty spot, against Tottenham Hotspur in October 1976.

Matthews, Tom Finney, Wilf Mannion and Len Shackleton, and for me the immaculate Leon Leuty. All of these giants of the game were tied to maximum wages of £8 per week plus win bonuses of £2. Years later Tommy Trinder at Fulham FC made Johnny Haynes the first £100 per week footballer and later still the redoubtable Jimmy Hill obtained freedom of contract for all registered FA players. From these milestones the current 'sky's the limit' scene evolved with players' agents patrolling the Bosman front both at home and abroad, obtaining unbelievable salaries of which those old-time legends could only dream.

Former Rams player Francis Lee.

On the spectator front, a remarkable game in 1966 saw a sea-change in crowd behaviour at the Baseball Ground. Manchester United, with their team of current stars, Dennis Law, George Best, Bobby Charlton, Pat Crerand, Harry Gregg, etc, were drawn against the Rams in the FA Cup. Their fans swarmed into the Pop Side and all together formed their own human amplification system with well-rehearsed mass obscenities loud and clear. This

Former Rams player Raich Carter.

broke the mould of previously well-dispersed groups all round the ground and was the very start of the 'visiting fans' syndrome at the Baseball Ground. Steadily it was to become, quite separately, an endemic police problem, rife to this day, all around the grounds.

Nevertheless, we've known our ecstasies and agonies aplenty down the years. From Third Division times upon a quagmire pitch to the heady days of a Division One championship win with Clough and Taylor. Onward then with the incomparable Dave Mackay to a second championship and a glimpse of Charlie George together with the mercurial Francis Lee. Heartaches to follow, before the Premiership became a reality under Jim Smith just in time for Pride Park.

Manchester United may well name Old Trafford 'The Theatre of Dreams', but the real field of dreams for me down 50 years of nostalgia has been the good old BBG.

The chants of 'Eanor' and 'Sharples'

WRITING in the *Derby Evening Telegraph* on the day of the Queen's visit, John Atkin recalled his memories of the old days at the Baseball Ground.

'IT was enough to bring a lump to your throat.

As a schoolboy armed with only a Rams scarf and vivid imagination, walking to the Baseball Ground offered an emotion-packed opportunity to stroll into Derby County's heritage.

These intimate houses, chippies, pubs and corner shops surrounding Shaftesbury Street were the same ones which once rattled to the cheers of huge crowds celebrating triumphs of days gone by.

By the early 80s, when I tucked my juvenile season ticket into my stylishly-flared jeans and cycled the eight miles to catch a bus from Mickleover to the game, the glory days were gone.

Handed-down tales of the likes of 'Dally' Duncan and Raich Carter had painted a picture in my adolescent mind of footballers as giants, legends to whom the likes of Alan Biley and Derek Hales would never match up.

But by now Leeds and Chelsea had brought their boot-boys to the Baseball Ground, and the seats rained down on the pitch.

The Pop Side gleefully spilled out through the cages and on to the side of the pitch for the last few minutes of a crucial match against Fulham.

Visiting winger Robert Wilson was kicked by a fan, the final whistle went early – and the Rams were still up.

The lukewarm 'pies' were barely edible, and you stood little chance of visiting the loos without having to stand in a pool.

When the Heanor Rams chanted their '"Eanor" battlecry, the rest of the Pop Side still responded: "Sharples!"

Barnsley came, and the Hovis theme tune was hummed. Andy Gray, now the voice of Sky TV's soccer coverage, was left in no doubt that the supporters had read the tabloid stories about his marital dramas.

And I may be wrong, but I think the sun shone at every game.

Gone now are the days when football was played on a Saturday afternoon – a man's game, unless you were a lad standing on an orange box and waving a rattle.

Football rubs shoulders with big business, so clubs like Derby need corporate headquarters to match.

To many die-hard supporters, Pride Park will always be Chaddesden Sidings, just as Foresters Leisure Park is always going to be Normanton Barracks.

The Pop Side was reshaped in 1995, the first major change to the Baseball Ground since the Ley stand was built in 1969.

The Queen, with Rams manager Jim Smith, meets the players on the pitch of the new Pride Park Stadium on July 18, 1997.

But since Derby County's directors announced the move to a new stadium, their foresight has created an air of excitement in the city.

Jim Smith's players did their stuff, catapulting the Rams back into the big time at least a year earlier than expected.

Then they did it again, finishing in a respectable mid-table position when the pundits had Derby down as relegation favourites.

Now the fans have done it too, with season tickets sales already breaching the 20,000 mark.

The FA Cup winners of 1946, some of whom wiped away a stray tear in the new Toyota Stand today, will always be special.

So too, will the heroes of the championship years who turned Derby from unfashionable East Midlanders into the pride of England.

The names of Clough and Taylor became as comfortable together as gin and tonic.

And Dave Mackay, bursting with thunder and grace on the pitch, showed he was equally stylish in a manager's sheepskin coat.

Pride Park's open spaces may be muddier than the Baseball Ground on a rainy Tuesday in February, and Gasworks Terrace still remains a more appropriate name.

But standing in the near-empty ground watching the red carpet being laid and the seats wiped down, there was an unmistakable feeling that the ghosts of Derby's greats have finally put up their seats in the old Ley Stand and taken up comfortable positions here.

The stadium may have been opened by the Queen – herself appearing visibly moved after stepping out of the players' tunnel to a cacophony of noise.

But there was no mistaking the fact that this was a Day of the People.

The Queen unveils the name plaque at the stadium opening on July 18, 1997.

Hand-lettered rosettes and painstakingly-prepared banners proved how excited pupils at schools across Derbyshire have been in recent weeks. And 10,500 children's voices raised in unison in response to Rammie, icon of football's rediscovered family image.

As a grown man armed with only a notebook and a vivid imagination, walking to the Pride Park Stadium offered a peek into the future of a proud football club.

It was still enough to bring a lump to your throat.'

Storer restored pride with quality signings

by B D Oxey, Waterford Drive, Chaddesden

I STARTED watching Derby County in 1948. Raich Carter's last match against Blackpool was my first.

I started seriously the following November when the club paid a record fee £25,000 for Johnny Morris from Manchester United. A lot has been written about the Cup Final team, and later Billy Steel before Morris.

At this time the team was still a force in the First Division until the demise in 1953. Players in this era not talked about are Jack Parry making his debut and scoring, Jack Lee from Leicester, a tall striker, and little Jimmy Dunn from Wolves. Ken Oliver and Norman Nielson, a South African centre-half. Albert Mays, Tim Ward and Colin Walker, Colin Bell, wing-halves; Bert Mozley, Geoff Barrowcliffe, Keith Savin, Roy Patrick, Rex Osman at fullback. Numerous dodgy keepers, including Billy Townsend and Harry Brown, Hughie McLaren or Cecil Law on the left wing and several more reserves.

The demise to Division Two and Three North brought other poor players to the club until Harry Storer brought the pride back to the town in 1955 with signings like Reg (Paddy) Ryan and Martin 'The Bull' McDonnell and Dennis Woodhead, and the emergence of young players like Frank Upton, Ray Straw, Glyn Davies and Ray Young.

Tim Ward was appointed in 1962, and brought in some mediocre players, but persevered with some youth players who went on to serve the club in its glory years under Cloughie. Players like Colin Boulton, Pete Daniel and Ron Webster. The rest is history.

Balmy nights under floodlights were great atmospheric occasions.

I was brought up in Glossop Street not too far from the ground, and got 'the bug' from my father.

This was just after the war before the ordinary man had a car. People came from the out-of-town places like Alfreton, Ilkeston, and Burton. All the buses used to be parked around the streets near my house and near the Rolls-Royce factories. You could hear at our house if the

Raich Carter scoring against Blackpool in his last match for the Rams.

Rams had scored and could note the goals from our garden.

The excitement of the fans going over Elton Road bridge and surrounding streets was a memory to treasure. And the fans coming back was a great atmosphere, especially if the Rams had won.

Cycles were stored near the ground and kids made their pocket money this way by looking after them.

Programmes were sold from the front room of a terraced house at the bottom of Harrington Street near the ground.

I have watched the Rams for over 50 years through thick and thin.

A Rams fan for 67 years

by Alan Hawkes, Minster Road, Bath

I STARTED following the Rams in 1932 when I was four, when my father, who was a fanatical Rams supporter and a more than useful winger with Town Mission (Traffic St) FC, took me to see my first match.

Even though I moved from Derby many years ago, I have remained a firm fan of Derby County to this day.

I used to stand on the Pop Side with my father in the early days, and when big crowds were in attendance, young lads were passed over the heads of the crowd to the front to view the match through the railings, which were on the top of the wall at that time.

Two matches which I recall well prior to the war were against Stoke in the FA Cup in, I think, 1937, and Chelsea in the League in November 1938.

In the Cup match Stoke, including Stanley Matthews, were leading 2-1 with a few minutes to go. Me and my mates were in the boys' pen at the corner of the ground and we decided to leave a couple of minutes before time to beat the crowds and play football along the streets and through the Arboretum on the way home to Dashwood Street.

As we left the ground, a big roar went up and we assumed that Derby had equalised. I was home before my father, who had been on the Pop Side, and when he came in, I said: "They didn't play too well, did they?" He said:

An aerial view of the Baseball Ground.

"No they didn't", and I then said: "I can't see them winning the replay can you?" He said: "What replay?" to which I replied: "We equalised just before the end, didn't we?" My father replied: "Dai Astley got the ball in the net but was ruled offside."

You have never seen a more crestfallen boy in your life as I was at that moment.

In November, my father took me to London to see Derby play Chelsea. What a thrill. My first visit to the capital, and to see the Rams play. The only drawbacks were that, first it was a typical foggy day in London and we saw little of the play, added to which the Rams lost 2-0!!

League football as such ceased during the war and my father was away in the Army for much of the time in France/North Africa and in a prisoner-of-war camp from the fall of Tobruk in 1942 to the cessation of hostilities in 1945.

There was a Midland League in operation during the latter part of the war and it involved lots of local teams,

Fans invade the pitch after Rams against Arsenal, the last match at the Baseball Ground in May 1997. Arsenal beat the Rams 3-1.

NEXT MATCH
CENTRAL LEAGUE
WEDNESDAY, SEPT. 6
v
HUDDERSFIELD
KICK-OFF 6·0 P.M.

NEXT MATCH
LEAGUE CHAMPIONSHIP
SATURDAY, SEPT. 2
v
ASTON VILLA
KICK-OFF 3·0 P.M.

Members of the armed forces going in to watch Derby County at the Baseball Ground in October 1939. The entrance price was 6d.

and I remember trips by train to Nottingham, Chesterfield, Sheffield, Mansfield and Rotherham, to name but a few.

In June 1945, just after my father returned home, Derby played Aston Villa in the Midland Cup Final at the Baseball Ground. Clubs in those days had the services of locally-based military personnel, and Derby were fortunate to have Raich Carter and Peter Doherty playing for them. Anyway, we played Villa and won 6-0. Villa tried to play the offside trap that Peter Doherty beat many times which resulted in centre-forward Clarrie Jordan, a Rotherham player on loan, scoring five goals. Peter Doherty scored number six from a penalty.

The year after, the Rams played Charlton in the cup final and won 4-1 after extra time, thanks largely to a Jackie Stamps extra time hat trick.

We didn't have TV in those days, and as we couldn't get a ticket, we sat with our ears glued to the radio throughout the whole 120 minutes. I also remember going to the town centre to welcome the team home with the Cup. What an occasion that was.

In the following years, I recall going straight from work at the loco at 8am on a Saturday morning to queue to get into the ground for visits of the big teams. We also queued from 9am on Sundays to obtain Cup tickets.

Sadly, as the years went by, the Rams were relegated to first the Second Division, and then to the Third Division (North).

Shortly after that, in 1957, I left Derby to work first in the north-west until 1970, followed by a move to the West Country, where I still reside.

I have always looked first for Derby County results through good times and bad, and was delighted when Second Division and then First Division football returned

Wounded soldiers watch a wartime match at the Baseball Ground in September 1943.

to the Baseball Ground in the Clough era.

I was equally delighted with the championship wins of the 1970s and the involvement in European football.

I have seen Derby play home and away quite a number of times over the years including Liverpool at Derby in 1965 in a Second Division match with Bill Shankly's great team which went on to win promotion in the spring – and the rest is history, as they say.

I also saw Derby play Liverpool and Everton on Merseyside, in the 1960s, Swindon Town in a cup match at Swindon in the 1970s, and Bristol City home and away in the early 1980s, when both were in the First Division.

A couple of years ago, I was delighted to be able to attend the last match at the Baseball Ground against Arsenal. A great occasion, despite the fact that Arsenal won 3-1. My memories went back to that day in 1932 when I first saw the Rams, and

Rams legends Roy McFarland and Dave Mackay on the pitch at Derby County's new home – Pride Park – before the first game at the stadium against Sampdoria in August 1997.

it was a very emotional experience. Recently I was privileged to visit the new Pride Park Stadium to see the Rams play, and beat Liverpool 3-2.

A fantastic day out – a great stadium and so aptly named – and the right result. What more could a man want?

Away day peril for a couple of Rams fans

by S J Flint, The Nook, Holbrook, Derby.

IN Brian Clough's reign as manager of Derby County, my parents John and Dorothy Flint travelled to every home and away match possible.

Money was tight, yet they always found enough to follow their beloved Derby County. I would like to tell you of one away match they will never forget.

The match my father recalled was away to Blackburn Rovers on a Saturday. Derby County were in the old First Division, the season he thinks, was 1969-70. During their journey to Blackburn in dad's

Brian Clough parades the League Championship Trophy after the 1971-72 triumph.

Rams manager Brian Clough on the touchline during a match.

trusty old black car the engine blew up on the motorway. But luck was on hand when a dustcart pulled up and towed them to a scrapyard, just outside Wigan.

The scrap man told them the car was past repair and only fit for scrap. Dad took £40 for the car and headed off to Wigan by bus. And from Wigan they caught a taxi to Blackburn. When they arrived at the ground 15 minutes of the game had been played and the score was 1-1. There was no further score, so they missed both the goals. Outside the ground they caught a bus to the railway station. They caught the train to Stoke where they had to change for Derby.

They were thinking things weren't too bad, when the train caught fire halfway to Derby. Mum and dad had to stand and wait an hour for a replacement train in the rain. They finally arrived back in Derby at 11.30pm.

After this experience they spent the next four days in bed with the flu. Their only regret was missing both the goals.

What a day!

**by Peter Collins,
Derby Road, Chellaston**

Great players, great days at the Baseball Ground

I FIRST went to the Baseball Ground as a young boy with my late father in 1933 to see Derby play Everton. As you can imagine, the whole atmosphere was terrific on a first visit. The one thing I always remember was seeing the great Dixie Dean playing for Everton, what a great player he was between then and 1939.

As my father usually worked on a Saturday, an uncle took me to most reserve team games with odd League matches as well for various treats.

In those times I saw some wonderful players for Derby: Hughie Gallacher (one of the greatest), Charlie Napier, Jack Bowers, Reg Stockill, and what we all called in 1938 the million pound forward line of Crooks, Dix, McCulloch, Astley and Duncan.

Rams manager Brian Clough and long-time partner Peter Taylor in the dug-out.

When wartime football commenced in 1939-40, I then became a regular as I was now at work. During the war I saw some wonderful games and great players as Derby, over those years, had a lot of guest players to make up the team.

Then in 1943, we had the first appearances of Carter and Doherty, who were both stationed at RAF Loughborough, and also a very good centre-forward in Colin Lynam, of Spurs, who was also stationed there. Another fine player we had at that time was Frank Bowyer, of Stoke City. The team in those years was also made up of older players who were on war work such as Jack Nicholas, Ralph Hann, Sammy Crooks, Dally Duncan, Jack Bowers, Peter Ramage, plus a number of young local players such as Tommy Powell, Leon Leuty, Jack Parr, Fred Tapping, Geoff Knight, Arnie Grace and Tommy Jones.

There were some great games in those years. Besides friendlies, there were league and cup matches. Derby were in the Football League North. The best match I saw was the second leg of the Midland Cup Final of May 1945, when Derby County beat Aston Villa 6-0 and Peter Doherty scored five of them. He virtually played them on his own. It was a wonderful display of inside-forward play.

It was then 1946 – FA Cup Final year. My outstanding memories were of the semi-final and final. We went to Sheffield on the Saturday and drew 1-1 with Birmingham City. Everyone was worried because Leuty was injured and would miss the replay. This was at Maine Road, Manchester, on the Wednesday and a crowd of us went by train. Everyone was so confident we were going to win. One chap even took his piano-accordion to have a sing-song on the way back.

There were more than 80,000 at the game, a record, and just before the kick-off it was announced that Jack Howe would play centre-half. He had only just arrived home from service in the Far East and he played a blinder. He then played left-back, his normal position in the final, because, sadly, Jack Parr had broken his arm.

One outstanding moment was a brilliant save by Vic Woodley, from Bodle of Birmingham, at a crucial part of the game. Then the Cup Final. I didn't get a ticket until the Friday, and we stood behind one of the goals. Wembley in those days was mainly uncovered.

And what a day it was. First 1-1, then the ball burst,

then came extra time when Jack Stamps was unbeatable, scoring two goals. I've still got my programme, price 6d.

Then came the peacetime years and I purchased my season ticket in the Normanton stand in May 1946 when league football started up again in August 1946, and I kept the same seat until 1991 when the game became more expensive as by now I had retired.

In the post-war years I saw some great football and plenty of highs and lows. We were relegated from the First Division to the second and then the third. Then came the great comeback years that started with Harry Storer becoming manager and building a team that took us out of Division Three, with a great captain in Paddy Ryan and support from players like Martin McDonnell, Tommy Powell, Ray Young, Jack Parry, Jesse Pye, Les Moore, Bill Curry, Glyn Davies, Gordon Hughes. All such good and loyal players.

Also, just after the war we had some great players and matches. One match that stood out was in December 1950 when we beat Sunderland 6-5 on an ice-bound pitch, which today wouldn't even start, but it was a superb game. Jack Lee scored four for us and Trevor Ford scored a hat-trick for Sunderland. Again in those years we had great players such as Johnny Morris, Billy Steel, Tim Ward, Ken Oliver, Hughie McLaren, Jack Lee and Frank Broome.

I was one of the first people to join the Derby County Supporters Association when it was formed in 1956 from a small office in Friar Gate and then moved to The Spot. I was an agent for many years.

Then came the great years under Brian Clough and in those years I also went to most away games. Every one of those years was fantastic. Winning the Second Division championship and then into the First Division, plus wonderful European games. Two matches that stand out for me are the League Cup game when we beat Chelsea 3-1, in October 1968, when the old ground was alight with a roaring crowd, and in October 1975 beating Real Madrid 4-1 with Charlie George getting a hat-trick.

I saw many great players in that era, such as Kevin Hector, Roy McFarland, Alan Durban, Henry Newton, Archie Gemmill, Dave Mackay, a great captain.

Over the years, I've got to know a lot of players and some have become friends. Sadly some have passed away, such as Tim Ward, Leon Leuty, Tommy Powell, Ken Oliver, Jack Stamps, Ken Oxford, all I knew very well.

I'm still a great supporter and hope one day to go to Pride Park as it looks a wonderful stadium and we have a very good manager and team.

But I look back at the old Baseball Ground with great affection for the wonderful memories I've had in the 48 years I spent there. The great players I've seen and the matches. They'll live on forever.

**by Ivan Lower,
Collingham Gardens, Mackworth**

Goodbye – and good riddance – to the Second Division!

THE last game of the 1968-69 season against Bristol City, saw the visitors clap the Rams, already the winners of the Second Division championship trophy, on to the pitch.

That day, a hat-trick from Alan Durban was the highlight of a 5-0 win.

Again the attendance at the Baseball Ground topped 30,000 as the Rams said goodbye to the Second Division where they had bobbed about for 12 seasons.

Victorious, the team displayed their trophy on an open-topped bus through the centre of Derby, packed with cheering fans.

Members of the Voluntary Civil Aid Service were draughted in to act as stewards at home games, here during a match against Nottingham Forest.

Crowds outside the Council House cheer on the Derby County team, winners of the Second Division championship trophy in 1968-69.

First memories of a perfect day with the Rams

I WAS born in Milford in 1931 and my first memories of Derby County was at the age of 13 when my father, who was on leave from the Army, took me to watch them. We had to catch a bus from Milford to Derby bus station and walk from there. I can always remember Ivy Square on the way to the Baseball Ground.

The match was Derby County against Rotherham on December 16, 1944. I still have the programme and many more. The reason we went was because Len Slack from Bargate was playing and my father worked with his dad Jack at Gee, Walker and Slater in Uttoxeter Old Road, Derby. Len was a well-known local footballer

by
Patrick J Spencer,
Kilbourne Road,
Belper

and cricketer for Openwoodgate. Derby won the match 4-0 with two goals from Doherty, and ones from Carter and Slack. There was no finer sight than Carter and Doherty going down the field passing to each other and finishing with either Raich slamming it in or Peter flicking it in. Doherty was a master of taking penalties. Derby County had many players guesting for them in those days.

Looking through my programmes, one match stands out. On November 16, 1946 Derby lost 1-4, they had a full team out but Balmer, the inside right, scored four. Bob Paisley played left half for Liverpool. Another match I can recall was when Tommy Lawton scored a great header for Chelsea in a one-all draw. I can also remember the likes of Ted Sagar in goal for Everton or the enormous Mapson for Sunderland in the 1946-47 season.

If we were late getting in the ground the police would

Rams legend Peter Doherty (right) in action against Birmingham in the 1946 FA Cup semi-final.

walk the youngsters across in front of the Pop Side and drop us in front of the crowd so you would get a good view and you also got a good booing from the crowd. Derby won the Football League (North) and the Midland Cup in this period.

I started work at 14 as a joiner's apprentice and was lucky to win a Cup Final ticket at work. To get there I had to borrow a bike and cycle from Derby to home at Milford, to get up early Saturday morning and cycle back to catch the bus to Wembley. I stood behind the goal and saw the goals go in. I have been to Wembley since when Derby were there but the impression was never the same as the first time.

Following that season I started playing football for Milford as a goalkeeper. We won the Derby Sunday School League, DFA medals and cup in those days. I still have a photograph of the teams when Leon Leuty, the Derby County centre half presented us with trophies. I played locally until 1956 and then retired. I can remember going to see Derby County's Ralph Hann with a knee injury. I played for Gee, Walker and Slater on the Old Meadow behind the Cattle Market, which is now the site of the new Pride Park. Tommy Hateley the father of Tony played for Gee's – he was a good footballer.

In 1955 I started working for Bowmer and Kirkland until my retirement. During that time I came into contact with Derby County in a different light. Jack Kirkland, my boss and a Derby County director, took me to the Baseball Ground when he started all the alterations

under the main stand. He introduced me to a young Stuart Webb, in my opinion one of the best signings Derby County ever made without paying a fee. Under the stand there used to be long dark corridors with the old players' photos on the walls. At this time I was working on the bench as a joiner and dyed all the timber that cloaked the beams, often putting my name on the back side of the timber.

All the rooms and corridors, and players' lounge were then panelled. I met most of the managers from the Clough to Cox era. I remember having to purchase timber in a hurry to replace seats in the stands after the Leeds and Chelsea matches in following weeks due to damage caused by hooligans. I watched most of the matches and went into the Sportsmen Club where I met many famous players past and present such as Billy Wright, John O'Hare, Gerry Daly, little Willie Carlin, Roy Mac and many more.

One particular player stands out in my memory: Steve Buckley would stop in the street and chat with you, as would Jack Parry who was in the same class as me at the old Derby Tech College in Normanton Road. Also in my memory when modernising under the stands is when Brian Clough told one of the apprentices to get his hair cut or not go to work there the next day. He never did have it cut. Once, when in the Sportsmen Club, Lou Macari was watching horse racing on the TV before a Manchester Utd match. I asked him what would happen if I kicked him before the match. His reply was "I would kick you back," which I found amusing.

I have lots of old press cuttings, programmes and photos of old players. I stopped watching DCFC when the hooligan element crept in. I listen to every match on Radio Derby. Even when Derby County clash with a match on TV, I watch TV and have headphones on to listen to Derby. Barry Ecclestone was a good commentator, as is Graham Richards. And I like Eric Steele's comments against Ian Hall, who I think is better at cricket.

The game has changed considerably from the old leather ball with all the new equipment. I have lots of happy memories of Derby County. My grandchildren have purchased a brick for me at the new Pride Park stadium – a lifelong Rams fan.

The victorious 1946 FA Cup winning team were driven through the city on the back of a lorry.

Doing the rounds

by Audrey Dawson, Caroline Close, Alvaston

THIS photograph was taken when Derby County were doing a whistle-stop trip round the town after their FA Cup success in 1946.

It was taken outside the Blue Peter at Alvaston.

I am one of the faces in the crowd (I was 15 at the time) along with some of my friends.

Rams among first to help the blind

by Phil Matthews, Stanstead Road, Mickleover

DERBY County have been responsible for a number of innovations during their history – shirt sponsorship being a prime example – but, despite their proud and rightful boast of being part of the community, one of their most noble contributions is all too frequently overlooked.

In 1952, Derby County became only the second club in the country to provide commentary to their own blind and partially-sighted supporters in the ground.

Just for the record, Portsmouth were actually the first, but the time span between the two is so short that Derby could not be accused of jumping on the bandwagon, just taking a little longer to convert thought into deed.

It was a new venture, and with no role model everybody wanted to ensure that things were done right.

A short-list of half-a-dozen or so volunteers were invited along to a reserve fixture against Preston where they sat alongside John Arlott and Harry Walker from the BBC sports department. The trainee commentators were put through their paces

Jackie Stamps in action for Derby County.

and given advice by the professionals before the Derby County directors, who were listening in, chose the four who would make up the commentary team.

Amongst the trialists on that day was Roy Christian. "I had done a limited amount of broadcasting whilst serving in the Navy and wrote a letter of application. It seemed that I was the only one with any experience which obviously gave me a head start.

"The game was very dull, and I was given first crack at commentating, and luckily the only goal of the game came very early on while I was broadcasting. They offered me the job (which has always been unpaid and voluntary) and I was therefore the first ever voice heard on commentary for the club."

Roy remains an essential part of the commentary team to this day, and has a service record broken only by holidays and the occasional cricket match which at the time of writing runs to 47 years, surely making Roy the longest-serving commentator, professional or otherwise, in the country.

Also chosen as part of the initial four was Bertie Mee, a promising Derby County reserve whose footballing career had been terminated before it had started due to injury. Bertie was a physiotherapist at Etwall and progressed to the post of physio at Burton Albion. From there he moved to Arsenal where he was ultimately promoted into the

manager's chair. He was in charge of the very successful Arsenal side of the early 1970s.

Since those early days many volunteers have picked up the microphone, too many to mention here, although they know who they are and form part of a proud lineage.

At times the crew have been joined by well-known names such as BBC Radio Derby's Ashley Franklin, and on one occasion a truly famous one in Bill Shankly, who had been invited to do a brief half-time interview. He then insisted on doing some second-half commentary. Despite his extensive knowledge of the game, his broad Scottish accent unfortunately rendered the majority of his broadcast incomprehensible.

When Radio Derby Link, the Derby Hospital Radio service, was formed in 1974 one of the first things that they did was to hook into commentary, and it is something that has been provided for the hospitals ever since.

Commentators have set the scene for all Derby County home games and have been part of all the great nights of European football, championships, cup runs, and also, sadly, relegations.

I am a relative newcomer to the team. I have long

Jackie Stamps goes for a header.

watched the Rams as a season ticket holder, but had never harboured a desire to communicate my passion to others until an old school friend of mine, Alan Flintoft, approached me one Saturday afternoon. Alan always used to speak to me when popping down to see his uncle in the row behind. Alan would then disappear to his own seat – I knew not where.

This one particular day he made a beeline for me, explaining in a croaking rasp that he was due to commentate in a few minutes, but had lost his voice, and would I like to take over.

With no time to have any doubts, I was thrown in at the deep end. For the rest of that season and the next one I became first reserve when any of the regulars were unavailable. I was then promoted to full-time member and was quickly made aware of what an honour and privilege it was to be part of the service.

Since then I have had great days and bad days with Derby County, and have been lucky enough to meet the audience that we provide the service for. People like Jackie Stamps, the FA Cup-winning forward whose loss of sight was attributed to repetitive heading of the old case balls. He was a regular at the Baseball Ground until his death and became dependent on our service for his fuller appreciation of the matches.

Commentary started in the front row of the directors' box and moved over the years to its current location in the Press area. Between us we have seen and reported on almost every player and manager to be part of Derby County. I know that down all the days the broadcasts have been appreciated by so many.

It has all been made possible by the foresight of the club secretary all those years ago, Cyril Annable.

Squeaky singing in the kids' corner

by Mark Winson, Mill Lane, Belper

I CANNOT honestly recall the opponents the Rams faced on my first visit to the Baseball Ground. It would have been the 1967-68 season, and I was a totally overwhelmed eight year old. I guess it must have been an evening kick-off because I can remember the staggering amount of blue-grey cigarette smoke which billowed and rose above the stands and terracing to be penetrated by the shimmering and dazzling floodlights. I recall the game switched from end to end with unaccustomed regularity and had more pattern and purpose than the strain of football I was familiar with in the playgrounds and parks of my childhood.

My attendances were irregular to begin with, dependent upon whether one of a group of men I travelled to matches with were ill or unavailable, then I would pick up their ticket for the game. This was an ideal introduction to the game for me. Through these middle-aged men I gleaned the rudiments of the great game that had bypassed me in the playground. I sat at first in the B stand and could gauge how well the Rams were performing by the number of times my arms were squeezed or the number of shoves in the back I received. If it was a poor game I would return home relatively unscathed, although a little nauseous owing to an overdose of Murray Mints.

Rams player Francis Lee is held back after hitting Leeds player Norman Hunter (number 6) in November 1976. The players were both sent off and started fighting again as they left the pitch.

Dave Mackay holds aloft the Second Division trophy to a packed Baseball Ground.

Side and join in their songs and chants. Unfortunately, due to our age and size we sounded like we had inhaled helium gas prior to the match and squeaked rather than cheered our team to promotion.

From the kids' corner I witnessed the arrival of my first hero, Dave Mackay. This man seemed to possess everything needed to succeed on a football field, in barrowloads. The sergeant major crop, the barrel chest, the confident swagger, and an arrogance tempered with tremendous skill. From that moment I decided that Desperate Dan of the Dandy was a mere charlatan and he was despatched to the dustbin swiftly. Dave Mackay was the real thing all right!

Eventually I outgrew the kids' corner and progressed to the famous Popular Side where all the noise and excitement seemed to emanate from. The Rams at this time attracted massive support and crowds of 40,000 were not uncommon.

I remember a gentleman, perhaps a steward or a police officer, although without a uniform, instructing the crowd through the aid of a megaphone, to push backwards to enable more fans to be shoe-horned into place. At times when the crowd surged forward due to a goal

After a few seasons of sporadic attendance I found myself hooked and progressed to watch most matches of the 1968-69 season from the kids' corner. This was situated at the corner of the Normanton end. From this vantage point we tried to emulate the big lads on the Pop

attempt, my feet regularly left the ground, and I was carried yards until the swell of the crowd subsided. As a result of this occurrence you sometimes would lose your friends for the duration of the match, only to meet up again on the train home to Belper.

In the early 1970s we witnessed many heroes and villains from the Pop Side. I remember a cup match against Arsenal when a young Charlie George was barracked mercilessly by the Derby faithful with a chorus of 'Charlie George superstar, walks like a woman and he wears a bra'. Political correctness was rare, and New Men were a little thin on the ground in the early 1970s. Charlie responded to our insults by scoring two goals in a two-all draw, and racing towards the Pop Side flashing a two-fingered salute which had nothing to do with the score line at all. Who would have guessed a few years later he would be wearing a Rams shirt and be transformed from villain to hero?

Occasionally a whole team of villains dropped in to see us. Yes, you've guessed it, Leeds United. Brian Clough had stirred up some ill feeling by publicly criticising manager Don Revie and his team methods. So from the moment Leeds trotted arrogantly on to the pitch you could feel the mutual hostility. Leeds didn't care a jot though and certainly didn't go out of their way to win your admiration. Their warm-up routine prior to the kick-off involved the whole team forming a line and going through what looked like a keep fit class, that would not have looked out of place at a women's institute. Oh, and who can forget those sock pendants each displaying the player's number, an innovation never seen before and thankfully never witnessed since. Some years later, two players, Norman Hunter and Francis Lee tried to settle their differences via a bare knucklefight. Both players were led away bloodied but unbowed. The result a draw.

Derby County were now entertaining all the top clubs at the Baseball Ground and the sheer volume of the crowd could be deafening. I could swear we could alter the nature of a game by our tremendous enthusiasm. "ATTACK, ATTACK, ATTACK, ATTACK, ATTACK!" we chanted, and frequently the Rams responded and delivered our reward as Hector skipped past two defenders and slid the ball home.

By this time the Baseball Ground had become a fortress and to be there was an honour, you hardly ever saw the Rams lose! Our formidable home form coupled with fine defensive performances away from home could bring only one thing, the League Championship. First Brian Clough's team brought the trophy to the Baseball Ground in 1972 and two seasons later Dave Mackay's Derby were champions again.

The reward for winning the Championship was, of course, the European Cup competition, bringing some of Europe's greatest teams to the Baseball Ground.

I remember my father dropping me off one Sunday morning at 6.30am outside the ground to queue for a ticket for the visit of the mighty Benfica. Tickets were issued via the turnstiles, I don't recall a ticket office.

The atmosphere changed at the Baseball Ground after the ground became all-seater in 1995.

It turned out to be a legendary night, when Benfica including the great Eusebio were thrashed 3-0 with exceptional performances by McFarland and Todd. I have never heard such applause for two central defenders.

Of course, jealous people would remark that we had an ally that aided us in our victories: Derby's infamous pitch. But I prefer to look back in wonder at the fantastic football played on a surface which occasionally resembled a black forest gateau.

When the pitch was dug up at the end of another 1970s season, small pieces were sealed in plastic and mounted on a commemorative plaque and sold. I think it's now safe to admit that I sneaked on to the pitch, snatched a lump of mud containing a few strands of green and plunged it into my pocket. When I got home I transplanted the sod into my parents front lawn, where I'm sure it has enjoyed its healthy and lengthy retirement.

As a young lad I was at my most impressionable in the late 1960s and 70s, and because of this it has to be my favourite period at the Baseball Ground.

There have been good times since, of course, great players have come and gone, with many false dawns, promotions, relegations, play-offs. But now there is a feeling of genuine optimism. We have a good manager in Jim Smith and the club seem to be moving in the right direction.

Who would have thought that the Baseball Ground could conjure up one more fantastic memory. But it did, of course. On April 28, 1996, we met Crystal Palace. If we won we were promoted to the Premiership. With just half the fans in the ground compared to the 1970s due to seating replacing terracing, we made an awesome din, willing our team on to another famous victory.

The thing that made this victory sweeter than any other, though, is the fact that I shared it with my son Joe who was 12 at the time. When the final whistle blew and I looked round at him I saw myself, 25 years earlier, my silk Rams scarf tied to my wrist punching the air in celebration.

Of course I feel great sadness at leaving the old Baseball Ground, but Joe and younger fans like him can look forward to watching a great team in a fantastic new stadium, which will I hope bring them just as many wonderful memories as I have recalled from the old Baseball Ground.

Robbie van der Laan celebrates with Matt Carbon after scoring the winning goal against Crystal Palace in April 1996.

The FA Cup Final – April 27, 1946

by Alan Atkin, St Mary's Close, Newton Solney

I HAD been a Derby County fan from a very early age. My father took me to the Baseball Ground when I was about six years old to see Derby County Reserves play. I remember that Jack Bowers was in the Derby team, having just recovered from injury.

The FA Cup in 1945-46 season was a two-legged affair and I saw all the home games that took the Rams to the final. We were told not to apply for tickets to Wembley until a notice was published.

The *Derby Evening Telegraph* carried the notice which my mother drew to my attention as soon as I arrived home. I immediately wrote asking for two tickets and the long wait began.

I had asked a friend of mine, Bill Chammings to go with me if we obtained tickets and we were bitterly disappointed when the *Derby Evening Telegraph* announced that if we had not received tickets we were unlucky.

But two tickets arrived in the post the following morning!

The next problem was to get the Saturday morning off work. In those days, almost all businesses worked on Saturday morning and it was a very nervous junior clerk who approached the management to request the morning off to see the Rams at Wembley. Fortunately, permission was granted!

We travelled to Wembley on a special train which left Derby at around 8am. We arrived at the stadium in good time and were standing behind the goal that Charlton were defending in the first half. The teams received a tremendous reception when they came out to meet the King prior to the kick-off.

Derby dominated the game, with Leuty outstanding in the middle of Derby's defence, and Carter, Doherty and Stamps posing many problems for Charlton.

With nine minutes to go Derby scored when Turner, the Charlton right half, put the ball in his own net. We had hardly stopped cheering when Charlton equalised, with Turner, taking a free kick near the edge of the Derby penalty area, hitting the ball against a Derby defender and into the corner of the net.

The score remained at 1-1 at full time and so extra time was played for the first time in the Cup Final. Derby scored through Doherty in the first minute, with Stamps adding another after 11 minutes and a second about six minutes later. Derby had dominated the game, especially the extra time and were without doubt the better team.

After the game, we made our way back to St Pancras Station to catch the train for home. On the platform we met Mr Mason, a teacher at Kedleston Road School and a keen football supporter who had also been to Wembley. We discussed the game and all agreed that the best team had won!

The following Wednesday the team paraded through Derby on an open coach, with the FA Cup on display. There were thousands of people along the route to welcome the team, but unfortunately I could not join them as I was taking my banker's exams at the Westminster Bank in the Corn Market.

Names add to stand ad

**by Roland Lane
Norfolk Road
Long Eaton**

THE first match I saw at the Baseball Ground was the first time Jack Kirby played in the first team, taking over from Henry Wilkes.

We used to stand in the bottom of the Osmaston Stand before the main stand was extended.

On the end of the main stand was an advert for the Ideal Building Society, and it read:

"Don't Dally or Ramage
In other Groves, be Keen
To secure your Ideal Bowers",
referring, of course, to Dally Duncan, Peter Ramage, Arthur Groves, Ike Keen and Jack Bowers.

Jack Bowers, by the way, was the best centre-forward Derby County ever had.

A club that has always been the heart of the city

by Gerald Mortimer

CHIEF Sport Correspondent Gerald Mortimer has clocked up more than 29 years service with the *Derby Evening Telegraph*. Here he recalls memories of the Baseball Ground.

"It was the smell that used to distinguish the Baseball Ground, especially at night matches. Derby County's home was up against Ley's Malleable Castings and the smoke from the foundry gave, to young nostrils, a characteristic flavour to football. Even in Derby's European Cup days, sparks flew from the neighbours and soot settled.

Victorian football grounds were inextricably linked with industrial conurbations. If they did not live cheek by jowl with factories, they were surrounded by the homes of the factory workers. The Baseball Ground used to be hemmed in, Ley's on one side, Shaftesbury Crescent on the other.

Private enterprise flourished. In the days when more people used bicycles, they could be stored in alleys between the houses in Shaftesbury Crescent for a modest fee. When there were queues for big-match tickets, tea and soup were served by the residents. A shop at the Normanton End corner saw trade rocket on match days and former chairman Sam Longson used to moan that the owners made a fortune from the club. It sounded as if he thought that was his prerogative.

Football continued during World War Two, on a regional basis with guest players frequently used. Those stationed near a club could usually find a game, especially if they were as good as Horatio Carter and Peter Doherty. The war shaped Derby's most famous day. Carter won the League and the FA Cup with Sunderland, Doherty was a League champion with Manchester City and they were certainly among, probably the best inside-forwards of the 1930s.

They played for Derby as guests and, in 1945-46, manager Ted Magner persuaded them to sign full time. Derby had to pay, £6,000 each, and, significantly, they were eligible for the FA Cup. The war was over but not in time for the League to resume business. For the only time, the Cup was played on a two-legged basis and, in terms of talent at their disposal, the Rams were ahead of the game.

Carter and Doherty were the catalysts. They attracted crowds to the wartime regional League South and I paid my first visit to the Baseball Ground in January, 1946. Derby beat Millwall 8-1 and I was hooked for life. The nearest I came to the Cup Final was a shop window in the Spot, to see the team, on the back of a brewers' dray, parading the trophy through the town.

It was the first major prize Derby had won, although they were among the 12 original members when the League was formed in 1888. They reached the Cup Final in 1898, 1899 and 1903, losing each time. Their 6-0 defeat by Bury in the third final went into the record books as the biggest drubbing and the story that they were cursed by gypsies, angry at being displaced when the Rams moved from the County Ground to the Baseball Ground in 1895, gained currency. They rented the land from Sir Francis Ley, who had laid out a recreational area for his employees. On a visit to America, he was much taken by baseball, so that became one of the available sports and gave a name to Derby County's home.

They always had good players. Steve Bloomer, whose scoring record of 332 goals for the club will stand for ever, was one of football's early greats and was prompted by John Goodall, an England captain amazingly signed from Preston North End, champions and Cup winners, in 1889. In the 1930s, Derby were one of the top teams, but the way they could keep stars like Sammy Crooks, Jack Barker, Jack Bowers and Scotland winger Dally Duncan used to puzzle football.

In 1941, a joint League and FA commission provided some answers as they found Derby guilty of paying illegal bonuses and inducements when there was, of course, a maximum wage. George Jobey, manager for 16 years, and five directors were suspended from football. Stuart McMillan was manager by the time Derby beat Charlton Athletic in the 1946 Cup final but, when peacetime football resumed, he found it hard to replace Carter and Doherty after they moved on.

Derby tried hard enough. They twice paid British record fees, £15,500 to Greenock Morton for Billy Steel in 1947 and £24,500 to Manchester United for Johnny Morris a little under two years later. The Cup success was followed by a progressive decline and, in 1953, the Rams lost the First Division place they had held since 1927. Worse was to come because, in 1955, Derby slid into the Third Division North, the first time they had been out of the top two divisions. The lowest point came in December, 1955, when they lost 6-1 at home in the FA Cup to Boston United of the Midland League. To rub in the humiliation, Boston included six former Derby players, including Reg Harrison, a member of the 1946 Cup-winning team.

Harry Storer, a former Derbyshire opening batsman as well as Derby County and England footballer, stopped the rot. The two years in the Third North were fun because Derby scored freely, 110 and 111 goals, and crowds at the Baseball Ground averaged 19,000. I remember watching Derby beat York City on the night before I reported to Normanton Barracks for National Service in the Sherwood Foresters and I was back at the Baseball Ground on the day after being released from the Army in 1957.

By then, Derby County played an important part in my life but, after they won the Third North with a cannily-experienced team, there was little to stir the pulses for another decade. Storer's management ended on a muted note and his successor Tim Ward, another former Rams international, found the directors equally parsimonious.

It had become an unambitious club, swimming along in the Second Division and unlikely to go up or down. Managers had to make do and mend until, to widespread astonishment, Ward paid Bradford Park Avenue £40,000 for Kevin Hector. The Rams had a star, but even Hector's goals could not keep Ward in the job beyond the end of that 1966-67 season. Brian Clough and Peter Taylor were to gain the benefit from Hector, Alan Durban and Ron Webster, signed or developed under Ward. Clough and Taylor changed perceptions at the Baseball Ground while igniting the town and county with their enthusiasm. Supporters, unhappily accustomed to tepid fare, knew something good was happening even though, in the first season under Clough and Taylor, the Rams went down a place in the League.

In summer 1968, they signed Dave Mackay from Tottenham Hotspur. Mackay was 33 but his status was legendary. Other players in the Spurs Double team of 1960-61 reckoned Mackay was the most influential player in the club. He was ideal for fostering a young Roy McFarland, John O'Hare, Alan Hinton, John Robson and what became an exciting team. Clough and Taylor bought an experienced midfield player, Willie Carlin from Sheffield United, and were ready to take off. The feet on Shaftesbury Crescent had an eager beat again, the crowds were back and, the thing that attracted Clough and Taylor, a football town had come alive.

Derby soared out of the Second Division in 1969 and promptly qualified for Europe. Equally promptly, they were banned because of payments to Mackay for programme articles, something outside his contract. It was an administrative blunder and Derby brought in a more alert secretary, Stuart Webb from Preston. Supporters felt the blow keenly but, in 1971-72, the Rams were League champions for the first time. Within 12 months, they were European Cup semi-finalists, ultimately knocked out by Juventus. Juventus at the Baseball Ground – that would have taken some believing when the European Cup started in 1955 and Derby were playing Accrington Stanley, Halifax and Workington.

As Derby proved in the 1940s and 1950s, they are most at risk after a major success. With Clough and Taylor in their pomp, all should have been set fair. Sure, Clough was prone to sound off on television and upset the men in boardrooms, not only at his own club, but that was not an adequate reason for Longson, the chairman who appointed them, to become so set on shifting the management. He succeeded, too, and 18 months after winning the title, Clough and Taylor were out. Longson and his cronies could afford to chortle as Clough floundered at Brighton and Leeds. Then he went to Nottingham Forest, revived his partnership with Taylor, and created a great club at the City Ground. Twice they won the European Cup, to the distress of Derby fans who reckoned they should have been celebrating.

Mackay returned as manager in 1973 and had a tough time from Clough's supporters, in the dressing-room as well as the stands and terraces. Mackay and his assistant Des Anderson gradually turned it their way. They, too, bought well, Bruce Rioch and Francis Lee. Derby were champions for a second time in 1974-75, a terrific achievement for Mackay, and back in the European Cup. This time, it was Real Madrid at the Baseball Ground. Incredibly, Derby repeated their error by getting rid of another championship manager 18 months after he'd lifted the trophy. They tried to lure back Clough and Taylor – and failed. The outcome, inevitably, was a downward spiral as Derby went through a string of managers, Colin Murphy, Tommy Docherty, Colin Addison, John Newman and Peter Taylor. All the time, their finances were also in freefall.

Nine years after the second championship, Derby were on their way back to the Third Division, where they would celebrate their Centenary. They were fortunate to be alive because, in 1983-84, they had to negotiate a winding-up petition in the High Court. They emerged with the help of Robert Maxwell, the millionaire publisher who owned Oxford United. To stay within League regulations, his son Ian became Derby chairman but everybody knew whose pocket contained the cash. Derby appointed a new manager, Arthur Cox from Newcastle United, and were ready to take off again. Cox, with McFarland as his assistant, supervised two successive promotions and, when the Rams hit the First Division in 1987, Robert Maxwell succeeded his son.

At first, it looked good. Peter Shilton and Mark Wright were signed to add the class necessary to stay up and, the following season, Dean Saunders arrived from Oxford for £1m. It was money changing pockets rather than hands. Derby finished fifth, their best position since Mackay left and, again, all should have been set fair. Supporters did not like Maxwell and his rare visits to the Baseball Ground were not marked by the adulation he felt was his due. He was also overstretching himself financially by moving into American publishing and making overtures to other clubs. The money box was closed, the club was increasingly difficult to handle and relegation hit them in 1991. Maxwell wanted out: the sale of Saunders and Wright to Liverpool paid him off. It became a shabby episode and Maxwell was heading for financial scandal

when he was lost at sea, over the side of his yacht. His death caused much speculation.

Cox's best days – and they were very good – had gone but the Rams were ready for another U-turn when Lionel Pickering bought the club. Here was a local man prepared to invest heavily but it was not all plain sailing. Cox spent heavily before resigning because of back trouble. McFarland succeeded him but, despite an unlucky play-off defeat by Leicester at Wembley, could not take the final step. Pickering finally took the chair, appointed his own board and, in 1995, brought in Jim Smith as manager. Success returned. Smith won promotion at his first attempt and survived in the Premiership, the acid test for clubs going up. Top-half finishes coincided with the first two years at Pride Park Stadium. It was an emotional wrench to leave the Baseball Ground and a brave decision to move after more than 100 years. The obvious success of Pride Park should not blind anybody to the risks involved.

As the century nears its end, memories are revived. Some supporters can still recall the 1930s, while for others the two championships are in a distant past. The players parade past, from my schoolboy memories of Raich Carter and Peter Doherty through to Igor Stimac, Mart Poom and Jacob Laursen. Tommy Powell's skill stood out in bleak days, then shone in the Third North winners. He was a Derby man and never moved. Brian Clough and Peter Taylor brought in heroes, who were tutored by Dave Mackay, then established their own reputations. Was there ever a better defensive pairing than Roy McFarland and Colin Todd or a more elegant full-back than David Nish or a goalkeeper less prone to

Costa Rican international Paulo Wanchope celebrates after scoring the goal that secured a win over Liverpool at Anfield in November 1998.

Derby County's new home – Pride Park Stadium.

error than Colin Boulton? Kevin Hector and John O'Hare formed another great partnership, briefly replicated when Arthur Cox signed Paul Goddard to join Dean Saunders. Peter Shilton and Mark Wright went off to the World Cup with England in 1990. When the last tournament was played in France, the Rams had five representatives, none English. Horizons changed and the market place extended to Croatia, Costa Rica and Argentina.

Wherever they were born, players belong to the supporters who can savour Aljosa Asanovic's nomadic skills as readily as they warm to goalkeepers from Estonia and Coalville. Jim Smith is the most English of managers, but combines a traditional approach with a willingness to try new ideas. The club remains at the heart of the city, its successes governing moods. Football's audience is changing but, throughout the century, the game has been a social phenomenon."

A Life of Leisure

A seat for three in the cinema

by Miss J. Hill, Cannock, Staffordshire

WE were lucky in that in the days of the 1940s there was little traffic passing our houses other than post office vans, and we were, therefore, able to spend much of our time playing in the street.

The favourite games – naturally – were whips and tops (we became highly proficient at being able to whip the 'monkey' tops up into the air to land several feet away); marbles down the gutter; street cricket (with two bits of wood nailed together for a bat and wickets chalked on the wall); milk-bottle tops – the old cardboard ones, of course – which we skimmed from the pavement edge to the wall to see whose could land closest and snobs – which perhaps some people call 'five-stones'.

In addition, I recall that we often ran races round the block, starting from the corner of Hulland Street and Nelson Street, and going in opposite directions, so that we would usually pass one another in London Road, round about the chip shop.

Because the post office was just around the corner, we regularly came across the metal tags that were used to secure the mail bags. One of these, we discovered, if tied with string to the four corners of a handkerchief which was then scrunched up and thrown as high in the air as possible, made a nice little parachute.

If we wanted more room, to play football for instance (in those days with a tennis ball) or dodge ball (and didn't it sting when you were hit!), we would take ourselves up to St Andrew's Church yard, just at the end of the street. The vicar, Tom Parfitt, never seemed to mind us being there.

When we were a little older we would go up to Alvaston Lake, where we spent many hours on the swings and occasionally on the boating lake, or looking for newts in the pond. We would have been given enough money for bus fare, but it was not unusual for it to be spent on ice cream instead.

This sometimes gave rise to our only vaguely 'criminal' activity. When it was time to wend our way home and we were really tired, we would catch the bus, go upstairs to the very front seats, and hope that by the time the conductor reached us, found we couldn't pay and turned us off, we were already a good part of the way back!

Holidays were out of the question, being too expensive, but there was the occasional Trent bus mystery tour and, of course, the cinema. The nearest one to us was The Forum in London Road, and my favourite seat, when I went with my parents, was the one specially designed for three – a double and a single, side by side – on the right of the balcony. It was from there that I saw, among many other things, the newsreels showing the awful scenes from Belsen at the end of the war.

I recall that during the interval, while we waited for the B film to start (there were always two films in those days), one of the staff would come round squirting the 'flit' gun and we would all receive a light shower! Fortunately, I used to like the smell.

When we children went on our own we almost invariably tried to sit in better seats than we had paid for, sneaking into them under the cover of the semi-darkness once the film had started. Thereafter, each time the usherette's torch shone in our direction, we would sink as low as possible and hold our breath until the inevitable moment when we were discovered and shepherded back to our rightful places.

I think that at one point The Forum became The Cosy, and it was perhaps then, at its reopening, that it was visited by the film star Anouk. I doubt that I really knew who she was, but I acquired her autograph and signed photograph anyway.

For a more up-market treat we would go, on a Sunday, down to The Spot, to the Gaumont. It always seemed to be full, and when the lights went down the air of expectancy was palpable. Then came the strains of the organ, rising slowly from the pit, and we settled back to enjoy a satisfying evening's entertainment.

Later, in my teenage years, the Cavendish became a fairly regular venue, as well as The Normanton. At the latter cinema, the accustomed tickets were not in evidence, instead we were given large metal tokens, which we handed in as we entered the auditorium. The state of repair of the place was somewhat lacking and we soon discovered that a number of the seats, although still fixed to each other, were no longer properly secured to the floor and at a given signal we would tip ourselves forward, taking the whole row with us!

Peggy's double act proves a real show-stopper

by Ken Baines, Hillcrest Road, Chaddesden

APPEARING in Edinburgh, my act opened with Georgie (my main character) and myself being interrupted by Peggy, in spotty-faced St Trinian's-style with pigtails and wrinkled stockings, carrying a curly-headed little doll called Sammy. The part of the act ended abruptly when Sammy fell apart leaving her with just a piece of string in her hand.

A few minutes (and a quick change) saw her reappear with long sweeping hair, perfect make-up, and all sophisticated in a flowing kaftan, to work her favourite doll, Kathleen, for the rest of the act.

We took our bow to enthusiastic applause, when sud-

Working in cabaret in Tangiers, North Africa.

denly a broadly Scottish voice shouted: "That was ver' guid, – but why didna' that wee lassie take a bow as well. The one with the wee broken doll, – she was as good as you and deserves the same applause!"

What a lovely compliment. He hadn't realised the St Trinian's character and Peggy were one and the same! It goes to show that all parts of an act are as important as each other. It only happened the once, but it made our night.

Popeye and Hopalong on a Saturday morning

I STARTED going to the cinema in the 1930s, when I visited the Alexandra, which was situated at the corner of Hartington Street and Normanton Road, and which later became the Trocadero ballroom.

I used to go to the 'tuppenny rush' on Saturday mornings, where we saw cartoons featuring all the original Disney characters such as Mickey Mouse and Donald Duck, and also Popeye and Olive Oyl. These were usually followed by a cowboy film featuring Ken Maynard, Tim McCoy or Hopalong Cassidy.

My first visit to see a major film was to the Gaumont in London Road, at the time it first opened in, I think, 1937, when my parents took me to see Evergreen, starring Jessie Matthews.

During the war I became a regular cinema-goer and queued most Sunday tea-times to get into the Gaumont

by Alan Hawkes, Minster Road, Bath

with my friends to see the latest films, which by now were in glorious technicolour and featured all the glossy Hollywood stars of the time, which helped lift the gloom in what was a somewhat grey and bleak period between 1940 and 1945. Admission charges were one shilling (5p) or 1s 9d (9p) in the best seats at the back.

Among the many stars that we saw were Rita Hayworth, Alice Faye, Betty Grable and Carmen Miranda.

Leading men included Don Ameche, Robert Cummings and John Payne.

We also laughed at the antics of Abbott & Costello and enjoyed some of the early road films featuring Bing Crosby, Bob Hope and Dorothy Lamour.

There was also a regular supply of war films, usually relating to battles fought by the American forces in the Far East.

All of these films, both glossy and the war type, were, I suppose, made to help boost public morale in the USA, but they didn't do a bad job in raising the spirits of people in the UK either.

Betty Grable was everyone's favourite pin up, and I remember going to see her with Don Ameche in a film called Moon Over Miami at the Hippodrome, on an

Derby Hippodrome in Green Lane, Derby, pictured on April 5, 1937. The Hippodrome became a bingo hall in the 1960s.

Easter Monday in 1941 or 1942. In those days cinema performances were continuous and my friends and myself went in at 1.30pm, when the cinema opened and stayed to the end, which was around 9.30pm, to enable everyone to get home on the last bus.

The interior of Derby Hippodrome.

Cinemas and buses finished earlier in those days due to the possibility of air raids.

By the time we went home, we had seen the film three times.

Most, if not all, of the old cinemas have now been closed, pulled down or have other uses, such as bingo. This is sad, but I guess times change and people prefer to crowd into multi-screen cinemas or stay at home and watch TV.

In the 1940s and 1950s, I remember there being at least 18 cinemas in and around Derby, which were: The Gaumont, The Odeon, The Regal, The Empire, The Picture House, The Hippodrome, The Coliseum, The Cosy, The Cavendish, The Normanton, The Alexandra, The Cosmo, The Popular, The Majestic, The Gloria, plus cinemas at Alvaston, Allenton and Spondon. I can't recall the names of the last three, but think one at Alvaston or Allenton was called the Rex.

I have lived away from Derby for many years now, but it remains my home town and I hope readers will enjoy sharing my cinema-going memories.

---

by Margaret Hill, Queen's Park, Bournemouth

Chic of gravy browning stockings and blackout frocks

MEMORIES of walking to Chaddesden Park to inspect the bomb crater and look for shrapnel, at the same time stripping off socks and shoes and having a paddle in paddling pools.

Boating on Alvaston Lake and playing on the tennis courts.

Walking from Spondon to the Gloria and Majestic

cinemas and having to walk all the way home again afterwards.

Gravy browning applied to legs and a line being drawn to depict a seam.

Studio dresses made from blackout material for our dance class.

Blast walls, ack-ack guns, dried egg, parcels from America (we were lucky). Almost being evacuated to America before the ship carrying some children was torpedoed. Undies and wedding dresses made from parachute silk. Snoods and bangs for the hair.

The list is endless.

A small price to pay for peace and quiet

by Walter Ford, Yew Tree Close, Alvaston

I F YOU wanted to get rid of the kids for the afternoon you sent them to the cinema.

You gave them four pence in old money and for that they would get two halfpenny bags of sweets and a posh seat at The Cosy cinema or the flea pit.

It was always noisy when we went in but when the show was ready to start the boss would stand on the front seat and tell everybody to keep quiet.

Everybody would fall silent and then the boss would flash his light and it was on with the show. The noise was deafening. The show was nearly always the same – Flash Gordon and a cowboy film.

You could always tell where the kids had been afterwards. They were rubbing their eyes when they came out into the sunlight!

The Gaumont cinema was the posh one and it cost more. It was called 'the kiddies' club' and it cost sixpence to get in. The poor kids had to save up their pocket money to get in, so we did not go there very often.

If you had no money and you wanted to get in to the Cosy, you went round the back, down the alleyway between the house and cinema, went to the toilet and waited there till the show started, then you'd pick up a ticket off the floor and walk in.

If you got stopped you'd show them the ticket out of your pocket and then you'd go and sit down in a seat and watch the show. If your seat was not right you waited till no-one was looking and moved somewhere else. I did not

have to do that, as my dad got paid six pounds a week.

I also remember the Morledge and Cockpit Hill where 'Mad Harry' used to stand and give things away, especially to the kids. Great days they were.

What I used to like when I was young was to come home from school, rush home to get some bread and dripping and tell my mum where I was going (I had to or I would be in for a good belting). Off I would go down Canal Street to Siddals Road across to Scrappy Hills Yard and up to Fife Arches to watch the trains go by. My favourite was number 1000. It always seemed clean and smart. They used to go to places I did not know (I do now) and it was marvellous to see.

We used to go to Alvaston Lake on the tram. It used to cost a penny. It was great to ride on a tram.

We used to walk everywhere. I would walk to Markeaton Park from Derbyshire Royal Infirmary and for a young lad that was a long way. You could see the carnival with all the bands that took part, all in their fine uniforms. We used to march up and down with them. What a lovely day out.

Now this is going back some time, but in 1935 when King George V and Queen Mary came to Derby I stood outside Queen's Hall and watched them go by. I waved like mad and I knew they were waving back to me because I was the only one outside the Queen's Hall. All the others were on the other side of the road.

Shortly after this my dad brought me a book called the Royal Jubilee Book 1910-1935 and it was given to me in 1935. I've still got that book so it must be 64 years old and it's still in good order with wonderful pictures in it.

Joining the queue for potted meat and illicit nylons

by Margaret Hill, Queen's Park, Bournemouth

Q UEUEING for hours for Joyce shoes that had arrived at Barlow Taylor.

Buying broken biscuits

from Joyce's biscuit stall in the Old Market Hall.

Theaker's delicious potted meat from the Market Hall. More queues for a few Bird's cakes and possibly some sausages at the shop in St James' Street.

Walking every Saturday morning as a 12-year-old from Spondon village to Barron's Nursery in Borrowash for a quarter pound of tomatoes, then on to Mill's Provisions shop for a pound of slab cake, either plain or fruit, then walking back home again.

Becoming a regular for under-the-counter nylons at a market stall in the bus station market and walking to Sadler Gate from Siddals Road in my lunch hour to have them invisibly mended at 1s 6d for a small ladder, rising by 1s depending on the length. You could also purchase 'laddered' nylons, which were also much sought after.

Neglected and derelict but memories live on

by Geoff Moore, Stenson Road, Littleover

I WOULD like to share memories of a long-forgotten institution of the history of Derby, the canal system that once existed, particularly in the Nottingham Road and Erasmus Street area.

The era I refer to was in the early 1960s when the system had been allowed to fall into dereliction and decline, and the once-busy waterway had become neglected and overgrown and was a potential health hazard.

I recall that at the south end of Erasmus Street, at the junction of Darwin Terrace, was the White Bear public house, and over the wall at the side could be seen the remains of the lock gates at the canal basin.

Next to this, and also in a state of dereliction, was Long Bridge, still spanning the River Derwent at the top of the weir. I remember that the bridge had warning notices to keep people off, but we still crossed it for a dare despite the possible consequences.

At the north end of Erasmus Street was a smaller basin which was always a lure to the local children, as in the winter the water froze over, and in the summer a rope swing from a nearby tree was the main attraction.

Borrowash lock on the old Derby Canal in February 1960.

At the end of Erasmus Street was a small shop, and the street led to Pegg's Bridge and Nottingham Road beyond. To the right and down towards Clarke Street was a yard that used to display memorials. I believe this was a business run by a family named Garratt and the headstones were manufactured on site.

The area at Erasmus Street was a busy one due to the comings and goings at the fruit wholesale market where, at the end of the day, we were allowed to help ourselves to the over-ripening fruit. Needless to say we never fell victim to constipation in those days!

The old Derby canal bordering Nottingham Road. It shows the infilling of Phoenix lock in 1963 to make way for a 500-space car park. St Mary's Bridge can be seen in the background on the left.

Sadly, and perhaps inevitably with the decaying canal, the nearby river, and the fruit market, the area became a playground for rats. They could be seen on a regular basis in search of food.

The Derby system of canals was extensive. From the area I have just mentioned, the waterway ran down to its source at St Mary's Bridge, and in the other direction along Nottingham Road following the route beside Nottingham Road Cemetery where the A52 now lays, past the Courtauld's works at Spondon, and out towards the systems beyond.

At the junction of Nottingham Road and Stores Road the canal veered off, under the road itself and ran along the end of the Racecourse, in front of Aiton's and across to the Great Northern Railway arches towards Breadsall.

In the other direction from Bass Recreation Ground it ran along Siddals Road, where it veered off and along the back of the locomotive works, past the gas works, under Deadman's Lane and London Road and across to Harvey Road and Brackens Lane. It then proceeded to Shelton Lock, where remains can still be seen today.

Where beautifully decorated canal boats once adorned the city, nothing or very little now remains of what was once the nucleus of Derby's transportation system, and industrial archaeology can only be seen if you know where to look. But in recent years in the fight for relieving congestion on the overcrowded roads there has been talk of reintroducing a canal system and the conservationists have already started this in certain areas.

I am confident that reintroduction would enhance the beauty of the city and would give recreational opportunities to many. It would be impossible to recreate the waterways in their original positions, but I would suggest Pride Park would be a great place to recreate a new marina. Thus the people of Derby could again relieve the a transportation system from a bygone era.

The basket makers.

Denis and Mary Hudson, Whangaparaoa, Hibiscus Coast, New Zealand

Life's a basket of cherished memories

HERE ARE a few photos that may provoke more memories for your readers. This faded photo (top) of the Basket Makers is one my father cherished of his father Henry Hudson (my grandad), proudly displaying his workmanship for all to see. My grandad is the guy in shirt sleeves above the letter 'O' on the big basket. The photo is about 75 years old, so I doubt anyone can put other names to grandad's mates.

The Boys' Brigade.

The photo of the Boys' Brigade (above) was taken outside the Ashbourne Road Congregational Church in about 1942-44. I can remember only a few names. The corporal on the right side of the photo is Bill Bull, the famous Trent bus driver. His brother, John, is the private on the very left of the photo. The Corporal two to the

The camp at Kelstedge on visitors' day.

right of John is yours truly, and to my right is Alf Haslam. To the right of Alf just behind the vicar is Henry Bull, brother to Bill and John.

The officers seated are from the left: Mr Hall, The Reverend Earnest Walton, Captain Mr Mansfield, Pop Evans and an unknown visitor from another company. The rest of the company all look familiar but I can't put names to them.

The third photo (left) was taken in about 1945 when we were all at camp at Kelstedge on visitors' day.

Derbyshire fast bowler took six wickets in seven balls!

ALTHOUGH I have lived away from Derby for many years now, I still have lots of happy memories of cricket in Derbyshire, both before and after the war.

My father started taking me to see Derbyshire play cricket in the mid-1930s.

In those days, almost total silence was maintained while the game was in progress, apart from when a wicket fell, a maiden over was bowled, or a player or his club reached a milestone in the innings, such as 50 or 100 – so unlike it is today!

During the intervals, small boys would play cricket about the boundaries, using a pop bottle as a bat and a tennis ball, which was great fun.

I remember Derbyshire winning the championship in 1936 and also an amazing match in July 1937 against Warwickshire.

The match stated at 11.30am on the Saturday and 98 deliveries and some 65 minutes later Warwickshire were all out for 28.

Derbyshire's fast bowler Bill Copson took eight wickets for 11 runs and in the process, took the last four wickets in four balls. He also took two wickets off his first three balls in the second innings – which meant he had taken six wickets in seven balls. An outstanding effort indeed.

Derbyshire batted and made 227, Warwickshire totalled 291 in their second innings, leaving Derbyshire to get 93 runs in their second innings, which they did for the loss of five wickets.

by
Alan Hawkes,
Minster Road,
Bath

Incidentally, Copson scored 30 in Derbyshire's first innings – which meant he, batting number 11 I think, outscored the whole of the Warwickshire team. Truly a memorable match.

The team at that time featured several England players and included Denis Smith, Albert Alderman, Stan Worthington, Leslie Townsend, The Popes – George and Alf – Harry Elliott, the wicket keeper 'Dusty' Rhodes, Tommy Mitchell, a wonderful spin bowler and, of course, Bill Copson, who but for ill health and the war, surely would have represented his country on more occasions than he did. A. F. Skinner, an amateur player, skippered the side.

The war altered many things, with little or no cricket to watch, my father away in the Army, and it wasn't until 1946 that things began to get back to normal, when some victory internationals were played.

In 1947, the South Africans toured and Compton and Edrich scored over 3,000 runs each, in what was a long hot summer.

In 1948, it was the Australians' turn and when they played Derbyshire at the County Ground, E. J. Gothard, an amateur, who captained the team at that time, bowled the great Don Bradman for 62 runs.

The New Zealanders

Tom Mitchell, April 1934.

Uncle and nephew walk out to umpire. On the left is Harry Elliott, the former Derbyshire wicket keeper, and Charlie Elliott, the former Derbyshire batsman. Charlie was also the Rams' chief scout.

Derbyshire's Denis Smith.

followed in 1949, and in 1950, the West Indies came with a team which included the three famous Ws, Weekes, Worrall and Walcott.

They also had a couple of useful spin bowlers named Ramadhin and Valentine.

I watched the West Indies play Derbyshire at Chesterfield and it was a real treat to see so much talent gathered on a cricket pitch at the same time.

I played cricket myself for a few years after the war with the Loco Works No. 8 shop team and had modest success as a slow off-break bowler, even getting a mention in the Green sports paper for taking six for 29 against West Hallam Whiterose CC.

Freddie Brown captained the team, Dave Constadine kept wicket and Sam Roberts and Albert Varley were both good medium fast bowlers.

We played our home matches on a pitch in the outfield at the County Ground, but not of course, on or near the hallowed central square.

I am now 70, and have thus been a Derbyshire CC fan for more than 60 years and I always check their results and progress before any other clubs.

It would put the icing on the cake, as it were, if they could win the championship again while I am still around to see them do it.

**by H.W. Foulds
Alvaston, Derby**

Football team needed pedal power

S HARDLOW ST JAMES FC team in the 1934 to 1939 season consisted of players living in various areas such as Derby, Sawley, Draycott,

Castle Donington, Aston-on-Trent and Long Eaton.

The manager Ernie Barton showed great dedication towards the success of the club. Ernie who biked to Spondon, where he worked, would go home and then cycle to and from the above places to make sure he had a team.

I joined the club in the 1935 season. At that time it was difficult for managers to contact players. It wasn't just a matter of picking up the phone to make arrangements, personal contact was more often the only way.

Shardlow St James FC 1936-37 season (from left) H. Foulds, W. Halford, L. Maddocks, A. Pickering, D. Porter, F. Bowler, E. Fineren, F. Eccleshall, A. Mynett, D. Pickering, A. Wheldon, E. Barton (manager).

1938-39 season (from left) H. Foulds, D. Porter, A. Pickering, N. Chambers, A. Wheldon, W. Stringer, F. Eccleshall, A. Mynett, A. Bosworth, F. Birds, E. Barton (manager).

The Story of the Rural Domestic Economy Centre (Home Crafts Education Service)

by Mary Moore (née Blagg), Henry Street, Derby

HOW MANY readers recall walking up a driveway from Duffield Road in Derby to the RDE Centre to attend a demonstration or practical class in one of the domestic arts?

The Rural Economy Service was a fairly unique part of adult education provision which served both borough and county. Many Derbyshire women, and some men too, used this valuable service in the mid to late 20th century.

The first members of staff were appointed at the end of the war and worked from Community House, Kedleston Road. Derbyshire County Council soon took over responsibility, building a new purpose-designed centre in the early 1950s from where it operated until 1991. The building was situated in the grounds of Park Grange (formerly a doctor's house) which initially became the Schools Museum Service and was then used as a day centre by social services. It was also next door to Queen Mary Maternity Home. The name was changed to Home Crafts Education service

Entrance to Park Grange and Home Crafts Education Service (RDE) off Duffield Road, Derby.

in 1978 before reaching its demise in the cutbacks of the early 1990s.

Many of those attending the RDE Centre will remember Miss Edna S J Williams, the senior instructress, and the first staff appointed as assistant instructresses – Mrs Dorothy Cox and Miss Marjorie Warrington. Initially, they were employed by the Ministry of Agriculture, Food and Fisheries and then by Derbyshire County Council. Indeed some of those experiencing Edna Sarah Jane's rigorous approach to instruction will remember shedding a few tears as they struggled for perfection.

Flower arrangements by Mary Blagg.

In the early days of RDE, food was still rationed so the preservation of food was vital. The highlight of the year in many homes both urban and rural, was the killing of the fattened pig for providing welcome winter meat.

Edna and Marjorie, who were trained at Smithfield Market, London, in the curing of bacon and preparation

of pork products, travelled to the outlying farms to teach rural women how to make the best use of all parts of the pig. Imagine the intrepid instructresses setting out in a little Ford car with cans of petrol, a paraffin cooking stove, knives etc, starched white overalls, a packet of Woodbines and with an overnight bag. They would be met at the farm gate and often asked by the farmer's wife in hushed whisper 'Are you menstruating?' If so, they were turned away as rural superstition believed that the pig meat would go bad. All in a day's work in the 1940s!!!

If they overcame that hurdle, gathered in the farmhouse kitchen, wives and daughters of local farmers would perfect their skills in the preparation of sausages,

On location in a farmhouse. Mary Blagg teaching flower arranging with a group of Chaddesden WI members at Brook Farm, home of Eunice Morton, standing on left of picture.

black puddings, chitlings, scraps, pork pies, haslet and the laying down of the bacon and hams in salt for curing. They had to complete the task within two days as there were no domestic refrigerators available, only cold stone slabs in cavernous pantries in those post-war days.

Margaret Roddis (née Blagg), of Highwood Farm, Whitwell, remembers as a young girl her father sharpening the knives in readiness for cutting up the pig at one of these courses held in their kitchen, and Marjorie cut her finger.

Did anyone attend the WI communal canning sessions held under the watchful eye of Miss Williams? Not only did they can at The Centre in Duffield Road but the instructresses were prepared to go out to the village halls with the equipment and can trays and trays of fruit with the local WI members.

Another aspect of work at The Centre and in the

county was the wide range of soft furnishings that were made under the expert tuition of Dorothy Cox. Everything from lamp shades, curtains, covers and even eiderdowns were made or recovered and even reclaimed. (Long before duvets were popular.)

The interior of the multi-purpose practical and demonstration room for cookery or craft.

At the centre, there was only one practical/demonstration room plus a preparation kitchen used by the staff preparing to work out of centre and a small office. Both cookery and craft classes had to be dovetailed into the teaching space. Were any readers there on the day that Miss Williams arrived at the RDE Centre to prepare for a cookery demonstration, only to find everywhere covered

in down and feathers from the eiderdown session the night before?

In spite of the limited facilities and small budget the RDE Service served the whole county and continued to travel to village halls, other adult education premises, libraries, health clinics and meeting venues of all sorts until it closed. All that had to be provided in situ were a table, a tap and a three pin plug! Eventually, to ensure countrywide coverage additional out centres were established in other county council establishments in the north east and north west of the county, but the staff were still part of the Derby team.

The peripatetic teaching staff were intrepid drivers facing country roads, dark nights and all weathers to meet their commitments. They were also proficient furniture movers; packing and unpacking boxes of pots and ingredients or equipment, and organising the furniture around the table and plug. At the end of the day or evening there was the clearing up, re-packing and returning to base to repeat the process once more!

There will be many readers who remember the spectacular Christmas demonstrations, whether they packed into the centre in Duffield Road or went to a county venue when the team were on location: Hope Valley School, Long Eaton or Clay Cross Adult Centre, Ripley Co-op Room or Library, Alfreton Hall, Chesterfield Guide Hall or Swadlincote Town Hall. These required

A typical audience for a Christmas demonstration at the centre.

tremendous staff dedication to prepare all the displays and the live cookery demonstrations, and there were no spares or retakes in case of error! For many years the whole lot had to be transported from place to place by county council van with a driver and assistant. There was everything from the demonstration table with overhead mirror to the traditional, decorated Christmas tree on board.

Dorothy Oliver (food and nutrition lecturer) at the end of a Christmas demonstration, ready for 'tastes'.

In spite of the rigours, the nature of the work suited staff and they stayed for many years.

The centre was initially looked after by Mr and Mrs Moss (Jack and Gwen) of Chaddesden. He agreed to look after the boiler on a temporary, part-time basis and stayed on for 19 years.

Courses differed from those in adult education because they were nearly all short sessions, one afternoon, an evening or a day that focused on a specific aspect of cookery or craft and did not require a long-term commitment. Nevertheless, over the years the same people returned many times and there will be readers who will remember coming to classes as a young engaged couple, returning regularly throughout their lives and still

coming when their grandchildren were grown up. Men, too, were not neglected and before equal opportunities prevailed there were specific men's cookery classes.

Out and about at Bakewell Show with a 24ft display.

The teaching staff responded to the changing domestic scene and were able to update people with such things as the introduction of:

Wash codes to care for fabrics and domestic refrigerators in the 1960s;

Freezers, mixers and latex foam upholstery in the 1970s;

Microwave cookers, duvets and Austrian blinds in the 1980s.

Some of the themes from the 1950s to 1980s, showing changing topics for changing times.

Cookery went from coping with rationing in the 1940s and early 1950s to the richness of Cordon Bleu cookery using pints of cream in the 1970s and responding to the regime of NACNE and COMA reports for healthy eating in the 1980s.

Many listeners to BBC Radio Derby will remember the Two Dorothys' (Dorothy Cox and Dorothy Oliver) weekly Friday morning advice phone-in programme in the 1970s which answered queries on all aspects of cookery and home management.

As well as providing courses to update the general

End of an era on July 4, 1991. Mary Blagg (second left) with members of the WI singing Auld Lang Syne. The Home Crafts Education Service closed at the end of July and the centre emptied.

demonstrating a subject (cookery or craft) and to qualifying as a judge.

This route of opportunity encouraged people's untapped ability and encouraged some to train as teachers. For example, several highly-respected local teachers of sugar craft started via this route, and several of the technicians who started work at the centre eventually became teachers. Through in-service training links, school home economics teachers used the service as a resource to update information and collect new recipes.

Changing policies for care in the community and in adult education opened another door in the late 1980s enabling people with special needs to take their first steps to independence and participate in education for adults.

Many households in Derbyshire will have boxes of recipe and instruction leaflets developed by the lecturing staff and technician, typed and printed by the secretary and often collated by the ancillary staff. The leaflets are still in use today because they 'worked'. Sadly there are no replacements available as the service closed in the county council's economy cuts of 1991. To this day people we meet regret the closure of this unique facility.

public, there was a commitment to train members of the Young Farmers' Clubs and Derbyshire Federation of Women's Institutes. There was a series of proficiency tests enabling people to progress from a basic knowledge to

When Elsie Tanner had lunch at Ranby's

by Judy Jones, St John St, Wirksworth, Derbyshire

MY HAPPY MEMORIES of shopping in Derby are around the early 1960s. On a Saturday my mum and I would wait for a bus to Derby from Derby Road, Wirksworth at around 9am.

We would get off the bus in the Market Place by the underground toilets. We would look around Barlow & Taylor's (now the Derbyshire Building Society), I think this was the first shop where I went in a lift.

We would walk up to East Street and go into Williamson's cake shop. People would be queuing for cakes. I remember all the square tins with loose biscuits in. We would go in the back to the cafe and have a plate of yummy cream cakes, chocolate eclairs, buns etc, and a cup of coffee. All served so nicely by the very smart waitresses.

We would go to all the usual shops, Marks & Spencer, Woolworth's, Midland Drapery, Co-op etc. Then on to Ranby's (now Debenham's) for lunch. We would go to the restaurant with waitress service, and usually sit at the same table. The waitress that I remember best went to live in Australia.

People used to always sit in the same places. Often we would have ladies modelling the latest fashions, holding cards with the prices on. We were once having lunch and Elsie Tanner from Coronation Street (Pat Phoenix) came

Ranby's department store, now Debenham's, in Victoria Street, Derby, in Jan 1962.

in with the management for her lunch. She must have been on a promotional day.

We would go up Green Lane to Central Education and down towards the market by the bus station. There was no Eagle Centre then. We would watch a man selling bedding and towels at knockdown prices. Mum still has things she bought from him.

Then on to the bus station. I always had a magazine from the stall in the bus station. We would wait for the bus in the ladies' waiting room. At this time the Wirksworth bus started from opposite here. We would get home around 4pm. Days went slower then, life was more gentle. These are very happy memories.

Love of jazz sparked by movies

by A Hawkes, Minister Way, Bath

THROUGH being a keen filmgoer during the war, when I was a teenager, and seeing many of America's top bands in films at the time, I became very interested in dance music and jazz. As a result of this I felt that I would like to become a musician, and when my father returned home from war service in 1945, I persuaded him to help me to buy a set of drums.

I then started practising at home in the spare bedroom, which wasn't too easy for my parents or the neighbours. I also took some lessons from a good friend and work colleague "Hadge" Pritchard. After a while I felt that I had mastered the rudiments and began to look round for a band to play with.

Fortunately at that time, a near neighbour's son, Ken Hetherington, wanted a drummer for his Hawaiian band, so I joined up with him and Len Gwinnutt on accordion, Ron Keeling on piano, and Syd Brown on rhythm guitar. Ken played the Hawaiian guitar.

The Ken Hetherington Hawaiian Serenaders during a concert at the Majestic Cinema, Chaddesden, in 1947.

I stayed with this band for around two years, during which time we played at many venues in and around Derby, including the local Majestic cinema in Chaddesden, where we did Sunday concerts. We also had an audition for BBC Radio in Birmingham, which although unsuccessful, was a great experience. We made a record (self financed) at the Victor Buckland Studios in London Road, and appeared for a week at the Grand Theatre on the Bryan Mickie Discoveries Show. This entailed going straight from work each night at 5.30pm and performing twice a night for the whole week. This was quite a hectic week, but all in all not a bad time for a bunch of young musicians.

I did want to get involved in the local dance music and jazz scene, so I left the Hawaiian band and started doing

Alan Hawkes aged 19, in 1947, on stage at the Majestic Cinema, Chaddesden.

Alan Hawkes – aged 26 in 1954.

Kyte; Assembly Rooms – Freddy Sharratt; Rialto – Jack Wood; Ritz – Wally Mellors; Central Hall – New Mayfair Dance Band; Kingsway Drill Hall – Rhythm Aces; and Trocadero – Jimmy Monk

In addition, the pool in the baths in Queen Street was boarded up in winter to enable Saturday night dances to be run and Billy Joyce and Wylie Pryce were both resident with their bands for several seasons.

After a while I decided to form my own band, and around 1952 I recruited some fine musicians, namely Denis Tatham/Albert Day on piano, Joe Powell on bass,

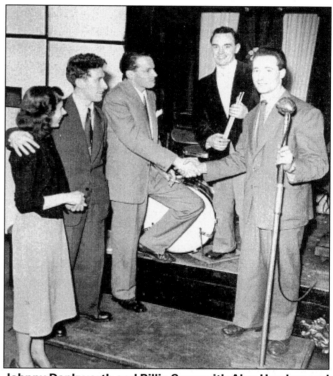

Johnny Dankworth and Billie Sage with Alan Hawkes and the couple who ran the Dancing School which housed the Modern Music sessions. Sorry I am unable to remember their names.

gigs and depping jobs for many of the bands who were operating at that time, around 1948-1950.

In all there were some eight or ten dance halls in Derby operating several nights a week, so there was usually some work to be had.

Dance halls and bands I can remember were:- the Plaza – Ken Turner/Jimmy Monk; Churchill Hall – Syd Arkell/Billy Joyce; Albert Hall – Harry Hopkin/Harold

Johnny Dankworth, plus his pianist Bill Le Sage. Together with Joe Powell on bass and Alan Hawkes on drums at The Derby Modern Music Club in late 1952.

Alan Hawkes Dance Band at the Grandstand Hotel, Nottingham Road, Derby in 1954. Pete King trumpet, Wally Mellors clarinet/alto sax, Joe Powell, bass, Albert Day, piano and Alan Hawkes, drums.

Alan Hawkes quintet at the Derby Modern Music Club in late 1952. Bob Buggs tenor sax, Dennis Keenan trumpet, Maurice Butterworth piano, Joe Powell bass and Alan Hawkes drums.

Wally Mellors on alto sax, and Pete King on trumpet.

With an enlarged band I auditioned for Sol Lux when he started running dances at the Albert Hall, but lost out to Harold Kyte. Harry Hopkin also had a prolonged spell at the Albert Hall and had a fine band including Charlie Hannaford, Joe Tomlinson and Harry on saxes, Dennis Keenan, trumpet, Harry Preston, bass, Alan Walters, drums, and Maurice Butterworth, piano, perhaps the best pianist in the Derby area at that time.

I resorted to running a quintet for dance band work and enjoyed a few successful years on gigs and various residencies in Derby hotels, a Nottingham club and an American air force base in Lincolnshire. This latter job entailed leaving Derby at 5.30pm on Saturday and returning home around 4.30am on Sunday.

In 1954 the Rialto Ballroom became a dancing school run by Bernard Knight and Molly McKenzie and we spent several months there as well. It was a daunting experience having to play quicksteps, waltzes and foxtrots in very strict tempo and to a precise number of bars per minute.

In 1951 I decided to form a modern jazz quintet and I ran a jazz club for a while, initially at the Co-op Hall at the Cavendish, and later at a dancing school which was situated at the top of Sadler Gate.

I "borrowed" some absolutely outstanding musicians from local bands for our Tuesday night sessions and was proud to play alongside such talented players as Charlie Hannaford, Joe Tomlinson, Dennis Keenan and Maurice Butterworth from Harry Hopkins Band, plus Bob Buggs from Syd Arkell's Orchestra, together with Joe Powell from my own group. We did our own spot at the jazz club and accompanied visiting musicians who appeared for the night. The highlight of these visits was to accompany Johnny (now John) Dankworth and his pianist Bill Le Sage, when they appeared. I have remained a firm fan of John and his wife Cleo Laine to this day.

I stopped playing when work took me North in 1957

Dennis Tatham, piano, who also played with the Alan Hawkes Dance Orchestra in the 1950s.

and didn't play drums again until 1982, when I bought a new kit. I still have it and now play with others for my own enjoyment at various workshops and sessions which take place in and around Bath.

It doesn't seem like 53 years since I first started drumming, but it is and I have enjoyed every minute of it. Oh that I could put the clock back and do it again.

by Audrey Lockwood,
Park Lane, Sutton Bonington

My trips to my 'Mecca'

WHEN I WAS in my late teens in the early 1950s, Derby was the Mecca for me. I lived in the country but on a bus and a train route into Derby. On reflection, our entertainment was far more simple and less frenetic than it is now. The pace of life was slower.

Most Saturdays, my friend Sybil and I would go on a shopping and pictures trip to Derby. We usually took the same route – getting off at The Spot, and walking down to East Street for a wander around Midland Drapery with its labyrinth of departments. We each took out a budget account at £2 a month at the Midland and spent hours in the fashion department spending our account money many times over. This was followed by lunch or tea at the Midland's restaurant. Lunch was always Welsh rarebit and tea would be toasted teacakes with a pot of tea.

Sometimes we ate upstairs at Boots, across from Mid-land Drapery, and visited their library as well. Then it was on to Ranby's and finally to the pictures, usually the Black Prince in Colyear Street. I think it cost 1s 9d – in those days seats cost 1s 9d for years. Prices didn't seem to go up very often. I remember stamps always cost 2½d. The one film I remember seeing more than any other was Three Coins in a Fountain – so romantic.

Later, I remember a new shop opened. It was the latest 'with it' shop – Richards. I remember shopping there before I went on holiday – what sophistication!

Sometimes we visited the cinema in the afternoon, depending on the buses. If this was the case we would finish up at Cockpit Hill and then the open air market at the side of the bus station. There were row upon row of bargains to view. We always missed out the first two or three rows, they only had fruit, veg and meat. Finally we finished up at the Pot Lady. She was tall and blonde or grey and always wore an apron, I seem to think it was striped. She had a large stall at the side of the alley through to the bus station. She sold Cornishware and other T. G. Green seconds. Row upon row of blue and white striped crockery. When I went to college I bought some square red and white gingham cups, saucers and

The Black Prince cinema in Duckworth Square, Derby, in September 1960.

Ranby's department store, later to become Debenham's, in Victoria Street, Derby.

Midland Drapery in East Street, Derby.

plates. Very contemporary it was. Everything had to be contemporary in those days, although I'm not sure we really knew what it meant.

Then the final dash through the alley to catch the bus, often meeting the bus driver rushing the other way. They were going to three rows in the market we had ignored. Even in those days freezing and cold storage was more difficult, especially on a Saturday. A friend told me her bus driver father would bring home a joint of beef for 1s 6d and tomatoes at 2d a pound.

I have other memories as well. I used to play hockey for British Rail. I would arrive at Derby station having changed at Trent Junction, then take a walk down to the pitches along a path parallel to Siddals Road. After the game we entertained the opponents at the Railway

Institute – sandwiches, tea and cakes – kunzle cakes, if my memory is accurate.

Young Farmers' dances took place in a dance hall above the Odeon. Our escorts used to park their cars in the garage next door. People in the know drove up a long passage to the work area at the back – quite a convenient arrangement. I don't know what they paid for this.

I moved away from the area and visited very infrequently. The town altered so much and not necessarily for the better. And what had happened to the market?

A few months ago I had to walk through Derby to search for an estate agent. What a busy, thriving place it has become, with a great variety of shops and entertainment. It's all so different, of course, but I noticed one thing still remains – Richards.

The man who used to put us in the picture

I STARTED working at the Popular in Mill Street, Derby, about 1948, as a projectionist. I really enjoyed this life in entertainment.

I remember the Black Prince starting up as the Cinemascope age took hold. As the Popular belonged to ABC, all the staff were told to go to the Black Prince and buy a ticket to go in, but were not allowed to stop

by Don Harrison, Cromarty Close, Sinfin

in there for more than an hour. A couple of hours passed and another member of the staff would go in and get another ticket.

This went on throughout the run of The Robe to see how well the ticket sales were going.

Then the Regal in East Street started with 3D films. This was very interesting as the Regal was also ABC. We were allowed to go down and see how this was achieved.

They had to do all the altering to the projectors after the normal showing of the films. When all this was achieved, the big night arrived for all the staff to watch. The best 3D film made was the House of Wax.

We watched this film at one o'clock in the morning. It was a hit in Derby.

I used to like working at the Gaumont as well, as they had live shows, such as Cliff Richard's one-night stands.

I left Derby to go and work at the Regal cinema in Chesterfield. This I really liked, as we had live shows every other month. We had the likes of comedian Jimmy James and company. This show had, if I remember, the great Roy Castle on the bill.

Then there was Peter Brough and Archie Andrews, also David

In the foyer of the Cavendish cinema during 21st birthday celebrations. Mr Hall, the manager, (left) is pictured with two usherettes and Don Harrison.

The Cavendish cinema in Derby Lane, Derby.

Whitfield, Lonnie Donegan and his Skiffle Group, Johnny Ray and Ronnie Hilton.

I really liked this life. Then I went to work at the Ritz cinema in Matlock as chief projectionist. This was a lovely cinema and a cafe combined.

Then I came back to Derby to live and got married to Mavis. Then I got a projectionist's job at the Cavendish cinema, as a second operator. Then I got made up to chief projectionist.

I worked with David Larkin, and Mr Harold Hall, the manager, was a devoted man to the Cavendish. I remember him wanting to keep the cinema looking good as Rank would not spend money on decorating the cinema, so he got them to supply the paint and he did most of the decorating himself. He borrowed the big ladders from the fire brigade to do the auditorium. If I remember right, when he got to the foyer he fell off the high steps and broke his leg.

When the Cavendish closed in 1969, he went to the Gaumont, but he lived for the Cavendish. He didn't live long after that. I remember him making a 21st birthday cake out of hardboard and decorating it as if it was a cake to put on the canopy outside. He got on to the canopy, he pulled the ladder up that he was using, so that he could fix the imitation cake to the ladder, then found he could not get down. Someone called the fire brigade to get him

down, but he was a gentleman to work for and he was well liked by all the patrons.

I have such good memories of the cinema life.

In the rectifier room at the Cavendish cinema.

Sunday Trips to See the Animals at Cattle Market

**Dail Seaman
Spondon**

OFTEN on a Sunday morning, while mum was doing all the baking, my brother and I were taken down to the Cattle Market to see the moo cows. We thought this was quite exciting, even if it was a long walk for our little legs – sometimes we were carried a bit of the way back home.

We would go up Abbey Street, through the Little City – Burton Road area, with little jitties and alleyways where we could touch the walls either side of us, on to Cockpit Hill with all the cobbled pavements and there was the Cattle Market with all the pens for the cows. It was a bit smelly, though.

There was no worry about crossing the roads – there were hardly any vehicles, except maybe the odd bus or two, and if we saw a car everyone had a good look. There were plenty of pushbikes, but no-one ever thought of having to wear a cycle helmet then, and the men used to put cycle clips around their trouser bottoms so that they didn't get caught in the chain. After all this excitement and maybe a little walk around the River Gardens, where there were two big stone turtles and nice lily ponds to look at, we were very glad to be back home eating that lovely Sunday dinner – usually with homemade apple pie to follow.

Sunday afternoons had to be quiet. We were not allowed to play anything that was too noisy and usually went down to Sunday school. This was at Victoria Street Congregational Church – which was near to Woolworth's, the big shop selling nearly everything you could want.

On Saturday evening, we had been allowed to spend a little of our 6d pocket money on a few sweets, so we would eat them on the way home from Sunday school. No shops were allowed to open on a Sunday and all the streets were very quiet.

Not so on Monday mornings though. There would be Mr Boden going out with his horse and cart, and maybe an odd car or lorry. There was a slaughterhouse near to Hough's yard (which was nearly opposite the Spa Inn in Abbey Street) and a lorry would come every Monday with a load of pigs for slaughter. Their squealing was an awful sound.

You could still get a quart jug of beer from the Spa Inn public house – 'beer to go' ….

All the housewives would pray for fine weather on washday. Getting all the family's clothes clean was a long job, boiling the copper, ponching and dolly pegging the clothes and if it did rain, the washing seemed to be hanging about all week. No-one had invented tumble dryers then.

We had a lodger whose name was Mick. He had come to live in England from his home in Ireland just after the war. As he had no family in Derby he became a member of ours. Every so often, mum would ask him to find somewhere else to live, but dad would being him back home from work, Mum would give him dinner and he would stay again. But then there were many families like ours, everyone helped each other.

Cattle in pens at the Cattle Market.

Elton Road railway bridge.

On the right track

by Chris Canner, Macklin Street, Derby

PEAR TREE and Normanton Railway Station was where my railway enthusiasm first started, on regular trips to Burton-upon-Trent with my grandmother to see her sister in Newhall. I remember the engines that took us but cannot remember their numbers. I was only five and the year was 1952. The place to see engines go by was the 'jitty', which was a passage which connected Balfour Road and Elton Road. One character who used this passageway was the ice cream man George, who came along most evenings on his cycle, ice cream box on the front. George could not manage to push his cycle and box up the slope of Elton Road railway bridge. He always asked the trainspotters for help. We always said yes, but asked for broken wafers in return. He always gave the same answer, that he had none. But by the time we had pushed his cycle up the bridge, we always made sure there were broken biscuits when we reached the top!

My early days of living in Pear Tree Crescent with my grandparents was wonderful. I remember the Nissen huts between Pear Tree Crescent and Princes Street. The Army and RAF used them for barrage balloons during the Second World War.

We eventually left my grandparents' bungalow, and moved to the accommodation behind Flecknoe Brothers' shoe repair shop in Princes Street. I remember his bicycle and basket propped up in the street gutter outside the shop – no lock and chain in those days. Sadly, today, number 128 Princes Street is gone and the playing field for Pear Tree School is in its place. One character that lived in the area was 'Pigeon Percy', we all called him 'Pigeon'. A tall man, who always wore a long coat and often carried a pigeon in one of the pockets.

One feature of Pigeon was the way he rolled his head from side to side. He could often be seen sitting on the entrance steps of the Normanton Cinema, a pleasant man and a wonderful character.

Smith was a common name in the area, 'Bobby' Smith the policeman, 'Butcher' Smith the local butcher, Smith the grocers on Rutland Street and Princes Street. Miss Hatton the cake shop, Mrs Watson's haberdashery, where you could also buy your whip and top. I always seemed to get mine at Shrovetide. 'Butcher' Smith always seemed to do 'point duty' just like a policeman outside his shop when he had no customers. He would wave cars along as his shop was on the crossroads of Princes Street and Harrington Street.

On the corner of Coronation Street and Princes Street was Foster, Clay and Wards, a local hosiery firm, and alongside Clays, as we called it, was 'Bobby' Smith's police telephone box, painted blue with an orange flashing light.

Chris Canner, aged three years and nine months, with his grandad, George Beresford Leech, in September 1951.

Mr Pegg the local window cleaner, who lived in Pear Tree Street, always carried his ladders on a horse-drawn cart.

I well remember one character who came around each year was the man who stood on the street corner playing an accordion and blowing a trumpet. The last time I saw this man was when he was playing outside the Cavendish Cinema in 1960.

My grandfather and father both worked on matchdays at the Baseball Ground in the 1950s. My grandfather was on the invalids' entrance, and my father on the boys' enclosure. It was 9d to get in in those days. One job my grandfather did in those days was the half-time results. He used to put the half-time score up at the Normanton End.

George Beresford Leech (60) putting up the half-time score at the Baseball Ground in 1955.

There weren't many matches I missed in those days, and I even supplemented my pocket money by selling programmes. One thing I do remember about those early days of my life in Princes Street was the great number of people who went to work on push bikes. You often used to see one man with another bike in tow by his side, not recommended today by health and safety.

In 1960 on All Fools' Day we moved home again, this time to St Giles Road in Normanton. On leaving school in 1962 I decided to go into the hairdressing profession, and in March 1963 I became an indentured apprentice at Cyril Elkington's Salon on Upper Dale Road. My apprenticeship was for three years and I was an improver for two years. I spent 18 years working for Cyril Elkington, who in his time had served in the Royal Navy engine room branch. Many ex-servicemen came into our shop, and stories about their service life was then the conversation.

I always remember one customer who dressed in a very smart black suit, waistcoat, black socks, and shoes, black tie and always wore a black trilby hat, always had a profusion of hair growing out of his ears, and asked for the 'cemetery fluff' to be cut out of his ears. Even today nearly 30 years on I have heard it called 'cemetery mass'.

I even remember one customer wearing spats. Another customer came in a chauffeur-driven Rolls-Royce. The chauffeur would stand waiting by the car while his boss had a haircut. One day when the gentleman had had his hair cut, he went and sat in the back of the Rolls-Royce reading a newspaper and he waited while the chauffeur had his hair cut.

There were no yellow lines outside the shop in those

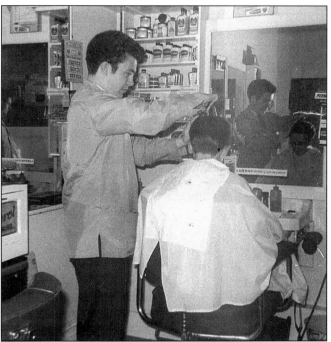

Chris Canner cutting hair at Cyril Elkington's in Upper Dale Road, Derby, during his first year apprenticeship.

days Many people came on cycles, we even had a cycle rack outside, made by local blacksmith Hector Horner – I think his workshop was in Stanhope Street.

When Cyril Elkington celebrated his 25 years at the Cavendish shop, he managed to have a barrel of beer set up in the shop for the weekend celebration. I don't think I've seen so many customers go home so happy.

In 1964 I joined the Derby Roundhouse Club, a train-spotting club which attracted members from the Derby area, and the trips were organised throughout the year. Membership was 3s per year, and our first trip was to Carlisle, departing Derby Market Place at 1am and priced at £2. Trips were on a regular basis over the next two years – June 1964 to June 1966, and in July 1965 a week's holiday to Scotland was attained.

Fourteen people including the driver went on this trip. The price for the week including accommodation breakfast and travel was £19-0-0d.

An inter-club cricket match was organised between Chaddesden members and Cavendish members on a cricket pitch at the Race Course. The winners were Chaddesden, and some injuries did occur.

During one of our visits to Crewe in 1964, I visited a

most unusual shop on Crewe Station bridge: Alan Thelwall's Mini Market shop, selling cigarettes, pipes, tobacco, everything for the smoker, sweets, chocolate and fancy gifts, but, most important, Ian Allan ABC spotters' books. In 1957, Alan Thelwall first opened his business selling confectionery, and by 1959 realised there was an outlet for selling railway books, notelets and pens.

By this time soft drinks in a can could be obtained. Many visits to Alan's shop were made for my spotting books, but in 1966 his shop was to be closed as British Railways wanted to demolish it for a station car park. Luckily Alan had another shop in Earle Street, Crewe, similar to his Mini Market shop, so we were able to go and buy books from there. From his idea of a combined sweet, confectionery and book shop came the idea for the Railway Bookshop. In 1981, when I opened my first Hairdressing and Railway Bookshop business at the Cavendish, it was Alan who supplied me with some of the books, and I will always appreciate the help he gave to me.

When I opened my Hairdressing and Railway Book-shop in Macklin Street, Derby, in 1988, some bright wag said it should be called Short Back and Sidings!

1989 was a memorable year for rail enthusiasts in Derby when the Midland Counties Railway 150th anniversary celebrations were held to commemorate the opening of the Midland Counties Railway in 1839. I was invited to have a travelling bookshop on all the special trains which were run. With my trusty helpers, Dennis and Janet Bosworth, Dave Greensmith and Ian Beacock, we looked forward to the forthcoming events. The first special was the 'Denby Dawdler' on April 22, 1989, Derby to Denby and Wirksworth, followed on May 6, 1989 by the 'Jolly Collier' from Nottingham to Cotgrave and Calverton colliery branches. I think the proudest moment of the celebrations came on May 23, 1989, for Alan Dance and Stuart Smith, the organisers, and the Midland Counties Railway 150 committee, when brush Type 4 class locomotive No 97561, resplendent in red livery, was named Midland Counties Railway 150 1839 to 1989, at a naming ceremony at Derby Station.

There were trips to Central Wales, Bristol, Bath and Scarborough, with 'Green Arrow' covering the journey from York, and Carlisle with steam in the form of class 8F locomotive No 48151 over the Settle and Carlisle section. On Friday June 2, 1989 a celebration dinner was held at the Midland Hotel, which both my wife Marian and myself attended.

The Commemorative Special ran on Sunday, June 4, 1989, making ten trips, five in each direction, between Nottingham and Derby hauled by BR HMT 2-6-4T 80080 and Jubilee 4-6-0 45596 Bahamas.

As we waited on platform one with the station trolley full of books to take over to platform two where we were

Locomotive number 48151 on Ribblehead viaduct on the Settle to Carlisle railway.

to join the train, Dave Greensmith had an idea to ask the station master if the train could be diverted on to platform one to make loading the books on to the train easier.

His request was granted, and to this day it is one of Dave's proudest moments, as he says, getting the train diverted specially for him. Sure enough, 45596 Bahamas arrived on platform one at 9.26am prompt. We calculated on our journeys we did a mileage of 1,916 miles 06 chains.

Today the hairdressing salon and railway bookshop offer the customer the chance to come and browse through the books and videos and have a chat about days gone by. Jack Wallis, a friend who used to be an engine driver at Slack Lane loco shed (Friar Gate Shed), came into the shop one day with a small coiled spring with prongs. When I asked him what it was for he promptly clipped it on to the end of a shovel and said: "There you are, a toasting fork, simple but effective."

Jack was a true engineman, with many stories to tell, always prompting a smile. Sadly Jack's beloved Slack Lane (Friar Gate) loco shed was demolished during March 1999, having been opened in October 1878.

From my early years of trainspotting at Pear Tree and Normanton station, my apprenticeship in gents' hair-dressing, my membership of Derby Roundhouse Club, and my move to Macklin Street with the hairdressing Railway Bookshop, my interest has not waned, and even today many ex-railwaymen still come into my shop, and tell of their tales on the footplate.

When Richard did his first Saturday run

by Richard Wood, Bowbridge House, Mackworth

TODAY I did my first Saturday run. Previously my brother had always done it, but as he is now 15, grown up and works on a Saturday, I have to do it. My first trip was to Corden's, just down Abbey Street from where I live. They have a greengrocer's under the arch. It is stacked full of potatoes, cabbages, bananas and suchlike. Mum says you couldn't get bananas in the war but now you can.

I gave Ma Corden my list. Although Pa Corden was there with young Ted, I had always been afraid of him and daren't give him the list. We had always got the same from Corden's for more than 20 years – no spuds, peas, beans or greens because dad grew them himself. It was carrots, lettuce in season, onions and very occasionally some fruit.

Ma Corden loaded up my brown canvas bag for me, the carrots at the bottom and the lettuce on the top, all loose. I gave her the two half crowns and she gave me one shilling and four pence change. She gave me the list back with the prices written against what mum had ordered.

Having taken them home to mum my next trip was to the Co-op Bakery, just up the street. Mr Potts the manager was my friend Raymond's dad. He has an Austin Seven car, in fact I think he was the only person in Abbey Street with a car. He keeps it at the Spa Inn yard. Sometimes, on a Sunday he takes Raymond and I to Little Eaton, where his mother lives. It's nice to go into the countryside. Sometimes we have dinner there. Do you know they put pepper on their chips!

Our divi number is 43252. I remember it as forty-three, twenty-five, two. Mum uses the divi to get us new shoes and clothes. During the week, Mrs Potts serves behind the counter, but on Saturday Mr Potts serves with a neat pinny over his suit. In fact I don't think I have ever seen Mr Potts without his suit on.

Raymond always brags that they are the only family in Abbey Street with the use of a phone. I ordered two sliced loaves and paid one shilling. While Mr Potts was filling in the divi slip he told me that sliced bread had first been made in Derby by the Mosley Family, but one of them had done something naughty before the war and nobody talked about them now. I took the sliced bread home and had a drink of water before starting the long run.

First stop on the long run is the Co-op store for tins of beans, lard and marg. The lard and marg are cut off a large block with a wire with a wooden handle at each end. Sometimes, the man doing it would heat the wire over a candle to make it cut faster. Mum had issued instructions that if he did that, I was to ask that he poured the molten marge or lard on to the block we were buying since we had paid for it.

A burning ambition

A FIRST night at the Playhouse in Sacheveral Street in 1956, the new venue for the Repertory Company of Derby that had moved from the Little Theatre in Becket Street. And I was there backstage, where I had all my life intended to be getting ready to go on – in the star role of course.

by Janet Grundy, Aspen Cottage, Mickleover

At 17 years old and with stars in my eyes it did not seem to matter too much that as ASM (assistant stage manager to the uninitiated) I was rushing about finalising the props in their correct places. I had spent the previous week cadging the props from local traders in return for having their names in the programme!

I was running errands for the company, answering the call of my boss the stage manager, with everything from what won the 4.30pm at Haydock to getting a large whiskey from the bar and rehearsing 'my line' – well, the voice of a caller on the telephone from offstage.

I would get there one day, I just knew it. My ambition to be a famous actress had started longer ago than I could remember, but I was told by my beloved daddy that I danced in my cot and was a proper little show-off and acted to get my own way before I could walk.

Repertory, however, in a town where the patrons are usually the same each week, is a strange way of life. I had found that if one played a downtrodden little person one had so much sympathy from the public in shops and in the street, but woe betide you if you played a lady of easy virtue or a marriage wrecker – it just was not advisable to pop into Boots or Sainsbury's for the run of that play!!

The play we were presenting that week, The Wick and the Wax, was not exactly a popular one with the cast. The stage director, Stuart Routledge, hated it, constantly muttering under his breath about the lighting and how impossible it was to expect a repertory company to stage it with just a week's rehearsal...

After a hectic night and then trying to learn my lines for rehearsal of next week's play, (yes, I had a small part

The old Playhouse in Sacheveral Street, Derby.

in the forthcoming production. I told you I would get there) I drove off to the theatre. This sounds pretty grand, but in fact it was in a 1939 Singer Nine that daddy had lent me for my time at the Playhouse, mainly for getting home late at night, provided I stood the cost of running it. This was a poser, as on 10s a week, maintenance costs were out of the question, and it was all I could do to put two gallons in the tank, buy ten Benson & Hedges and have a little over for coffee and sandwiches!

However I remembered my old friend Sam – a car mechanic – and we did a deal. I accompanied him to the dog track (when my busy life allowed) and he sorted out my precious little Singer when it broke down.

I arrived in Sacheveral Street, and to my horror there were fire engines, police, and crowds around the theatre. I could hardly believe my eyes, the empty shell that only the night before had been the keeper of my dreams…

With some of the rest of the cast, I walked through the charred remains of the auditorium and the stage. The dreadful truth began to dawn on us – no work, how do we pay the rent? – how do we eat? I was one of the lucky ones, as, being a Derby girl, I was living with my parents, but it was an earth-shattering blow to the rest. There was no dole or equity minimum for out-of-work actors in those days. With nowhere else to go, we gathered at my house in Littleover where mummy provided a bottomless pot of coffee and sandwiches for all.

However, what to do now? Flicking through the *Derby Evening Telegraph* I noticed that Caroll Levis, the star-maker of the 1950s, was coming to the Derby Hippodrome the next week (Derby actually supported two live theatres at that time). With nothing to lose, I went to the audition, and with my confidence abounding I went on stage and sang!! I will never be a Maria Callas or even a Vera Lynn, but as I was to find out throughout my life, being in the right place at the right time could turn failures into successes. As Caroll's manager was just saying: 'Yes dear we will let you know – don't call us', a voice from the auditorium called: 'I wanna see that girl'. It was Caroll. I went to his dressing room – number one of course – and we talked, then Caroll tried to get fresh with me. I recoiled in horror, saying vehemently: "I am going to be a star, but on my talent alone". I cringed in the

The old Playhouse after the fire in March 1956.

The building was demolished in 1988.

silence that followed – I thought I'd blown my best chance. The next minute he roared with laughter – "You will do for me, girlie", he said. He offered me a contract to replace Violet Pretty, for whom he had secured a contract with J Arthur Rank.

The next two years must have been some of the happiest of my life, travelling with Caroll, getting star billing, and most important, learning my trade from a master.

Although my days at the Playhouse were short-lived I shall never forget them. To me, as a 17-year-old, the lovely little theatre in Sacheveral Street was second only to the London Palladium.

Nothing over sixpence

by R. Stevens, Gurney Avenue

IN the early 1920s, Woolworth's store in Victoria Street boasted nothing over sixpence. A bucket, a kettle, whatever, at that price.

And this is the reason I remember it so well. Woolworth's was just a ground-floor store, until one weekend my father working for, and with, Henry Bestwick, opened up a stairway on the left at the bottom end.

Apart from the railing and side pieces all the stairs were cut in the cellar of our house in Princes Street, and I had the job of numbering all the pieces ready for assembly.

When the store closed one Saturday night, my father and Mr Bestwick worked all night and the following day, and the job was completed ready for the fixtures in the upstairs to be fitted. No doubt there are people who can also remember this. I'm 89 years of age.

Dad gets a punctured ego

by Dail Seaman, Spondon

WE HAVE A car and a television … When it was Coronation Day most of our neighbours crammed into our little room to watch it on our new television set. Then one summer evening, mum told us they had bought a car.

All excited, my brother Richard and I ran down the entry expecting to see a lovely pale blue Morris 1100 or something like that. We stopped dead to see a dark green square thing with a great big boot which stuck out on the back. We giggled a bit trying to hide our disappointment. The seats inside were real leather, though, and we were told it was a Singer and went like a bomb. Having been told tales about the war by our older brothers and sister, we were a bit worried about this, and wondered what Vera Lynn had to do with cars and whether we would get blown up.

Come the weekend we all got ready in our best clothes to go for a 'spin'. Everyone laughed when mum put her umbrella next to the picnic basket. "You won't need that now, Ann", said Dad. She had the last laugh, though, because three or four miles down the road we had a puncture. Of course it was raining, and mum and I were quite dry under the umbrella while the men of the family set about changing the tyre.

Derby Regalia Carnival Band marching towards the municipal sports ground in the 1950s.

Carnival capers in the 'fifties

by Mr Dennis Leonard, Matlock Road, Chaddesden

Members of Derby Regalia Carnival Band in the 1950s: Barry Spiller, Alan Day, Dennis Leonard and Norman Theobald. The two girls are Beryl Mason and Anne Pell.

THESE PHOTOGRAPHS are of the Derby Regalia Carnival Band in the 1950s. One shows Derby Carnival street parade coming down Osmaston Park Road to the municipal sports ground. The girl throwing the mace is Brenda Bird and the two small mascots are Maureen Withey and Arthur Cholerton Jnr who in later years became the drum major of Derby Serenaders.

There were about 12 bands in the league and we went out to competitions most Saturdays. After the competitions we would all march back on to the arena to await the results. On the way home to Derby we would sometimes stop at a pub for a drink.

Derby Regalia Carnival Band band members (from left to right) Alan Day, Joan Chambers and Dennis Leonard.

---

by A. B. Groome, Woodstock Close, Allestree

Bless this house

'THE Lord Loveth the Gates of Zion'. During the long sermon my eyes would trace these words painted across the chapel wall. I knew every twist and turn of the long blue scroll, with its capital letters picked out in gold.

The chapel was simply furnished with hard, shiny wooden pews, and tall rectangular windows flooded the place with light. The floor was bare except for the strip of brown linoleum, with its Greek maze patterned border, stretching up the aisle to a communion table covered with a pristine white, crochet-edged cloth.

Up two steps and behind the blue-and-golden wrought iron rails were the choir pews and pulpit. Beyond these were two matching arched, maroon baize-covered doors, one of which was imitation, the other leading to the choir vestry.

My grandparents, Henry and Alice Hodgkinson, were staunch members of Mount Street Primitive Methodist Church. Originally from Flagg, Henry came to Derby as an apprentice butcher before setting up his own business. His brothers, Arthur and Moses, were also members along with their families. Indeed, it seemed that half the congregation was related in some way or other.

Quite a few members from both sides of my family were in the choir and great uncle Arthur was the organist. The organ, or harmonium, had stops to pull out and treddles that had to be kept moving. I know this because a surprised, but beaming, Uncle Arthur had to vacate his seat when I was called to play Rousseau's Dream from my piano tutor, at the Sunday school anniversary.

On these occasions the menfolk would put up the platform a week before the service. It consisted of a series of benches surrounding the pulpit and stretching from floor to ceiling. Originally everyone dressed in white and all the words printed on the special hymn sheets had to be learned by heart. On one occasion my brother, Roy, reluctantly recited My New Braces, and was later rewarded by the Rev Goldstraw, a minister and family friend, with a brand new pair of braces.

Mostly sacred songs and poems were performed on the Sunday, but Monday evening was the fun night when one of the most popular items was 'The Chickleham Estate', a sort of version of Old MacDonald. This was led by the choir sitting at the very top of the platform, with Uncle Charlie, a fine tenor, delighting us with his animal noises.

There were other annual occasions such as the Whitsuntide Treat, when everyone was issued with a ribbon bearing the name of their Sunday school before embarking on horse-drawn drays and processing through the town. This was followed by a field day at Borrowash with races and lots to eat.

Harvest time was special. The chapel would be bursting with bright flowers and mounds of fruit and vegetables. The pulpit was decked with purple grapes and strings of orange crab apples. I always looked out for the large loaf of bread in the shape of a sheaf of corn. I loved all the harvest hymns, and my favourite line was 'The valleys stand so thick with corn that even they are singing'. It seemed to sum up all the joy of the occasion.

Monday was the evening when all the produce was auctioned off. Large boxes of rosy apples and stripy marrows were passed over the heads to successful bidders, and the children too were given a chance to bid for single items. Roy always chose a pomegranate, from which he picked out seeds with a pin.

On one occasion Grandpa gave a sausage and mash supper in aid of the poor and needy. Roy sat next to old Mr Fletcher and likened his red nose to the tomato-flavoured sausage he was eating, for which he got a strict telling-off. Sometimes games evenings were held for the younger generation, when the collection plate was pressed into service for 'spin the platter'. For 'all change' the name of a local railway station was given to everyone.

Sacrament was a serious occasion in which the young took no part, but Roy and I would sneak round to the back door of the choir vestry to see if there was any cordial left over in the tiny glasses after the service.

I dreaded prayer meetings. We sat there, heads bowed in heavy silence broken only by the sound of a creaking pew as some member stood up to deliver a fervent prayer. Though small, I found the outpourings of emotions embarrassing and unsettling. I much preferred the reassurance of a normal service surrounded by 'a thousand tongues' singing to the tune of Diadem, guided by a 'Great Jehovah', and 'anchored firm and deep in the Saviour's love'.

We attended chapel three times a day on Sundays as well as other events on weekdays. Mother, though shy and retiring, dutifully ran The Women's Friendly Circle, where I remember performing Three Blind Mice on my toy harp. On one occasion mother invited one lady to tea. I was persuaded to nurse her baby while the two of them chatted, only to be rewarded by a warm sensation on my lap and a clammy wet gymslip.

Mount Carmel was part of Derby South circuit and we would often visit other chapels, where I was sometimes prevailed upon to recite. Auntie Lily had a lovely soprano voice and would sing a medley of songs such as Trees and Bless This House, her particular favourite.

Lily was the eldest of the children followed by my mother, Clarice, then Florence, then later the two boys, Harry and Donald. After living on the corner of Midland Road, the family moved to 106 London Road. There was a private side entrance, but when visiting we always went through the busy shop. Mother used to tell the tale of a favourite cat which would sit behind the open door ready to thwart any unwary dog that dared to enter. Out would come a lightning paw and the intruder would retreat with a yelp and a sore nose.

I remember white tiles on the floor and two stout supporting pillars just right for clinging to, and playing 'Round and round the mulberry bush'. Highly-polished brass rails spanned the windows and there were two long counters on either side. Left was the pork side and beef was on the right. Between the counters at the back was the office, behind which was the huge walk-in fridge. As this was forbidden territory it was an adventure in itself to experience the blast of ice-cold air when the heavy door was opened to expose the meat hanging on either side.

Uncle Arthur had his domain 'in the back' where the mince and sausages were made. The floor was covered with clean sawdust which we stamped off on a grid before ascending the well-worn wooden steps to the pie chamber, a long narrow room with a wide bench running along one side. The pie machine and various sizes of moulds were congregated at one end waiting to be clothed in pale pastry, converting them into what resembled rows of sandpies. The finished products were sent to Williamson's to be baked.

The pie chamber led into the dark scullery, usually occupied by Mrs Bunting and Mrs Maskery. From here the dark, back stairs led up to a box room housing the treasures of yesteryear, such as wooden jigsaws, farm animals, a clockwork railway and conjuring set. Most used was the stout wooden fort, its infantry with broken rifles, many headless and some reincarnated with the aid of matchsticks. The cavalry had certainly seen battle, particularly the horses, many of which had to be propped up on three legs. I cannot remember any girls' toys, but I did eventually inherit Donald's geriatric teddy bear, hairless and wobbly-ankled.

There were four other rooms and a bathroom on this third storey, but my favourite spot was the landing on the front stairs, so light and airy because of the large window patterned with stained glass. From here was the start of the slipper bannister which descended in three right-angled twists to the side passage below.

The living room, with its heavy mahogany furniture, was the largest room. Two rocking chairs stood either side of the fireplace, next to which was a fascinating speaking tube with its whistle for communication with the shop below. On the walls were ornately framed pictures of highland cattle. A door opened on to a confined leaned roof space which grandma endeavoured to enliven with shelves of potted geraniums. One side sloped steeply, and we could clamber up to peep through a small lattice fence at the back gardens of Regent Street before sliding down again.

During the 1930s, my grandparents left London Road to live at Allestree, leaving Uncle Harry and his wife Olive in charge. Uncle Donald went with them and would sometimes pick us up on a Sunday in the old 'Star'.

Outdoor games were not encouraged so we resorted to quiet board games, such as Halma and Peggity. On warm days we would sit in the sun parlour surrounded by grandma's Goss china collection and weird African artifacts given to her by various missionary friends. My favourite was a musical instrument made from a small gourd with an attachment of flat metal prongs. Fascination also lurked in the lounge in the shape of a lion skin rug, complete with a head large enough to perch on. Sometimes we played the gramophone and I can still remember most of the words of grandpa's favourite record, Smilin' Through.

Reading matter consisted mainly of old annuals and a series of temperance booklets, the subject of which was John Barleycorn, who came to grief through the demon drink. I still have a picture in my mind of his matchstick figure bent double over a sack of barley, huge teardrops falling from his eyes.

Eventually rules were relaxed and Uncle Donald introduced clock golf and croquet, much to the delight of the younger generation. Annual Whit Monday visits to Biggin Grange, where grandpa started his working life, continued and the Christmas celebrations at Allestree remained the highlight of the year. As usual, summer holidays at the seaside included the extended Hodgkinson and Harvey families.

All this was soon to end when Derby Corporation requisitioned the site of Mount Street church and the final service was held in 1939. A new church was built at Blagreaves Lane, in Littleover, and named New Mount, many of its original members being scattered between other churches. Ironically, the old chapel remained in situ many years after.

I was between schools when war broke out and the summer holiday was extended. Both my uncles, now married, joined the Air Force and my father, William Harvey, a First World War veteran, had been called up for service and was stationed at the barrage balloon site in Chester Green.

Lily was now living in Crewe with husband Harry, but all other members of the family, including Madge, Don's wife of six months, were helping out at the shop. Mother gave a hand there most days, so Roy and I became latchkey children for the first time in our lives. Flo's husband Ted joined the LDV, later the Home Guard, but worked in the shop during the day.

It was a huge blow when Harry was killed on a training flight. Shortly after, Donald was reported missing, following the fall of Singapore. The family continued to write encouraging letters to him and were overjoyed at the beginning of 1944 to hear that he was still alive, although a prisoner of war. Sadly, unbeknown to the family, he died a few weeks later at the notorious Kanchanaburi prison. Letters which had failed to reach him were returned after the war.

106 London Road is now part of Derbyshire Royal Infirmary. I often wonder if there is anything left inside of the old days. Perhaps they have divided up the large living room where a young Donald turned the chairs upside down to make a cattle market. What happened to the fearsome, long-horned cattle heads that adorned the passage where Florence ran, tripped and broke her sister's new doll? Who now gazes from the drawing room window where Harry's granddaughter waved to King George V and Queen Mary, as they passed by in their landau?

The site of Mount Street Methodist Church is now a

car park. No place for ghosts, only passing memories of some of the people who made up its congregation; Allison, Alvey, Barnard, Basford, Berrill, Bilson, Carvell, Chambers, Cuthbert, Fletcher, Flux, Harvey, Hodgkinson, Mather, Milner, Moorcroft, Morley, Rowe, Talbot, Woodward, Yeomans – on the roll call at the 'Gates of Zion'.

Big Screen Memories Relived Over Bowl of Pasta

by Caroline Morrow-Brown

THE elegant Cameo Cinema opened on December 18, 1913, as the London Road Cinema, but quickly became known as the Cosy. By the time it closed in 1959, it was called the Cameo, and had also briefly been known as the Picture House and the Forum.

A novel feature of the Cosy was that it was the first cinema in Derby to have indirect lighting, described at the time by the *Derbyshire Advertiser* as "restful to the eyes".

The Cosy had an added advantage in that it was sited very near to the railway station. A large advert in the

Gianni Rossi was struck by the grandeur of the old cinema.

station informed travellers waiting for connections where they could while away an hour or two most pleasantly watching a film.

The cinema was no flea pit. There was a quiet grandeur about the Cosy's appealing frontage with its Baroque-style ornamentation and spectacular metal balcony above the pillared entrance.

The interior decoration was impressive to say the least – the Derbyshire Advertiser once again waxes lyrical, finding it "particularly bright and attractive".

Sam Winfield, in Dream Palaces of Derbyshire, describes how the interior had very much the atmosphere of a theatre, with a horseshoe-shaped balcony extending around three walls and "curving gracefully towards the screen".

This effect was greatly enhanced by the ornate plaster work, including "busts reminiscent of the female figureheads of old sailing ships".

Sadly, by the 1950s, all this elegance had become more than somewhat faded. One regular customer, Bill Doyle, remembers the Cameo (as it was by then known) as coming into the category of cinemas with "ill-fitting carpets and rickety seats".

The Cameo cinema pictured in 1960.

Then as now, children were important cinema customers. Joan Moore, who was brought up in Canal Street, vividly recalls her visits to the Cosy as the highlight of the week.

She said: "When I was around eight years old I used to go every Saturday afternoon. If you were among the first in the queue you could get a seat on the first two rows at the front for 2d. The other seats were 3d or 4d, and the balcony seats were 6d.

"My dad used to give me and my younger sister 6d each and we could have sweets and ice cream and pay the entrance fee for the films as well.

The spectacular interior of La Tosca restaurant, showing the original architecture.

"When I see the films of today I feel the character and exciting atmosphere is no longer there. Oh, there are beautiful seats, chrome and glass and wonderful films too, but I don't believe audiences appreciate films as we used to."

The ornate plaster work including 'busts reminiscent of the female figureheads of old sailing ships'.

Current owner of the building, now La Tosca Italian Restaurant, is Gianni Rossi.

Mr Rossi recalls his first sight of the building, which had been in disuse for some time: "I was very impressed with how it looked from the outside. Inside it was a bit of a mess, but I remember being struck by the grandeur of the auditorium and the really high ornate ceiling. I could see its potential as a restaurant straight away."

The happy ending to this story is that although the much-loved Cosy is no longer a cinema, much of the original architecture and decoration has been preserved. And nearly 100 years after it was purpose built as a place of entertainment, people are still going there to meet friends and enjoy a good evening out.

Many of La Tosca's customers can still remember it as the Cosy. Over a bowl of spaghetti they love to relive those happy days of Fred and Ginger, Bogey and Ingrid Bergman, Roy Rogers and John Wayne. Those days when stars really were stars, when villains were villains, heroes were heroes and even married couples slept in twin beds.

"I remember Mrs Osbourne, the ticket dispenser. She was also the manageress, I believe. She had long, black hair and wore thick lens spectacles with thick, black frames. She always looked very stern and I was a bit afraid of her. She wouldn't stand for noisy children pushing and shoving each other.

"I used to like the weekly serial Flash Gordon, played by Buster Crabbe. He was left on a cliff hanger each week, so we had to see if he escaped next time…